YORKSHIRE POTS AND POTTERIES

CONTENTS

LIST OF ILLUSTRATIONS

PLATES

7

IN TEXT

INTRODUCTION

Pottery has been made in Yorkshire since the earliest times. In the Middle Ages and post-medieval period the art was developed and a wider range of items made. Peak production was reached in the nineteenth century, when over 100 potteries were operative in the county and products were exported far afield. Few of these potteries are still working; the majority closed in the face of competition from the Staffordshire potteries.

Until the mid-eighteenth century pottery was produced to meet local requirements only, many potters working singlehanded and employed only part-time in pottery-making. The potworks were situated where raw materials were readily available. Products were hawked from door to door round the neighbouring villages, and sold in the nearest market.

As transport facilities improved, with the opening of canals and railways, it became possible to import raw materials and export finished wares. Thus potteries spread to areas where access to transportation was of paramount importance and the availability of local clay and fuel less so. The Staffordshire potters were also able to transport their wares farther afield, which included Yorkshire, and the competition, together with the growing popularity of finer factory-made wares, caused the decline and closure of many of the traditional Yorkshire country potteries.

With the advent of the Industrial Revolution and the rapid growth of urban communities, the potteries developed to meet the increased demand of the townfolk. Businessmen built factory potteries and shares were issued. These gentlemen, not necessarily potters themselves, employed large numbers of workpeople, each having a particular job on the production line. Modern machinery was installed, fine clay and flint were imported from the south and from Norfolk respectively, and fine pottery in the latest taste, equal to that made elsewhere in the country, was produced.

In the first half of the nineteenth century many more potteries were opened to meet growing demand, but by the end of this period taste was declining, mass production was the order of the day, and transfer printing was at its height of popularity; piracy of designs was commonplace and workmen moved from pottery to pottery with great rapidity, taking with them expertise and the secrets of former employers. Thus by the mid-nineteenth century the products of one pottery differed little from those of another, and it is virtually impossible to tell them apart. Adding to this difficulty is the fact that a large number of pottery owners went bankrupt, and neighbouring potters took the opportunity of buying up their unfinished wares, moulds and copper engraving plates cheaply—thus marketing almost identical goods. Pottery owners, too, often moved from one pottery to another or worked two or more potteries at a time.

The majority of the early Yorkshire potteries were situated in the West Riding. The availability of coal there afforded cheap and easily accessible fuel, fireclay found in the coalfield was used for the production of wares, and the thickly populated area (the most heavily populated in Yorkshire) supplied a ready market nearby.

Yorkshire pottery made before the mid-eighteenth century is rarely to be found for sale, and as such cannot be considered to be 'collectable'. For this reason the early potteries are mentioned only briefly in this book, but sources of information are listed for those interested in studying the subject further.

There has been speculation for some time that tin-glazed earthenware may have been made in Yorkshire, despite the high cost of transporting tin there. Until recently evidence was lacking, but it is now known that tin-glazed earthenware was made at Middleham in the North Riding. There is reference to delft ware at the Rothwell Pottery, but this may simply have been the local term for pottery. The term 'galley pots', originally used to describe delft ware and later a name given to ointment pots or chamber pots, is used at both the Rotherham Old Pottery and the Swinton Pottery and raises the question as to whether this refers to delft ware. At Swinton, galley pots and chamber pots appear on the same bill.

The eighteenth-century country potteries were small, several often existing in the same neighbourhood, as at Potovens, Halifax, and Burton in Lonsdale. They were family concerns, worked in much the same way for generations, producing mainly utilitarian wares such as pancheons, crocks and jars, but also some ornamental pieces—puzzle jugs, cradles and money-boxes—when time permitted.

The factory potteries are best known today for their production of finewares, which have been treasured and thus preserved for the modern collector and student. Vast quantities of the commoner types of earthenware were also made. Export markets were established and pattern books issued by several potteries; those of the Leeds, Castleford, Swinton, and Ferrybridge Potteries are preserved to this day. Jewitt records having seen one from the Don Pottery, but it cannot now be traced.

The mass of mid-nineteenth-century urban potteries produced cheap white earthenware which was transfer-printed in a variety of colours. Mocha ware, slip-banded kitchen ware, lustreware, stone china, ironstone china and granite china were all made. Several factories, notably the Don, Ferrybridge, Holmes, and Northfield Potteries, experimented in porcelain production but never marketed it in quantity. The Rockingham Pottery, however, produced a superb soft-paste porcelain and was patronised by royalty.

From the second half of the nineteenth century up to World War II the production of stone bottles formed the staple product of several potteries, particularly in Hunslet near Leeds, Castleford and Burton in Lonsdale. These were made to contain a variety of products, ranging from whisky and ginger beer to furniture cream and ink. Cheaper glass bottles and plastic containers eventually killed the trade, and the potteries were forced to close.

At the end of the nineteenth century, art pottery became fashionable, with its highly coloured glazes and almost 'modern' shapes. This was made at Linthorpe, Burmantofts, the Leeds Art Pottery and the Woodlesford Art Pottery. Several manufacturers of firebricks and sanitary ware also made small quantities of decorative glazed pieces; examples are known from Wortley and Middleton, near Leeds.

Of the old potteries only the Ferrybridge Pottery, the Lindley Moor Pottery, and the Littlethorpe Pottery are still working today —a sad decline in a craft that once employed thousands.

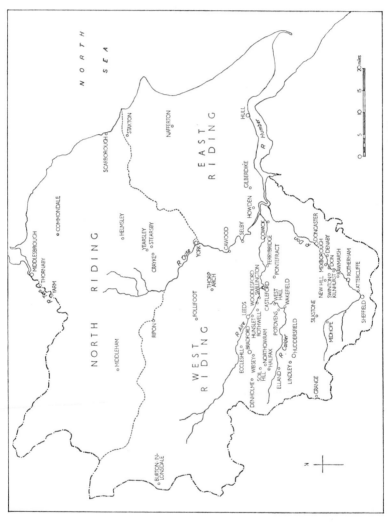

FIG 1   Location of principal pottery sites in Yorkshire

LEEDS AND DISTRICT

LEEDS POTTERY
Location: SE 302322

The Leeds Pottery, or Leeds Old Pottery, was built on Rushey Pasture on the northern side of Jack Lane, Hunslet, a mile south of Leeds. There has been some doubt about the date of its foundation, but recent research points to 1770. In that year Richard Humble, agent to coalowner Charles Brandling, bought 5½ acres of land called Rushey Pasture.[1] The deed states that there were stables and a holme on the land, but makes no reference to a pottery; though in the same year the local newspaper mentions a large earthenware manufactory being built near the town—an almost certain reference to this pottery.

A newspaper advertisement dated 1826, offering the pottery for sale, states that it has been 'extensively carried on for upwards of fifty years'.[2] Another advertisement, however, dated 1849,[3] says 'more than a century', which confuses the issue; but it is probable that men living in 1826 would be more accurate about the date, as it was within living memory of many of them. The pottery, valued at £1,000, was insured in January 1771 by Richard Humble, John and Joshua Green, and in the following October a further policy was taken out which included stock and utensils valued at £500.[4]

Savile Green was a partner in 1774,[5] the firm trading as 'Humble, Green & Co'. By 1776 William Hartley was a partner, and the firm became 'Humble, Hartley, Greens & Co'.[6] Notice of Richard Humble's retirement appeared in the *Leeds Intelligencer* in 1781, when the other partners are named as Henry Ackroyd, John Barwick and Samuel Wainwright.[7]

As to the confusion regarding the date of foundation, a Thomas Wilson wrote in 1854 that he had asked William Warburton, son of the owner of the Leeds Pottery, about the date of its establishment, and had been told 1760. From the tone of Wilson's letter it is clear that Warburton had little interest in the matter. Wilson learnt something 'from Mr Petty, son of a Mr Petty who in conjunction with one Rainforth, an apprentice of the Greens, established an adjoining Pottery in 1757'.[8] This would have meant that the Leeds Pottery must have been established by at least 1750, for Rainforth to have served his apprenticeship. But as far as the principal characters are concerned this date is impossible. John and Savile Green were born in 1743,[9] so they were only seven years old in 1750; Rainforth was born in 1764[10] and was an employee until the building of the Hunslet Hall Pottery in 1800 (see p 47); and the father of Mr Petty, referred to in 1854, was a bread baker at the beginning of the nineteenth century and did not become a pottery manufacturer until some years later. Thus it is clear that Warburton's statement is totally inaccurate, and nothing is to be gained by relying on his testimony.

Two important points, however, raise doubts as to whether the building of the Jack Lane Pottery in 1770 was the beginning of the firm, or whether it moved there from other premises: (1) several pieces of pottery judged to have been made before 1770 bear 'Leeds' characteristics, and (2) why did an important firm of enamellers, 'Robinson & Rhodes' (see p 79), set up in Leeds if there was no large pottery there?

Although thorough research has been made into contemporary source material, admittedly limited, no reference to an earlier pottery connected with any of the partners has been traced. Several facts that seem to confirm the 1770 origin of the pottery have emerged, however, and there are several plausible explanations for the earlier pieces with 'Leeds' characteristics. The Leeds Pottery partners could have acquired moulds and stock from another pottery—in 1769 Dennison's Pottery nearby was advertised to let, and it could well have been making fine pottery—and its workmen, too, could easily have moved to the new works.

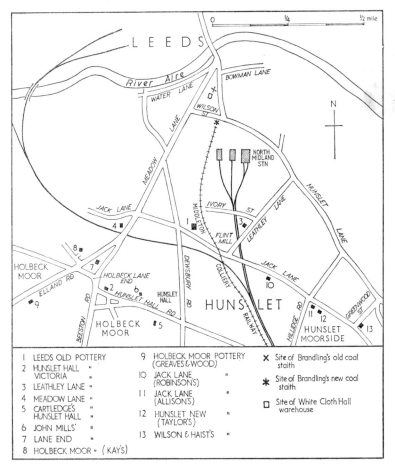

FIG 2 Hunslet showing location of potteries

Dennison's Pottery is not mentioned after 1769. The Rothwell Pottery was in financial difficulties in the early 1770s and the Leeds partners reputedly bought much of its stock.

A third possibility arises, but at this stage there is little documentary evidence to support it: the Green family came from Swinton in South Yorkshire and it is possible that at least one member of the family worked at Swinton Pottery before coming to Leeds; that being so it is possible that he brought ideas and designs from Swinton Pottery. Workmen from Swinton certainly moved to Hunslet in the early 1770s. An extant bill, undated but with others dated 1768, and concerning pots sent by Malpass & Fenney at Swinton Pottery to Earl Fitzwilliam, is signed by a John Green,[11] though such a common name it offers no conclusive evidence. The Leeds parish registers reveal many names of men from 'The Pottery' after 1770, but none before (see Appendix I). Who were the partners in this, the biggest and most important of the Yorkshire potteries?

Richard Humble, 1715–98, was agent to Charles Brandling, whose wagon-way ran through the pottery grounds. He probably had only a financial interest in the pottery, buying the land on which it was built. He married at Rothwell in 1757, Joshua Green being a witness. Although he withdrew from the partnership in 1781, his sons inherited shares in the pottery on his death.

Three members of the Green family were originally involved in the pottery (for their relationship see the family tree, Fig 3). Savile and Joshua were first cousins, Joshua being twenty-three years older than Savile, and John, Joshua's nephew, was the same age as Savile, both twenty-seven in 1770. Savile's son, Savile jr, married Rhoda Green of Swinton, daughter of William Green, probably Joshua's brother. Joshua's second wife, Judith, was sister to John Barwick, a partner in the firm.

Savile is first mentioned in connection with the pottery in 1774.[5] He was book-keeper at the pottery. Savile jr joined the firm, becoming its agent in Rio de Janeiro, where he died.[12]

John Green was born in London in 1743, the son of the Rev John Green of Soho. He must have been a partner in 1770, as he is first mentioned in connection with the pottery in January 1771 regarding the insurance of the pottery buildings. In an agreement concerning the flint mill at Thorp Arch, dated 1775, he is described as a potter of Hunslet. He is the only one of the early partners described as a potter, and it is assumed that he ran the works. During the 1790s he was in financial difficulties and sold his shares in the Leeds Pottery.[13] In 1800 he went bankrupt,[14] left

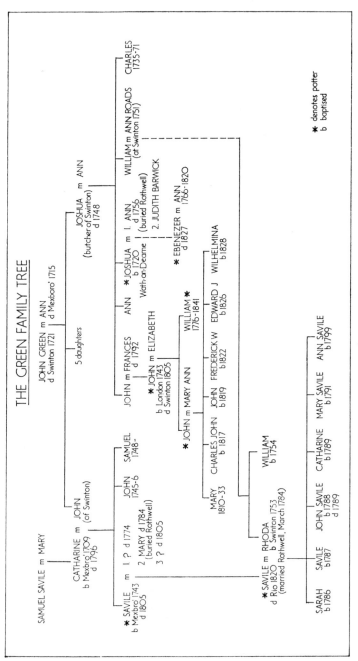

THE GREEN FAMILY TREE

FIG 3

Leeds, and settled at Newhill, near Swinton, establishing the Don Pottery at Swinton in 1801 and being joined there by his sons John and William.

Joshua Green, baptised at Wath-on-Dearne in 1720, had three brothers—the Rev John Green mentioned above, Charles, and William, probably the father of Rhoda. By 1757 he was living in the Leeds area, a friend of Richard Humble. In 1766 he occupied two closes in Meadow Lane, Hunslet, with Benjamin Russell, who at some unknown date built a pottery there, though no pottery is mentioned in the deed of 1766.[15] He lived in Middleton, south of Hunslet, being invariably described as a gentleman, and died between 1797 and 1799, when he lived at Upper Woodhouse, Rawdon. He too must have been a partner in the pottery by 1770 as he is mentioned in the insurance policy of January 1771. Ebenezer Green was Joshua's heir, probably his son, and worked at the pottery until his bankruptcy in 1820.[16]

John Barwick, a surgeon and apothecary in Leeds, presumably had only a financial interest in the pottery, possibly becoming involved through his brother-in-law Joshua Green. He was a partner in 1781, probably from the outset, and died between 1799 and 1802, his heir being his nephew William Barwick, then living in Russia in St Petersburg.[17] In 1804 two pottery shares, 'the property of a gentleman residing abroad', were advertised, probably William Barwick's. William sold one share to James Winter Butterworth in 1813, when he had returned from Russia to live in Norfolk. He probably had no physical connection with the pottery, unless he was agent for the firm in Russia, where it had a big trade.

Henry Ackroyd, yeoman, was involved with others in 1758 in selling land in Casson Close, east of the White Cloth Hall, to Charles Brandling for his wagon-way to the coal staith built north of the Hall.[18] The staith was about 170yd south of Leeds Bridge. Ackroyd bought a meeting house near the White Cloth Hall in 1763. The Hall was later used as a pottery warehouse, Joseph Humble buying it from John Green's assignees in 1800.[19] Henry Ackroyd married in Leeds in 1763, was a clothmiller in 1767, and had become a partner in the Leeds Pottery by 1781 at the latest. He died in 1788, and in the following year 'Miss Ackroyd, daughter of the late Henry Ackroyd, married the Rev. Mr Parsons', who became a partner in the pottery. Henry's widow, Sarah, and daughter Mary also inherited shares. Mary Ackroyd, described as earthenware manufacturer, went bankrupt in 1820 and left the firm.[16]

William Hartley became a partner in 1775 or 1776, when the firm's name was changed to 'Humble, Hartley, Greens & Co'. He probably came from Bradley, near Colne in Lancashire. His first wife died in 1797 and in 1800 he married Miss Hayes of Preston in Lancashire. William Hartley had died by 1813 and his son, also William, succeeded him at the pottery. William jr worked there until 1830, when he went to London. In 1820 he bought over $1\frac{1}{2}$ acres of land in Windmill Close, formerly one of the Dowbridge Closes, adjoining the Leeds Pottery.[20]

Samuel Wainwright (1747–1824)[21] was a partner in 1781, and probably earlier. Described as a gentleman, he lived at Thorp Arch at the turn of the century. His son, Samuel jr, became a potter, living at the pottery in the 1820s. He, William Hartley jr, and Ruperti were the partners when the pottery was sold in 1830;[22] and he remained at the pottery as manager until his death in 1834, in his early forties.[23]

Thomas Wainwright, postmaster of Ferrybridge, became a partner after 1781. In 1796 his daughter Jane married James Winter Butterworth and, following Thomas Wainwright's death in 1798, Butterworth became a partner in the pottery. A Kersey-mere printer in Leeds, he probably had a financial interest only. While living in Portugal in 1813 he bought one share in the pottery from William Barwick.

George Hanson, merchant of Manchester, was a partner by 1794, moving to Hunslet in the early 1800s and later living at the Pottery House. He is described as exporter of earthenware and earthenware merchant, until the mid-1820s.

Justus Christian Ruperti, potter, and Robert Nicholson, book-keeper, occupied the pottery in 1813 as managers and receivers appointed by the High Court of Chancery.[24] Ruperti later became a partner, living at the Pottery House, and remained until 1830.

Others who had a financial interest in the pottery, possibly as mortgagors, included William Wigglesworth, Nathaniel Clayton and Alexander Turner.

The pottery built in 1770 was a large affair with a flint mill on one of the Dowbridge Closes adjoining. In 1775 trouble arose over shipment of flint and the firm leased the Flint Mill at Thorp Arch, near Wetherby, until 1816,[25] when the windmill at the pottery was refitted and used for grinding flint.

By 1776 the firm was trading as 'Humble, Hartley, Greens & Co'. During the last quarter of the eighteenth century its products reached their height of perfection, and a large export trade was built up with Russia, Germany, Holland, France and Spain.

In 1785 agreement was reached with the proprietors of Swinton Pottery to amalgamate the two,[26] and John Green appears to have been in charge of both potteries. Then the original partners died, John Green, in financial trouble, left the firm in 1800, and a gradual decline set in. Friction arose between the Leeds and Swinton partners, the Leeds partners withdrew from Swinton in 1806 (see p 83), and the Leeds Pottery closed for a short time. John Brameld of the Swinton Pottery wrote and told Earl Fitzwilliam's agent in August 1810 that the closure of the Leeds Pottery had helped Swinton retrieve customers and obtain extra workmen.[27]

There was trouble in Hunslet, but by 1813 the pottery had reopened, and Ruperti and Nicholson were in occupation. The pottery continued but finances were strained, and in 1820 Ebenezer Green and Mary Ackroyd went bankrupt. The remaining partners —George Hanson, Samuel Wainwright, his son Samuel, William Hartley jr, and J. C. Ruperti—struggled on. Samuel Wainwright sr died, Hanson retired, and the others lost interest—advertising the pottery for sale in May 1826. There were four biscuit, eight glazing, and a corresponding number of hardening and enamel kilns, plus workshops, sliphouses, and the flint mill—'. . . The managing partners . . . being desirous of retiring from it . . .' The pottery was not sold until 1 May 1830, when William Hartley, J. C. Ruperti and Samuel Wainwright, 'surviving and containing partners . . . under the firm of Hartley, Greens & Co', sold it to merchants and other creditors of the firm.[22]

The pottery was again advertised the following August, but was not sold.[28] Samuel Wainwright jr remained until his death in 1834. Stephen Chappel took over as manager until January 1842, when he bought the pottery.[29] He was joined by his brother James and, employing Richard Britton as clerk, traded as 'S. Chappel & Co'. In the following December land which had held a reservoir for the use of the pottery was sold to the North Midland Railway Company.

In July 1848, after Stephen Chappel had died, a notice appeared in the *Leeds Mercury* requesting debtors and creditors to come forward and settle their affairs with his estate. The pottery was then run by assignees, Richard Britton remaining as clerk. The late firm was unable to meet its creditors and became bankrupt. Correspondence exists, dated 1849, from Samuel Warburton to a solicitor regarding negotiations for purchase of the pottery. Joshua Bower's offer of £5,000, however, was refused.[30]

In November 1849 the pottery was advertised to be sold by auction.[3] In the following January the stock, tools and utensils were also advertised for sale—15,000 to 20,000 dozen of manufactured earthenware, 'printed, blue edged, white, and yellow ware of very superior patterns and quality'.[31] Raw materials included blue clay, china clay, cream-coloured glaze and enamel colours, working and block moulds, and seventeen printing presses. The sale was expected to last 7 days.

The premises were bought by Richard Britton, who took Samuel Warburton into partnership, trading as 'Warburton & Britton'.[32] Britton ran the pottery, living at the Pottery House. Warburton died in 1863 and Richard Britton continued alone until 1872, when he took his sons, John Broadbent and Alfred, into partnership, trading as 'Richard Britton & Sons'.

The sons formed another, independent, partnership, trading from the same premises as 'J. B. & A. Britton'. In 1878 both firms went bankrupt,[33] the property being bought by the Middleton Estate & Colliery Co Ltd but remaining empty until taken over by 'Taylor Brothers', and run by Joseph Wilson Taylor, in 1881. Taylor also ran Petty's Pottery, the Leathley Lane Pottery (then called the Stafford Pottery), and Taylor's Pottery in Jack Lane. Taylor stayed for a few months only, and the pottery then closed for good.

A gasworks and industrial buildings now cover the area. Nothing is left to indicate that this was once the site of the biggest pottery in Yorkshire, producing some of the finest ware in the kingdom in the late eighteenth century.

Wares

A pottery working for over a century obviously made a vast quantity and variety of wares. The best period aesthetically ran from the inception of the pottery into the first decade of the nineteenth century. Later, taste deteriorated and pottery was just turned out to meet contemporary fashion. Luckily for the collector, it is the earlier products that have been treasured and a considerable amount survives to this day; the known products of later firms are far scarcer and, being rarely marked, are indistinguishable from the products of other potteries. The later products of the Leeds Pottery comprised almost solely domestic wares, which were not treasured and passed down the generations.

Early wares include red earthenware, saltglazed stoneware and reputedly glazed blackware of the 'Jackfield' type, although none has been identified as Leeds. Red stoneware was made in the early years, and several pieces are known with Leeds characteristics: an engine-turned coffee pot has recently come to light bearing Mark no 5a, a hitherto unknown mark.

By far the most important product was cream-coloured earthenware. The early pieces are in a deep cream, with a deep yellow tinted glaze covering the whole pot, and occasionally gathering rather thickly. Where it gathered, the glaze tended to craze, but generally the glaze was thinly applied without crazing. Crabstock handles and spouts, and strap handles with pinched ends, were soon followed by reeded, rope or double intertwined handles with leaf terminals, features now often associated with Leeds ware but used at several other factories in differing variations.[34] Knobs were often shaped like mushrooms, acorns or flowers, and the shoulders and bases of teapots often gadrooned or beaded. Much early creamware was left plain, but some was entirely covered with coloured glazes, including tortoiseshell, splashed manganese, green glaze and underglaze blue. 'Cauliflower' ware was also made. The most delightful products were the enamel painted creamwares, sometimes in manganese or green but more commonly in red and black alone, or with blue, green, yellow, pink or crimson tints.

In 1775, when William Hartley joined the firm, restrictions on the use of Cornish clay and stone were lifted and these were utilised in pottery production at Leeds, with a consequent lightening of the colour. Pierced work was then introduced. Neoclassical designs became popular, and elaborate tableware was manufactured. The pottery was light in weight and the glaze resistant to scratching.

In the last decade of the eighteenth century figures were made, some in plain creamware and some decorated in underglaze colours. The majority, however, were made in pearlware, which was introduced at this time at Leeds. The figures have a characteristic facial likeness, with snub noses and receding chins. The hollow-based plinths are deeper than those found on Staffordshire figures and the glazed interior is visible. Figures known to have been made at Leeds include 'The Seasons' (4), 'Skater', 'Falconers' (2), 'Boy with a dog', 'Musicians' (2), 'Sir Isaac Newton', 'Andromache' (see plate, p 34), 'Venus and Neptune', 'Bacchus', 'Air', 'Water', 'Minerva', 'Mars', 'Milton', 'Hamlet' or 'Prince Rupert', 'Couple with dog and foliage', 'Recumbent lion', and 'Woman with lamb'. A creamware figure of a flute player, incised underneath 'John Smith', has Leeds characteristics, particularly in the face.

Large quantities of 'Reproduction Leeds' creamware were made from about 1888, much of it impressed LEEDS * POTTERY or LEEDS POTTERY. Many figures were reproduced, together with others not mentioned above, namely a bust of Shakespeare 13in high, a group of sheep 5½in high, and a shepherd 8in high; these, together with 'Air', 'Charity' and 'Bacchus', are illustrated in a catalogue dated 1913. The reproductions generally have a greyish tinge and are often slightly crazed.

The well-known Leeds horses were made about this time, the majority being in pearlware, though creamware examples are known. Unfortunately, creamware horses have been reproduced in quantity from the original moulds. The reproduction horse illustrated in Slee's catalogue, mentioned above, has a deepish plinth, is undecorated and without harness and is 16½in high. Such reproductions could probably be decorated to order, and they were generally marked. In 1913 the horses sold at 30s new, but 'original' Leeds examples have recently sold for over £1,000 (see p 39).

Transfer printing on wares commenced at Leeds about 1780, and the use of black or brick red was followed shortly by blue. Several engravings include the words 'Leeds Pottery'. Scenes, personalities, and floral prints are known. In the early nineteenth century large quantities of transfer-printed pearlware were produced, much of it marked. The willow pattern, as elsewhere, was extremely popular, the early Leeds version showing two men on the bridge, with two small boats above and one large boat below, but no birds. Other known patterns include the following:

1 Man on horseback, two on foot with road winding to distant castle, and border of oak leaves and flowers.
2 Composite Eastern scene with palm trees, Spanish buildings, river, bridge with two figures, boat and fishermen.
3 'Scene after Claude Lorraine.' Two similar versions are known, and four differing border patterns, all depicting rural village scenes. Riley's of Burslem used a similar print (see plate, p 52).
4 The Great Wall of China (see plate, p 52).

5 The Wanderer—a man carrying a bundle on a crook, with a dog and a cottage. Illustrated by Coysh.[35]
6 'Cottage and Vase' pattern (see plate, p 52).
7 Floral groups (see plate, p 52).
8 Swans on a pond, surrounded by foliage and distant landscape.
9 Two cows in a ruined abbey or castle with a landscape background.
10 Cow standing in a landscape, with figures of Chinamen.
11 Chinoiserie scene, illustrated by Evans.[36]
12 'Chinese Junk' pattern.
13 Flowers and butterflies.
14 All-over shell design.

Transfer-printed scenes in black include more English views:

1 Church with trees and boat (see plate, p 69).
2 Cow in foreground looking at man fishing, lady on an island with distant windmill, and blackberry border.
3 Swan in foreground, tree, bridge and distant buildings (see plate, p 69.)
4 Goat looking at ruined castle, rose border.
5 Fishing scene (see plate, p 34).

Egyptian blackware tableware was introduced about 1800, but there is no evidence that ornamental blackware was made at Leeds. Many moulds for blackware were rescued from the site by the Kidsons, several of which are illustrated in their book.[37] Knobs used include a swan, lion, lapdog, and widow with barrel, again all used at other potteries, with variations. Blackware was sometimes moulded, the commonest design being a teapot with a strawberry motif round the waist; but more frequently it was engine-turned or had applied ornamentation (see Fig 4 and plate, p 34).

Prattware was certainly made at Leeds, but again was reproduced in quantity in the twentieth century. Some felspathic

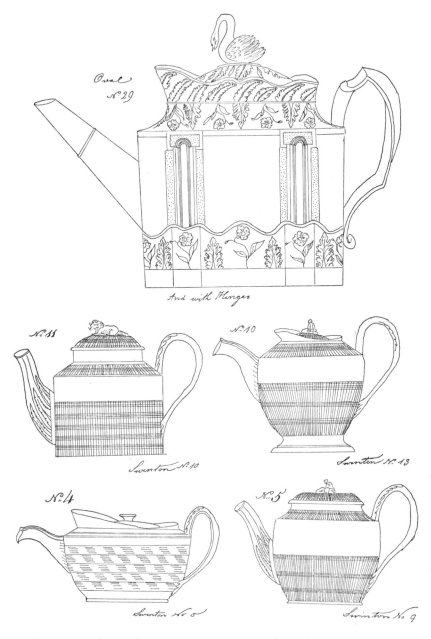

Oval
№ 29

And with Flanges

№ 11

Swinton № 10

№ 10

Swinton № 13

№ 4

Swinton № 5

№ 5

Swinton № 9

FIG 4 Tracings of blackware teapot designs from the Drawing Book
for Blackware, *c* 1800. Note that nos 4, 5, 10 and 11 are also Swinton
Pottery designs

stoneware of the 'Castleford' type was made, though it is rarely to be found marked.

In the nineteenth century several new types of decoration were introduced: Batavian ware was pearlware dipped in a café-au-lait glaze with reserve panels, left white, on which were applied transfers or paintings in underglaze blue or enamel colours; agate ware comprised differing coloured slips mixed together; and in encrusted ware, small particles of clay were fired on to a pot, usually as a central band, and it is often found on jugs and bulb pots.

Canary yellow ware, sometimes decorated with silver lustre, was made, but is rare. Drabware—pottery glazed in biscuit colour and often decorated with touches of silver or gold lustre and/or green, black and pink painting over the glaze, was also made, as were mocha ware, lustreware, and dip decorated ware.

It is difficult to cover the wares of the Leeds Pottery in greater detail. Fortunately there are many aids to identifying them, as drawing and pattern books still exist. Some teapot shapes and designs for plate rims traced from the drawing books are shown in Figs 5 and 6. Mr Towner, in his book *The Leeds Pottery*, includes tracings and reproduces the pattern book. There are four drawing books, Nos 1–4, giving a total of 351 drawings, a drawing book for blackware giving 90 designs, an enamel table service drawing book with 301 drawings, an enamelled tea ware book with 90 drawings, a handle drawing book with 27 drawings, and an ornamental drawing book with 29 drawings, at Leeds City Libraries. The original drawing books Nos 1 & 2, and a new teapot drawing book, with 78 patterns, are in the Victoria & Albert Museum's Department of Prints and Drawings.

There were two editions of the Leeds pattern book, dated 1783 and 1794, and both were reprinted. The title reads *Designs of Sundry Articles of Queen's or Cream-colour'd Earthen-Ware, manufactured by Hartley, Greens & Co. at Leeds Pottery: with a great variety of other articles. The same enamel'd, printed or ornamented with gold to any pattern; also with coats of arms, cyphers, landscapes, &c. &c. Leeds.*

There is also an agent's book at the Leeds City Libraries containing the first edition of the pattern book, priced in manuscript,

46 monochrome pen and wash drawings and 11 watercolours. Several designs do not appear in any of the known drawing books and this, together with other evidence, suggests that other drawing books existed but are now lost.[38] The keys to the pattern books were printed in English, German, French and Spanish. It is evident from remarks in the order books that wares were supplied to Swinton and Hull, and in such cases they were marked.

The serious student is advised to consult D. C. Towner's *The Leeds Pottery*, already mentioned, and J. R. and F. Kidson's *The Leeds Old Pottery*. A bibliography relating to the Leeds Pottery and its wares appeared in the Leeds Arts Calendar No 56 (1965).

Little is known of the products of the later occupants of the Leeds Pottery, but it is likely that this was utilitarian ware rather than ornamental. Five gloss, three biscuit, and four hardening kilns were operative in 1849 when the pottery was in 'full work' and capable of manufacturing nine gloss kilns of work per week. Materials offered for sale included blue and china clay, ground flint and stone, cream-colour glaze, soda, pearl ashes, underglaze and enamel colours, raw ochre, manganese, white lead and engravings—which gives some indication of the type of wares

———

Creamware: (*left to right*) Lidded creamware pot with double twisted handles; typical Leeds painting, knob and terminals; unmarked; *c* 1780; Leeds Pottery. Coffee pot with typical Leeds handle terminals and flower knob; unmarked; *c* 1780; Leeds Pottery. Terrine decorated in purple, yellow, green and dark red; unmarked; *c* 1785; Leeds Pottery. Dolphin candlestick; no 108 in the Pattern Book; unmarked; Leeds Pottery. Teapot decorated in black, iron red, having a central band of gilding with terminals picked out in blue, typical of the style of painting of the firm Robinson & Rhodes in Leeds.

Leeds Creamware: (*left to right*) Ewer; Pattern Book no 191; *c* 1790. Covered jar inscribed 'Leeds, 1817, Trade and Commerce'; painted in multicolours, edged in red-brown. Vase candlestick; no 116 in the Pattern Book; *c* 1785. Cup and saucer printed in black; typical Leeds terminals; unmarked; *c* 1785. Jug with twisted rope handles with typical Leeds terminals and flower painting in pink, iron red, green, blue, yellow and purple, with black outlines; unmarked; *c* 1780.

produced. Manufactured earthenware consisted of printed blue edged, white and yellow ware. Bricks were also made.

Jewitt states that Richard Britton made earthenware for domestic use, much of which was sent to London. He also mentions pearl white, which was used for toilet, tea and breakfast services and the bottoms of washing-machines. The pottery still made 'Rockingham Ware' (tea and coffee pots and other articles), Egyptian black glazed wares, and yellow earthenware in clay from nearby Wortley.

Marks

See nos 1–10, p 241.

REPRODUCTION LEEDS POTTERY, SENIOR AND MORTON

James Wraith Senior and John Thomas Morton are best known for their creamware, which is sometimes called 'Slee's Leeds.' In fact W. W. Slee was a Leeds antique dealer, not a potter; he marketed Senior's products but had no connection with Morton.

Leeds Pottery: (*left to right*) Splashed manganese decorated creamware coffee pot with typical Leeds terminals and knob; unmarked; c 1780. Pearlware figure of a musician; mark no 1; c 1790. Pearlware covered urn inscribed 'Jerusalem In Its Present State'; mark no 6 impressed in side of base; c 1810–20. Decorated in multicolours with red-brown edges. Creamware mug inscribed 'Enas Pattison 1802'; there were many named and dated mugs and jugs of this type made in 1802; unmarked, but typical of many with mark no 1. Pearlware figure of Andromache, painted in green, dark red, mauve, crimson, orange and brown with traces of gilding; mark no 1; c 1790–1800.

Pearlware coffee pot printed in black, touched up in green and yellow-brown; Don Pottery, mark no 85; tip of spout replaced. Pearlware sugar and cover; printed in black; unmarked, but other pieces in the service marked no 1; Leeds Pottery. Black basalt teapot; Leeds Pottery; no 29 in the Drawing Book for Blackware; unmarked. Black basalt jug; Leeds Pottery; mark no 1.

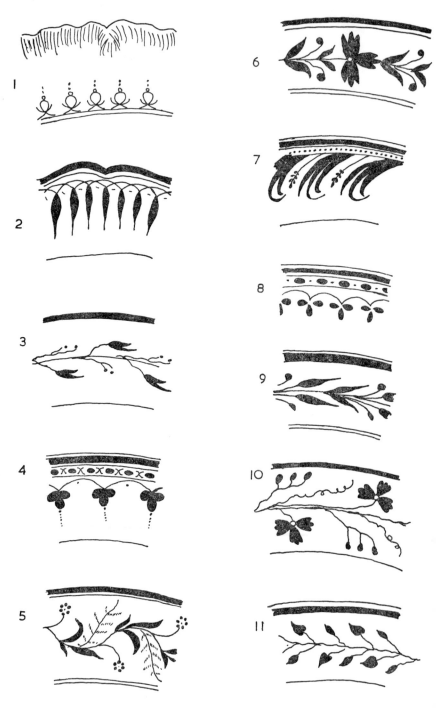

FIG 5   Tracings of painted designs for plate edges from the Enamell'd Table Service Drawing Book, 1800–20. No 1 comes from Drawing Book No 1, *c* 1780

Fig 6   Tracings of Leeds Pottery teapot shapes. Nos 324, 339, 340, 345 and 346 come from Drawing Book No 2, *c* 1803; nos 411, 412, 428 and 429 from Drawing Book No 3, *c* 1814

Most of the wares are reproduction wares from the old Leeds Pottery.

J. W. Senior, born 1854, started work at the Leeds Old Pottery in 1865. He worked at several potteries in Hunslet before starting up on his own, making pot boots and trinkets and using cast-off moulds from local potteries, including the Leeds Pottery. He was joined by his brother Jack for a short period, and in 1884 started the 'Hunsletesque Company' in Hills Yard, off Meadow Lane, Hunslet. Two artists from Burmantofts—Rowland Charles Brown and Harold Leech—joined the firm, which was renamed 'The Leeds Art Pottery', and made slipware and hand-painted tiles.

In 1890 the Leeds Art Pottery moved into the Leathley Lane Pottery (described by Morton as 'Taylor's Low Pottery'), where over forty hands were employed producing majolica ware, slipware, and tiles (mainly hand-painted). About 1892, Senior took some workmen from the Leeds Art Pottery and founded the 'Woodlesford Art Pottery', in the old pottery there, making the same type of wares. A few years later Senior left Woodlesford and started up again in a yard off Balm Road, Hunslet, where he made reproduction 'Leeds' creamware which was marketed by W. W. Slee.

In 1907 Morton joined the firm, followed by George Wraith Senior, son of the owner, in 1908. J. W. Senior died the following year and Morton left shortly afterwards. George Senior was joined by his brother James, and they continued making creamware, specialising in ornate pierced work.

In 1913 the firm published a catalogue with the royal coat of arms printed on the cover and the following words: 'Under The Patronage of Her Majesty Queen Alexandra LEEDS POTTERY'. The title page bears the coat of arms and 'Reproductions of Leeds Pottery, Queen's Ware. Decorated and Silver Lustre, Basalt, &c., &c. W. W. Slee, 30 Duncan Street, Leeds, Eng.' There are twelve pages of photographs, showing 89 items numbered between 502 and 628. Obviously there were other catalogues and a great variety of items must have been made. Pieces illustrated include highly pierced ornamental creamware vases, urns, plates, shell dishes, baskets, chestnut bowls, comports, candlesticks, a quintail flower horn, leaf dishes, sauce boat and puzzle jugs. The figures illustrated are 'Bacchus', 7in high; 'Venus' (called 'Charity' in the catalogue), 6½in high; 'Air', 6in high; a bust of Shakespeare on a pedestal, 13in high; a group of sheep, 5½in high; and the horse, 16½in high, already mentioned (see p 28).

Eight pieces of 'Prattware' are illustrated: six jugs listed as 'Hunting', 'Cricket', 'Admiral Nelson', 'Peace and Plenty', 'Volunteers', and 'Shooting' (6in high except the 'Cricket' jug, which is 6½in), plus a teacaddy called 'Beau and Belle', and a cream jug shaped like a lady's head. On the same page appear illustrations of a pistol and a cannon, both with silver lustre decoration. The last page gives a brief history of the Leeds Pottery and finishes: '1888 to Present Date The manufacture of Leeds Pottery revived in 1888 by W. W. Slee, employing workmen and using many of the original moulds and patterns obtained from the old works.'

G. W. Senior worked until 1957. He destroyed many of the old moulds, but gave some to the Abbey House Museum, Leeds. In an interview he said: 'This horse was made 65 years ago, and cannot properly be called a Leeds Pottery specimen, because it was fired long after the closure. But it looks the same, and if it fell into the wrong hands could be sold to an unsuspecting buyer as an eighteenth- or nineteenth-century piece.' Let buyers beware!

The creamware often shows a greyish tinge and crazing. Much is marked with an impressed LEEDS POTTERY in a straight neat mark, a copy of an early mark. A jardinière in brown slip is impressed ESQUE POTTERY HUNSLET LEEDS, and a low creamware candlestick GEO SENIOR LEEDS POTTERY, but these marks are very rare.

J. T. Morton, born 1875, started work with the Leeds Art Pottery in 1888 and in 1907 rejoined the Senior family; but soon he had opened his own pottery at 2 Rock Terrace, Harehills, Leeds, making similar wares to the Seniors. Morton and his son worked until the outbreak of World War I, when the pottery closed. In 1933 he built a pottery at Airey Hill, Filey, opposite Butlin's Holiday Camp on the Scarborough–Bridlington road, where he produced some beautiful examples of reproduction creamware and agate ware. The outbreak of World War II caused him to close, but at the end of the war he was able to reopen. Vibrations from nearby excavations, however, caused the perforated ware to crack while drying, and in 1947 he moved to Burniston, north of Scarborough, working there until the 1950s.

Mr Morton usually scratched his name underneath his products, and sometimes added the word 'Filey'.[39]

ROTHWELL POTTERY
Location: SE 343282

The second most important pottery in the Leeds area was built 4 miles south-east of Leeds, between the market cross and the beck in the centre of Rothwell.

In 1767 John Smith of Stainbrough, and John Pullen, a mason of Wath, leased the disused glasshouse at Rothwell from Sir William Lowther for 21 years at £15 per annum. They also leased Broomhill Close, Rothwell, for 17 years from 1772 at £7 annually. Smith and Pullen were permitted to dig clay 'for the making of Brick and other uses in the works of a pottery . . . in any such of the waste ground of the manor of Rothwell'.[40] An anonymous undated manuscript history of Rothwell states that 'The Glasshouse . . . was in the year 1768 converted into a house for the manufacture of Pots, such as are made in Burslem in Staffordshire and the trade is now very briskly carried on by Mr J. Smith, Paintor.'[41]

In 1770 Sir William Lowther leased to William Nield, gentleman,

that building commonly called the Glasshouse but now converted into a Pottery with three ovens in the same for the baking of Delpht-Ware, and . . . the Warehouse, the Hot-House, the

Turning-House, the Damp-House and the Slip-House, with a Slip-Pan and two stone Cisterns in the same, also two Sun Pans and a Slip-Pan and an Oven in the Yard.

Also leased were over 8 acres of land and buildings, including a flint mill, built on Breary Royd Bottom, for one year, renewable annually, at £34 per annum.[42]

On 29 May 1770 the following advertisement appeared in the *Leeds Mercury*: 'Rothwell Potworks. One third share of Rothwell Potworks to be disposed of. Any person intending to purchase, may apply to Mr Smith at Rothwell, one of the proprietors.' By the following September John Sacheverele had joined the firm, probably having taken the advertised share. Sir William Lowther wrote that he had demised unto John Smith, John Sacheverele and William Nield, Breary Royd and Breary Royd Bottom in Rothwell.[43] John Pullen is not mentioned again, but James Ramsey became a partner.

By 1772 the pottery was working at a loss, and John Platt, late of the Rotherham Pottery, was called in; his diary for December 1772 reads: 'At Rothwell valuing building and stock of John Smith ye Paintor and three more Partners of a Pottery at Rothwell near Leeds, which they gave up, the works not answering nor could they carry on without more capital spent.'[44] The valuation mentions James Ramsey as a partner, though he was recently deceased.

John Platt detailed the stock and buildings, valuing the pottery and contents at £449 and the flint mill and contents at £441 6s 5d. The buildings had cost a great deal more, but 'are valued at a price a purchaser need not scruple to give for them'. Although Platt did not put a price on the models and moulds, he commented that they had cost almost £200. Fineware was the staple product, but bricks were also made. There were 63 tons of Devonshire clay at 29s per ton, and large quantities of flint and white and red lead. Platt wrote: 'The mill with machinery (exclusive of all the materials) has not cost less than £600 and is believed to be the most compleat of the kind in England.'[45]

Assignees took over, but William Nield remained as agent in the warehouse. The whole concern was advertised for sale by auction in the *Leeds Mercury* on 13 April 1773:

Rothwell Potworks, in the county of York, situated within 4 miles from Leeds and 5 from Wakefield, 1 mile from the turnpike road leading to Wakefield, and within a small distance from the navigable rivers, Aire and Calder, the neighbourhood of which Pottery abounds with a great variety of clay and coal. The buildings consist of a large hovel containing 3 kilns, and capable of containing 4, with all proper conveniences; two large warehouses, and other convenient houses, for carrying the pottery business in the most commodious and extensive manner, wherein are a large quantity of Devonshire clays, and all tools and utensils necessary for workmen, with a great variety of original and working moulds in the newest taste.

All the buildings open into a spacious yard, inclosed and secured with a substantial wall. Also several dwelling-houses for workmen contiguous, all in the best repair and condition; together with a new erected flint mill, which works one pan of 15 feet, one of 5, and another of 3 feet diameter. Also a small pan for grinding of Enamel colours, and a pair of stones for grinding of palister, clays, etc., with conveniences for erecting a machine for slip and beating of clay. A dwelling-house for the flint-grinder, and 3 spacious rooms, well lighted and fitted up, for the Enamel work, and 2 reservoirs wherein are 25000 pecks of ground flint, and other suitable conveniences, and about 9 acres of very good meadow ground adjoining the flint mill.

The whole of the said buildings and grounds are held by lease for the term of 21 years, under Sir W. Lowther, Bart., at the yearly rent of £44, whereof about 19 years remain to expire, renewable at the end of 7 and 14 years for a further term of 21 years. Which lease, with the clays, utensils, moulds, and materials, and a stock of ware on the premises, are intended to be sold to the best bidder, on Tuesday, the 22nd day of June next, between the hours of 3 and 6 in the afternoon, at the house of Mrs Cooke, the Old King's Arms, in Leeds, according to conditions then and there to be produced, unless before sold by private contract, of which timely notice will be given. For further particulars enquire of Thomas Fenton, Esq., of Rothwell Haigh, and Mr Thomas Walker, of the Glass House, both in the parish of Rothwell, and Mr Samuel Keeling, of Rothwell, aforesaid, to whom John Smith & Company, the late proprietors of the said Pottery, have assigned the same, together with the rest of their copartnership effects, in trust for the benefit of their partnership creditors, and all such persons as do now stand indebted to the same copartnership are desired forthwith to pay the same to the said trustees, or they will be sued without further notice.

And for a view of the premises to be sold enquire at the Pottery. ☞ The works are carried on, and the warehouse open for sale, as usual.

The pottery was not sold and was advertised again from April to June 1774.[46] There was still no buyer, but reputedly much of the stock was disposed of, the Leeds Pottery being one of the main purchasers.

In January 1775 Thomas Carr, who worked in the pottery warehouse, was charged with stealing pottery from both the warehouse of the assignees and other pottery 'not the property of the above'. William Nield gave evidence.[47] Nield ran the pottery until his death in the late 1770s, when he was succeeded by his widow.

The *Leeds Intelligencer* of 11 July 1780 states: 'Sunday last was married at Rothwell, Mr Taylor of Thorp, near this town, to the agreeable Mrs Nield of Rothwell Pottery.' William Taylor then ran the pottery until 1785,[48] when he joined William Thompson at the Castleford Pottery, remaining there until it was sold to Dunderdale & Plowes in 1790. In 1791 a William Taylor, in all probability the same man, established the Swillington Bridge Pottery.

In 1785 the Rothwell Pottery was taken over by a woman, E. Medley. The following notice appeared in the *Leeds Mercury* of 21 February 1786:

E. Medley of Rothwell, Begs Leave to inform the Public, that she has purchased the Stock in Trade, and all the Utensils belonging to the Pottery at Rothwell near Leeds and has also taken the Potworks there, lately occupied by Mr Taylor. All persons who please to favor her with their Orders may depend upon being well supplied with the very best Articles, both in the Fine and Common Ware and at the most reasonable prices.

How long E. Medley remained is not known. The lease was due to expire in 1788; William Taylor is given as tenant in the Land Tax Assessments until that date, presumably subletting to E. Medley. The Land Tax Assessments for 1789–90 give Burton and Willans as tenants, but it is not known to what use they put the buildings. There are no further references to the pottery.

Wares

Until recently nothing was known of the products of the Rothwell Pottery apart from the information in the advertisements. It is clear that both local clay was used for coarseware and brickmaking and Devonshire clay for fineware. Three rooms were used for enamel work, indicating a large output of painted ware. John Smith himself was a painter. Several potters named in the Rothwell Parish Registers are later found at other local fineware potteries, ie Leeds, Castleford and Ferrybridge.

Sherds found on the site include white saltglazed earthenware; quantities of glazed and unglazed creamware; pearlware, notably the blue 'grass' border; some green glazed wares; and deep red bodied coarseware, glazed on the interior only, with a cream slip sometimes splashed with manganese brown. Other coarseware pieces had a very dark brown or black glaze.

The commonest wasters were pieces of creamware plates, revealing quite distinctive border patterns (see p 45), and several complete plates have been identified from these (see plate, p 51). Edges were often painted green, but many were left completely plain. The cream glaze has a yellowish tint, and occasional orange brown spots are apparent in it, particularly on the undersides of some pieces; this fault is also observable on some Castleford pieces. The two enamelled plates illustrated (p 51) are thought to

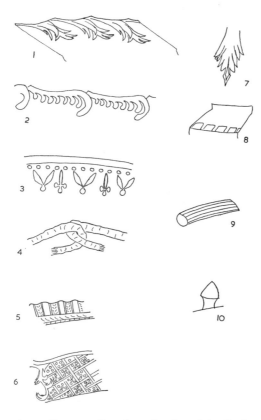

FIG 7 Drawings of wasters found on the site of the Rothwell Pottery. Plate rims nos 1–3 are illustrated on p 51. No 6 is saltglazed, no 7 depicts lower terminal of a handle, no 8 a teapot shoulder, no 9 a rope handle, and no 10 a knob

be Rothwell, since no other pottery is known to have used this exact 'feather' border of eight equally spaced barbs, though many factories used variations.

Other unglazed finds included rope handles, leaf terminals to handles, gadrooned and beaded teapot shoulders, double inter-twined handles, ribbing, basket work designs, and ribbed handles ranging from a single central groove only to a wide handle with seven grooves. The only knob found had a simple curved conical shape.

Decorated pieces were relatively scarce, but a quantity of un-glazed sherds were 'marbled' in black and brick red, on a white body, some having ribbed edges. Mottled manganese splashed creamware was found, both in brown on a deep cream glaze, and in grey-brown used in conjunction with green. Pieces of Rothwell are probably attributed to better-known factories.

In 1775 Thomas Carr was charged at Wakefield with stealing from the pottery 'Thirty Six Dozen of the best Plates called Queens Ware Several Pieces of Enamelled Ware of Different Sorts' and 'Earthen plain Table plates . . . three small painted Earthen Plates . . . Earthen Terene, Earthern Tea pots, Earthen basins, Earthen painted Juggs, Earthen picle leaf'. A jug found at Carr's house was identified, 'there being none of the kind made in this kingdom as he is informed and believes . . .'

Marks

There are no known marks.

SAMUEL SHAW'S POTTERY, ROTHWELL
Location unknown

It has been mistakenly assumed in the past that Samuel Shaw bought the Rothwell Pottery following the advertisement of May 1774, as on 21 June 1774 he advertised in the *Leeds Mercury* as follows: 'A New Pottery. This is to inform the public that Samuel Shaw of Rothwell, potter (late from Staffordshire), makes and sells all sorts of cream colour, red, yellow, and painted wares at his new pottery in Rothwell, where tradesmen and others may depend on being served at the very lowest prices, wholesale and retail.'

However, in an indenture dated 2 February 1774, 4 months

before the advertisement of the sale of the Rothwell Pottery, Samuel Shaw and his wife Hannah demised 'all that cottage . . . also a stable lately converted into a cottage or dwellinghouse with a barn or laith situate in Rothwell part whereof is now used as an Oven or Firestead for the burning of Potts or earthenware . . . now in the proper occupation of Samuel Shaw . . .'[49] Hannah Shaw inherited the property from her father; she married Samuel Shaw at Rothwell in 1771.

It is clear that this was indeed a new pottery, as stated in Shaw's advertisement, and was not connected with the Rothwell Pottery.

Samuel Shaw died in 1776, and in the July of that year the following notice appeared in the *Leeds Mercury*: 'To be Sold, By Wholesale or Retail, at the house of the late Samuel Shaw, in Rothwell, deceased. All sorts of Cream-colour'd & Painted Earthenware, also all kinds of Coarse Ware. The House, Workhouse and all the Tools and Implements belonging to the Pottery to be Lett.'

The two potteries in Rothwell apparently made similar wares.

HUNSLET HALL POTTERY, PETTY'S POTTERY, VICTORIA POTTERY
Location: SE 297319

Situated on the corner of Hunslet Hall Road and Beeston Road (a continuation of Meadow Lane) in an area known as Holbeck Lane End and just inside the Holbeck boundary, the pottery was known variously as Hunslet Hall Pottery, Holbeck Pottery or The Pottery, Holbeck Lane End; and later, when Cartledge's Pottery opposite Hunslet Hall became known as Hunslet Hall Pottery, one part was called Petty's Pottery and the other the Victoria Pottery.

In February 1800 Samuel Rainforth of Holbeck, potter, leased from Frances, Lady Irwin, of Temple Newsam, several houses and shops which he 'pulled down and thereupon erected a Pottery Oval and Warehouse' with another pottery warehouse adjoining. Rainforth was to pay £3 per annum, and the lease was for 21 years.[50]

Rainforth, born 1764, had previously worked at Swillington Bridge (see p 74).[51]

The 1809 *Leeds Directory* lists 'Rainforth & Co', Pottery, Meadow Lane. Rainforth's partner may have been Samuel Petty, but he is invariably described as a bread baker at this time. Rainforth died in February 1817, aged fifty-three, described as a pot manufacturer of Hunslet Hall Pottery.

The next occupants were Samuel Petty and Matthew Hewitt, who traded as 'Petty & Hewitt' or 'Petty & Co' c 1814–24. Petty's son, Samuel, joined the firm and from 1825 to 1845 they traded as 'Samuel Petty & Son'. John Dale was manager in 1826. They had a retail shop at 135 Briggate, Leeds, where they sold pottery and glass 'from the first manufacturers'; the shop was advertised to let in 1826.

In 1845 the premises were divided and George Leather and Charles W. Wardle, trading as 'Leather & Wardle', occupied part of the premises, which they named the Victoria Pottery. William Jepson occupied this part from 1849 to 1853, when John Mills took over.

In 1846 Petty left the pottery, advertising from July to September:

POTTERY TO BE LET and may be entered to immediately, that well accustomed Pottery, situate at HOLBECK-LANE END, near Leeds. On the premises are a steam engine of 10 Horse Power, for Grinding Flint, Two Sliphouses, Two Biscuit Ovens, Four Glazing Do., with Warehousing, workshops, very convenient and replete with Utensils and fixtures, Stable Yard with stabling and sheds. For Rent and particulars, enquire of Mr Petty, Moorville-Terrace, near the Works.

When Petty gave up, John Mills, who had worked another small pottery nearby, moved into Petty's section of the pottery, taking over the whole works in 1853. In 1861, however, Joseph Wilson Taylor occupied the portion called Petty's Pottery, John Mills keeping the Victoria Pottery, where he was joined by his sons John, James and William, trading by 1866 as 'J. Mills & Son'.

From 1867 the directories give 'Mills Brothers' or 'John Mills & Brothers'. They gave up the works between 1872 and 1875.

Joseph Wilson Taylor worked Petty's Pottery until 1881. He was also at the Stafford or Leathley Lane Pottery and in 1881 ran the Leeds Old Pottery.

Wares

Several pieces of pottery impressed 'RAINFORTH & C' are known; they include creamware of rather poor quality, but none the less attractive, painted both over and under the glaze. Blue and black transfer-printed earthenware is more frequently found (see plate, p 51). The pottery is of medium weight and the glaze on the pearlware a light blue. Examples can be seen at the Yorkshire Museum, the Victoria & Albert Museum, the Fitzwilliam Museum and Cusworth Hall Museum, Doncaster.

Until recently no marked examples of Petty's wares were known, but a pair of marked blue transfer-printed plates have now been found (see plate, p 51). Unmarked pieces with the same print are quite common, and one plate, identical to the marked ones, with an impressed crown, has recently been found on the site of the pottery.

Two plaster block moulds, the back of one inscribed 'Petty & Son 1841', depict Shylock and Falstaff; they were probably used for making reliefs for application to larger wares, or for making small plaques. From Petty's time onwards it is likely that only utilitarian domestic earthenware was made.

During the years 1848–51 John Mills is listed as an earthenware manufacturer and dealer in china and lustreware, and later as a manufacturer of Rockingham Ware. Before taking over the pottery he made yellow ware and Egyptian black, which he possibly continued making here.

Terraced houses now cover the site, but there is a vast rebuilding programme under way in the area, and when the site is cleared, further evidence may come to light.

As far as is known, Samuel Rainforth, the founder of this

pottery, was the only early potter in Leeds, apart from those at the Leeds Old Pottery, to make cream-coloured earthenware.

Marks

See nos 11–14, p 241.

CARTLEDGE'S POTTERY, HUNSLET HALL POTTERY
Location: SE 299317

Situated on the south side of Hunslet Hall Road, opposite Hunslet Hall.

The first documentary reference to the pottery comes in a deed dated 1809, which includes '. . . two houses with the workshops, warehouses, pott ovens, kilns, dryinghouse, stables and other buildings', and two closes called Cinnamon Fields, occupied by Thomas Cartledge and Samuel Thompson.[52]

Thomas Cartledge's father, Joseph, was a potter of Middleton, just south of Hunslet. In 1765 Thomas married Elizabeth Dennison, daughter of the Joseph Dennison who advertised his pottery for sale in 1769. In an indenture of 1782 Thomas is described as a potter of Middleton, but by 1799 had moved to Hunslet Hall and probably established the pottery there. By 1813 Thomas's son, William, had joined him at the pottery, and by 1823 they owned 'workshops, two kilns, bottle warehouse, pot shop, sheds . . .' and a clay pit.[53]

———

Rothwell Pottery: Creamware plates with border designs found on the site. The outer and top plates are edged in green. The top plate is painted under the glaze in manganese brown with touches of green and yellow; the centre bottom plate is painted over the glaze in green and purple. See p 44.

Hunslet Hall Pottery: (*left to right*) Blue printed mug; Rainforth & Co, 1800–15; mark no 11. Blue printed plate 'Gazebo' pattern; Petty & Co, 1817–45; mark no 12. Blue printed plate; Rainforth & Co, 1800–15; mark no 11. See p 49.

The pottery was advertised for sale in the *Leeds Mercury* in 1827, when it was described as a Black Earthenware Manufactory with valuable bed of potclay. It was not sold.

Thomas and William Cartledge had both died by 1830, and William's widow, Elizabeth, continued running the pottery until the early 1840s when she died, and her daughter Rebecca, the last of the family, ran it until her death. In May 1844 the pottery, now called the Hunslet Hall Pottery, was again advertised for sale, in three lots. Lot 1 comprised the pottery '. . . for many years past used for the manufacturing of Black Earthenware' and West Cinnamon Field, with 'valuable beds of white or firebrick clay, blue clay, and common clay, all very good quality and considerable thickness'. Lot 2 comprised land containing brick clay, supposedly over 10ft thick, and Lot 3 comprised six cottages.[54]

Lots 1 and 2 were bought by Thomas Nunns, an earthenware manufacturer of Hunslet Hall, formerly employed by the Cartledges. Two years later, however, the pottery was sold for £570

Blue printed plates: (*top row*) 'Buffalo and Ruins' pattern, Dunderdale & Co, Castleford Pottery, c 1810; mark no 172; also known in brown. 'Three Chinamen' pattern; Ferrybridge Pottery, c 1800–10; mark no 156. 'Reindeer' pattern; Don Pottery, c 1810; mark no 86; also known in black. 'Scene after Claude Lorraine' inscribed 'J. & S. Gott, 1819'; Leeds Pottery; mark no 6. There are two versions known from Leeds, and four different border patterns; also made elsewhere.
(*Bottom row*) 'Cottage and Vase' pattern, Leeds Pottery, c 1830; mark no 1. Tongue dish, 'Great Wall of China' pattern; Leeds Pottery, c 1800–20; mark no 1. 'Floral Sprays' pattern, Leeds Pottery, c 1820–40; mark no 1.

Swinton Pottery: (*top row*) Blue printed 'Don Quixote' pattern; mark no 50. Blue printed sauce-boat stand 'Castle of Rochefort' pattern; mark no 53 without the outer rim. Blue printed 'Llandig's Blackberry' pattern; mark no 50. (*Bottom row*) Blue printed 'Parroquet' pattern; mark nos 50 and 61. Chalk body plate painted in blue, green and red; mark no 50; note identical moulding on plate, p 88. Blue printed 'Twisted Tree' pattern, painted in orange, pink and green; mark nos 50 and 60. Blue printed soapbox lid 'Boys Fishing' pattern; unmarked; wasters found on the site.

to Robert Paul of York Road Pottery, Leeds. By 1849 Abraham Crossley was the tenant, remaining until the late 1860s. In 1865 Paul sold the pottery to builders, who kept much of the land but resold the pottery to John and Edward Meyers, earthenware manufacturers, in May 1870. They took William Greenwood into partnership, but in 1873 Robert Allison, potter of Hunslet, and William Lupton, grocer, took over the works.

Allison retired from the concern later in the same year and sold his share to Abraham Crossley. The latter died soon after and Lupton became sole owner.

The final transaction took place in 1896, when Lupton sold the pottery to a cab proprietor, already in occupation, and it closed.[55]

Wares and Marks

There are no known pieces. Stoneware bottles and black earthenware were made in the early years. It has been suggested that creamware pieces with the impressed initials 'HM' might have been made here, but it seems very unlikely that any creamware or fineware of the quality of the pieces so marked was ever made.

Later occupants are all given as earthenware manufacturers rather than potters, implying that domestic earthenware of a better type was made, predominantly white printed ware. Superficial investigations on the site confirmed this, though it has obviously been much disturbed since the days of the pottery.

LEATHLEY LANE POTTERY, LEEDS UNION POTTERY, HUNSLET NEW POTTERY, STAFFORD POTTERY, LEEDS ART POTTERY
Location: SE 304322

The pottery was built on part of Windmill Close in Leathley Lane, Hunslet, north-east of the Leeds Old Pottery, in 1824 by Reuben North, who traded with John North sr and John North jr as 'North & Co'.[56] In 1830 the works were known as 'The Leeds Union Pottery'. In financial trouble, the Norths sold the pottery to John Hepworth in 1832, and he, with his son John, changed the name to 'The Hunslet New Pottery'. Hepworth advertised as follows in 1835:

STONE BOTTLE MANUFACTORY, HUNSLET . . . JOHN HEPWORTH begs to call the attention of Porter and Spirit Merchants, Ginger Beer Manufacturers and others, to his highly improved STONE BOTTLES, which are warranted glazed inside and not to absorb . . . constitute his Bottles the first in the Trade . . .

In October 1837 Edmund Dawson, a colliery proprietor who had connections with the Leeds Pottery, bought the works and, taking in Stephen Chappel jr, traded as 'Dawson & Chappel'. Stephen Chappel ran the works, while his father and uncle were at the Leeds Pottery.

In 1842 a receiver was appointed and the stock and effects of the late partnership of 'Dawson & Chappel' were advertised for sale;[57] in the following year the pottery, then called the 'Leathley Lane Pottery', was advertised to let.[58] There were two biscuitware, two glazing, one stoneware, and two saltware kilns, plus hardening and enamelling kilns. Nearly new engravings, block and working moulds, and clay were included.

The pottery was leased by James Chappel, who was also, with his brother Stephen sr, at the Leeds Pottery; but they ran into financial difficulties and in 1848 the utensils, stock and James Chappel's personal effects were advertised for sale.[59]

The pottery was taken over by James Shackleton, Benjamin Taylor and William Gibson of the Woodlesford Pottery, trading as 'Shackleton, Taylor & Co'. Shackleton and Gibson lived in Hunslet, and Taylor lived in Woodlesford. The partnership appears to have been dissolved in the 1860s, for in 1866 'William Gibson & Co' are listed as operating at Leathley Lane and from 1861 B. Taylor on his own at Woodlesford.

In 1867 Joseph Wilson Taylor, son of George Taylor (of G. & S. Taylor, Hunslet New Pottery) was in occupation, trading as 'Joseph Taylor & Co' or 'J. Taylor & Co'. He bought the works in July 1871 and changed the name yet again to 'The

Stafford Pottery', but it was known locally as 'Taylor's Low Pottery'.

In 1890 the Leeds Art Pottery, run by Rowland C. Brown, Harold Leech and James W. Senior, took over the premises. After some disagreement, Senior, together with certain workpeople, left and founded the Woodlesford Art Pottery.

The Leeds Art Pottery became a limited company and the premises were bought by Rudolph Hauptman, the pottery manager, in 1895; he sold them in 1899 to 'The Leeds Art Pottery & Tile Co Ltd'. In the following year the company went into liquidation. The firm is listed in directories, however, until 1909.

Wares

In the early years blackware, stoneware, stone bottles and earthenware were made. By 1843, judging from the advertisements, goods produced ranged from fine enamelled and transfer-printed ware to stone bottles, saltglazed stoneware and tiles. Items advertised include figure moulds, 100 China tea and coffee services of various patterns, copper engravings, china clay, ball clay, bottle clay, ground flint, salt kiln bars, a lustre kiln and so on. The pottery was capable of making four gloss kilns and two salt-ware kilns per week.

Later occupants made transfer-printed and painted white earthenware, and blue glazed pottery with applied sprigged decoration in white. They also made banded ware, generally blue and black bands on a white base, and horizontally ribbed pottery. Blue 'grass' edged plates were made as well. The pottery, of white clay, tends to be thickish and fairly heavy, with a bluish glaze.

The Leeds Art Pottery produced fashionable art pottery, similar to wares made at Linthorpe and Burmantofts. Decorative tiles, hand-painted slipware and majolica ware in vivid colours were made, some of it being marked.

Marks

No marks are known and no pieces can be attributed to the early proprietors of this pottery. The Leeds Art Pottery sometimes impressed its name or initials or a combination of both (see nos 16–18, p 241).

TAYLOR'S OR HUNSLET NEW POTTERY
Location: SE 308318

Situated on Branson Nook Close on the south side of Jack Lane, Hunslet, adjoining Allison's Pottery to the west.

William Taylor, described as a potter in 1817, built the pottery before 1823, when he owned a dipping house, two pot kilns, slip-house, turning house, warehouse, shops and stables. (The name William Taylor is common throughout the area in connection with potters. In 1773 William Taylor of 'Pottery' baptised his son William at Leeds Parish Church; and another ran the Rothwell, Castleford and Swillington Bridge Potteries; but it is not known if all the William Taylors belonged to the same family.)

On Taylor's death in the late 1830s, his sons George and Samuel took over the pottery, trading as 'George & Samuel Taylor' or 'G. & S. Taylor'. In 1839 it was known as the Hunslet New Pottery.

G. & S. Taylor, with George's son James, bought the adjoining Allison's Pottery in 1854, and thenceforth ran the two works as one.[60] George died in the mid-1860s, but three of his sons—James, Joseph Wilson and Charles—continued in partnership with their uncle Samuel until he retired in 1866.

James Taylor retired shortly after, and the works were continued by Charles and Joseph W. Taylor for some years. Charles lived nearby, and probably ran the works, as Joseph was proprietor of the Stafford Pottery in Leathley Lane, Petty's Pottery and the Leeds Old Pottery during this period. Charles died in 1885. A James William Taylor is later listed as potter here, with Frederick Taylor as book-keeper. The pottery was closed in 1887.

Wares

There are no known pieces. Excavations on the site have produced quantities of white earthenware transfer-printed in blue, black and mauve, and some crudely painted ware, the majority in a dull tree green and red. Some banded ware was found, one piece with a crude leaf handle terminal, as was some brown stoneware, but the latter may have been made at Allison's Pottery. The earthenware was of medium weight and the glaze was the usual blue-tinted. Directories list the Taylors as potters or earthenware manufacturers.

Marks

No marks have hitherto been recorded for this pottery, but recently two pieces of willow pattern from local sources with marks (see nos 46 and 47, p 245) have been found, and it is possible that these relate to the firm of 'G. & S. Taylor'. Some confusion does arise, however, regarding mark no 46, as it appears on the same piece as no 157 (see p 171), used at Ferrybridge in the late 1840s. It appears that the Taylors of Hunslet bought biscuitware from Ferrybridge when the Taylors there ceased production.

ALLISON'S POTTERY, JACK LANE POTTERY
Location: SE 308318

Built on Branson Nook Close on the south side of Jack Lane, Hunslet, and bounded on the west by a lane leading to Hunslet Moor, later called Hillidge Road, and on the east by Taylor's Pottery.

The pottery was occupied in 1803 by Robert and Joseph Allison, when Robert mortgaged the land and two new houses, with warehouses, workshops and other buildings. The name of John Allison, potter, is recorded in 1807.

In the Hunslet Valuation List, 1822–3, John Allison is listed as owning a house, stable, pottery kiln, sheds, workshops, warehouses and sliphouse. In the following year he built another kiln, hothouse and sliphouse to replace some old buildings.

From the 1830s the pottery was called the Jack Lane Pottery. John Allison sold it to George and Samuel Taylor, who occupied the adjoining pottery, in 1854, and the two works were then run as one by the Taylors.

Wares

Brown and black earthenware were the principal products, and stoneware, particularly bottles, was introduced in later years. There are no known marks or identified pieces.

LANE END POTTERY
Location: SE 297321

This pottery is described in the nineteenth century variously as at Holbeck Lane End, Beeston Road or Elland Road, which has caused some confusion. In fact it was then situated on a triangular plot bounded on two sides by Elland and Beeston Roads, in an area known as Holbeck Lane End.

The pottery was built before 1776, when a close of land called the Croft and several newly erected cottages '. . . with the Pott Ovens . . . situate at Holbeck Lane End, occupied by John Halliwell, John Fletcher and Thomas Booth',[61] were mortgaged.

In 1816 John Clark was the tenant, and he remained until at least 1841, but by 1847 John Sykes was in occupation. He bought the premises, with its two kilns, in 1859, and was succeeded by his son John, who took Joseph Carr Dickinson into partnership. In 1871 Dickinson bought the pottery, which he occupied with Sarah Ann Sykes, spinster, and continued to trade as 'Sykes & Dickinson'. In 1892 Dickinson was trading alone, still under the old name and he remained active until early in the twentieth century. Miss E. L. Dickinson is given as occupant in 1907–11. In the following year 'Crossley & Co' took over, Joseph Crossley being listed in 1916 and Abraham Crossley in 1923. There are no further entries in directories.

Wares and Marks

Nothing is known of the early products, but probably traditional earthenware was made from local clay. John Clark made earthenware in 1817, and blackware, brownware and stone bottles thereafter; Sykes & Dickinson made blackware; and Crossley & Co made flowerpots.

There are no known pieces or marks.

RUSSELL'S POTTERY, MEADOW LANE POTTERY, HOLBECK POTTERY
Location: SE 298323

Situated on West Field Close, west of Meadow Lane and just south of its junction with Jack Lane, in Holbeck.

In 1766 two closes on the west side of Meadow Lane were occupied by Benjamin Russell and Joshua Green. Although there is no mention of buildings in the deed, this land probably became the site of Russell's Pottery,[62] which he occupied by 1791, when it was owned by James Smith. Russell's son William joined him, and they traded as 'Benjamin Russell & Son'. By 1809 William Russell was the sole occupant; he bought the property in 1814, enlarged the works and took in his son Charles.

William Russell died in the early 1830s, and Charles took in his son Joseph, who, after his father's death, was joined by his son Edward, trading from 1848 as 'J. & E. Russell' or 'J. Russell & Co'. Other Russells recorded as potters include John, Frederick, and the latter's son William.

The pottery closed in 1878. The site is now partially covered by a car saleroom.

Wares

There are no known pieces or marks. William Russell made blackware, brownware and bricks. Charles Russell introduced the manufacture of stone bottles in the 1840s. The firm is also listed as an earthenware manufacturer.

Investigations on the site produced a great variety of sherds, both biscuit and glazed. Blackware, brownware, and stoneware was found, as expected, plus creamware, pearlware, banded ware, white printed and painted earthenware, and blue 'grass' edging. The site has twice been disturbed for building since the pottery closed, and although sherds were collected at some depth, it is possible that earth containing sherds was deposited here from elsewhere in Hunslet.

DENNISON'S POTTERY, HOLBECK
Location unknown

Benjamin Dennison, born 1702, son of the Rev Benjamin Dennison, is described as a manufacturing potter of Holbeck. His brother Joseph, born 1704, owned a pottery which was advertised in the *Leeds Mercury* in March 1769 'To be Lett to enter to immediately, situated at Holbeck, near Leeds, the Pot-Works, Warehouses and a good House adjoining in the occupation of Mr Joseph Dennison the Owner, of whom further particulars may be had.'

No further reference to this works has been traced. Joseph Dennison died in 1783. His daughter Elizabeth married Thomas Cartledge, who later owned the pottery opposite Hunslet Hall.

The only reference to the products comes from Jewitt, who wrote: 'A kind of delft ware was made, and I have seen some very creditable copies of Oriental patterns, with salt glaze, also produced at these works.' This is the only information we have that delft ware was made in Leeds.

It is possible that the Leeds Pottery, built in Jack Lane in 1770, bought the stock and took on workmen from Dennison's.

ROBINSON'S or JACK LANE POTTERY
Location: SE 306319

Situated on Hebden Paddock on the south side of Jack Lane, Hunslet, half-way between the Leeds Pottery and Taylor's

Pottery, it was built by John Cooper, William Hardy, and William Robinson in 1840, when they traded as 'Cooper, Hardy & Robinson'. In December 1842 Cooper sold his share, the firm becoming 'Hardy & Robinson'. This partnership was dissolved in 1848 and William Robinson became sole owner, the pottery being known as either Jack Lane Pottery or Jack Lane New Pottery.

By 1866 William Robinson's sons, William and James Henry, had joined the firm, which became 'William Robinson & Sons'. The father died in 1884, the sons continuing until William jr retired in 1890. James Robinson sold the pottery to Thomas Richard Thompson, a Leeds earthenware dealer, in 1896, and Thompson retained the old name until well into the twentieth century.[63]

Wares

Cooper, Hardy & Robinson made earthenware and stone bottles, Hardy & Robinson added chimneypots to the list, and William Robinson made stoneware bottles, maltkiln tiles, chemical vessels, and water filters.

Marks

One mark is known, impressed in a stoneware bottle (see no 26, p 243).

WILSON & HAIST'S POTTERY
Location: SE 311317

Situated on the north side of Jack Lane, Hunslet, probably on the site of the houses later forming the south-east side of Greenwood Street.

A hitherto unrecorded pottery existed here in the 1790s on land owned by William Wilson. Shown on the 1791 map of Hunslet by Johnson & Sedgwick, it was occupied by William Wilson jr and George Haist.[64] A document dated 1792 mentions a 'new erected building used for a pottery in the occupation of

Messrs Haiste & Wilson'. In December 1799 the pottery was 'late in the occupation of Haiste & Wilson'.

There are no further records of this pottery. Wilson sold the land and unspecified buildings. Buyers included William Fazackerly and Joseph Todd, both potters, who built houses on their plots, which became the south side of Greenwood Street. The pottery was probably swallowed up in the redevelopment.

There is no record of what was made.

HOLBECK

Pottery was made in Holbeck early in the eighteenth century. The Ingleby Records in Leeds Archives contain two agreements between Sir John Ingleby and potters for digging clay on his land at Holbeck. One, dated January 1732/3, with John Davis of Hunslet, Mug Maker, was for digging clay at Holbeck for 11 years at £7 annual rent. Davis had to dig

> perpendicularly downward from the surface without dibbing into or undermining the rest of the grounds thereunto adjoining or any part thereof and Also shall and will before the thirtieth day of September yearly during the said eleven years at his or their own Charge fill upp and make levell and uniform all Such Pitts and breaches as Shall be yearly made or occasioned during the said Term by such Sinking or digging as aforesaid and Lay all the Corn mould uppermost.

Under the terms of the second agreement, dated 1732, Richard Wyre of Bradford, potter, was also permitted to take clay from land at Holbeck.

HUNSLET CARR
Location: SE 304308

Situated on the Carr Closes at Hunslet Carr, a hitherto unrecorded pottery is shown on the 1791 map of Hunslet by Johnson & S dgwick.

In 1784–91 it was worked by Samuel Brown,[65] who is listed in directories of 1817, 1823 and 1830 as a brown earthenware manufacturer of Hunslet Moorside; the 1826 directory records that he was living at Hunslet Carr, and the 1830 that he was at Hunslet Hall. It is not known what Brown made at Hunslet Carr, but it would probably be coarse brown earthenware.

TENTER CROFT POTTERY
Location: assumed SE 311312

A pottery existed on Tenter Croft, Hunslet, before 1846. In a deed of that date William and Richard Wilson sold 'all that building or pottery used as a glasshouse' to a firm of glass bottle manufacturers called Scott & Co. Their address in 1853 was Seven Arch Bridge, Balm Road, Hunslet, and was presumably on the same site.

MARSDEN'S POTTERY

J. R. & F. Kidson record that John Marsden made small ornaments for mantelpieces, such as figures, sheep, etc, at Bedford Row, Hunslet. They suggest he may have made pottery horses as well.

HOLBECK MOOR POTTERY
Location: SE 296321

Situated north of Elland Road in an area known as The Mint, bounded on the south-west by Holbeck Moor Road and on the south-east by Creskell Street, Holbeck.

Thomas Kay was established here by 1842, and was joined by his son Edward in the early 1870s, when the firm became 'T. Kay & Son'. Frederick Kay took over later, and in 1902 sold the works to William Green, a nurseryman of Garforth. Green was joined by his sons Charlie and Joseph, the latter 'of Holbeck Moor Potteries'. The sons bought the pottery in 1911 but continued trading as 'William Green & Sons' until 1914, when Joseph, then described as a pottery merchant and nurseryman, entered a deed of assignment and the property passed to Joseph Sharp, rag merchant.

It was a small pottery, comprising a house, potter's kiln, stable, warehouse, factory, 90ft chimney and other buildings.[66]

Wares and Marks

Thomas Kay made earthenware, horticultural wares, and chimneypots. The Greens made horticultural wares only. There are no known marks.

BRADSHAW & HEMINGWAY

In the period 1828–31 Richard T. Bradshaw and a Mr Hemingway worked the Holbeck Pottery, Meadow Lane, trading as 'Bradshaw & Hemingway'.

In June 1831 a pottery, 'situate at the top of Meadow Lane in Holbeck, lately occupied by Messrs Bradshaw & Hemingway', was advertised to let,[67] but which pottery this was is not clear, since there were several 'at the top of Meadow Lane' inside the Holbeck boundary at this date. It might have been the Holbeck Moor Pottery, worked by Thomas Kay in 1842.

JOHN MILLS' POTTERY
Location: 298319

Situated on the north side of Hunslet Hall Road half-way between Petty's Pottery and Hunslet Hall, in Hunslet.

In 1827 John Mills converted an old stable into a small pottery.[68] Mills moved into Petty's Pottery about 1846, and there is no further record of the earlier pottery, although Mills may have continued using the premises for some time.

In the early years Mills made yellow ware, and in 1839 was making Egyptian black earthenware. There are no known pieces or marks.

HOLBECK MOOR POTTERY
Location: assumed SE 293319

In the late 1840s Greaves & Wood had a terracotta works in Elland Road called Holbeck Moor Pottery. The chief product was chimneypots.

YORK ROAD POTTERY, SAVILE GREEN
Location: SE 318337

Situated on the north-west side of York Road on Pease Close, in an area called Savile Green.

In 1818 Garland, Kelly and Metcalf, bricklayers, bought the land formerly occupied by Hartley, Greens & Co. By 1829 James Northall, potter, had built a pottery and cottages on part of the land. Northall also built a pottery in Pontefract Lane nearby, selling both to Charles Naylor in 1839.

Robert Paul and Robert Towson occupied the pottery in 1842, Paul buying it in the early 1860s and working it until late in the decade; he also owned Cartledge's Pottery in Hunslet. From 1870 to 1872 John T. Schofield was in occupation. The pottery had closed by the late 1870s.[69]

Wares and Marks

All the occupants made black and brown earthenware and stone bottles. No pieces or marks are known.

PONTEFRACT LANE POTTERY
Location: SE 317335

Situated at Black Bank on the east side of Pontefract Lane.

In 1835 James Northall bought land and cottages in Pontefract Lane, and one of the cottages was occupied by Jesse Platts, a potter. By 1839 Northall had built a pottery, but he had left by May 1841, when it was advertised to let in the *Leeds Mercury*.

Directories list Jacob Patrick in occupation in 1842, Thomas Outhwaite 1847–66, George Jennings 1866–70, and John Wainwright 1867–83.

Wares and Marks

All occupants made black and brown earthenware. There are no known pieces or marks.

BURMANTOFTS, LEEDS FIRECLAY COMPANY (LTD)
Location: SE 318340

Situated north of Torre Road, off York Road, in north-west Leeds.

Bricks had been made at Burmantofts for many years, and in 1882 'Wilcock & Co' introduced pottery manufacture there. By 1889 the firm had become 'The Leeds Fireclay Company'; later it became a limited company, amalgamating with several other old established firms, making similar wares, still in existence today.

Wares

The pottery produced fashionable faience and art pottery in all manner of wares. At first three main colours were used in decoration—Persian blue, orange yellow and sang-de-Boeuf—but this practice was followed by more elaborate blending of colours. The results were sometimes quite attractive, at others almost grotesque.

Tall vases were extremely popular, and ashtrays, animal and human figures, plaques and pedestal urns were all made. Stipple decoration and sgraffito ware was introduced, and large quantities exported. Some employees from the Linthorpe Pottery moved to Burmantofts, and two of the founders of the Leeds Art Pottery came from there. The products of all these potteries, together with those of the Woodlesford Art Pottery, are difficult to distinguish unless marked, though Burmantofts did mark a large proportion of its products.

After the firm had become the Leeds Fireclay Company, there

was a gradual decline in the quality of the products and the venture was reputedly not a financial success. Production of art pottery ceased about 1912.

Pieces may be seen at Kirkstall Museum, Leeds.

Marks

Wares were often marked. Occasionally a piece has the firm's name on the upper side in raised letters. Other marks relating to mould pattern numbers may be found.

See nos 27–35, p 243.

WILLIAM INGHAM & SONS, WORTLEY
Location: SE 266328

Firebrick works were established in Upper Wortley by William Ingham in 1825. They had become 'William Ingham & Sons' by 1834, trading as such until amalgamation with the Leeds Fireclay Company at the end of the nineteenth century. In 1886 some statues, figures and vases were made, but the main products were bricks, tiles, and allied wares.

Black Printed Plates: (*top*) 'The Rat Catcher' pattern; Don Pottery, *c* 1820; mark no 86. (*Bottom row*) 'Bridge and Swan' pattern, rose border; Leeds Pottery, *c* 1800–20; mark no 1; see p 29. Two of a set of four creamware plates showing foreign animals; Swinton Pottery, *c* 1806–15; both mark no 50; see p 86. 'Church and boat' pattern, blackberry border; Leeds Pottery; *c* 1800–20; mark no 1; see p 29.

Pearlware 'Orange Jumper Jug' painted predominantly in red and orange with red-brown edging; inscribed (see p 100); Don Pottery, 1807; mark no 84. Teapot painted in green, blue and yellow ochre; Hawley, either Rawmarsh Top Pottery or Kilnhurst Pottery; *c* 1800–15; mark no 137; see p 111. Pearlware teapot painted in pink, yellow, orange, green and blue; Don Pottery; *c* 1815–25; mark no 83. Teapot painted in green, blue and yellow ochre; Hawley, Rawmarsh Top Pottery or Kilnhurst Pottery, *c* 1800–15; mark no 138, see p 111.

Several pieces impressed 'WORTLEY' are known, including a red terracotta engine-turned vase and glazed art pottery, in a sickly green and yellow decorated with frogs or snakes. It has not been established, however, which firm in Wortley made these.

See no 23, p 243.

JOSEPH CLIFF & SONS, WORTLEY

Established by John Cliff, firebrick manufacturer, in 1795, the firm had become Joseph Cliff & Sons by the middle of the nineteenth century, and amalgamated with the Leeds Fireclay Company at the end of the century. The pottery made architectural ornaments, vases, figures and busts from the 1870s, but the chief products were bricks and allied wares (see William Ingham & Sons, above).

Another branch of the Leeds Fireclay Company was worked at Hipperholme near Halifax in the early twentieth century. One of its products was a tobacco jar, with a roughly striated surface resembling bark and a panel of white clay through which is scratched 'A pipe lets take, For old times' sake. L.F.C. 1920' (see mark no 35, p 243).

Several other firms amalgamated with the Leeds Fireclay Company—Edward Brooke & Sons, Joseph Brook & Sons, Oates & Green Ltd. None are known to have produced any decorative pottery.

Blue printed pearlware jug and bowl 'Packhorse' pattern; Swinton Pottery; c 1810–20; bowl only marked no 50. Blue painted creamware jug and bowl; Leeds Pottery; c 1840–50; mark no 1.

Don Pottery: Pearlware dish overglaze painted in green and pink with red-brown rim; c 1815–25; mark no 83. 'Der Dey von Algiers' transfer-printed in black overpainted in green, blue, orange and yellow; c 1830; mark no 86. Saucer painted overglaze in pink, yellow, green, orange and blue with red-brown rim; c 1805–15; mark no 86. Pearlware plate printed in black, overpainted in green, pink, orange and yellow; c 1820; mark no 86; note identical border to coffee pot on p 34.

WORTLEY

Several other small concerns made coarse earthenware in Wortley. There were Benjamin Austin, early nineteenth century; C. D. Faber & Co of Blue Hill, Swinton, Upper Wortley, in 1826; J. Dean at Upper Wortley in 1861 and 1867; R. Baxendale at Upper Wortley Road in 1904 and 1908; William Walton at Upper Wortley, 1822–44, making black and brown earthenware; and Joseph Whitaker in 1838 and Jacob Whitaker in 1853, at Silver Royd Hill (which became the Farnley Iron Company in 1854), who made terracotta ornaments.

MIDDLETON

Several pieces of art pottery impressed MIDDLETON LEEDS are known. These were made by the Middleton Fireclay Company, Middleton, just south of Hunslet, Leeds, at the end of the nineteenth century.

Known pieces are rather crudely made art glazed vases, ashtrays, and small wall plaques.

WILLIAM WILKS

A treacle-brown glazed jelly mould impressed W. WILKS LEEDS is known.[70] It may be attributable to William Wilks, maker of terracotta and sanitary pipes at Cross Stamford Street, Leeds, in 1866, or to William Wilks, brickmaker of Kirkstall Road, 1853.

See no 20, p 243.

SEACROFT POTTERY
Location: SE 356361

Situated in the centre of Seacroft, 4 miles north-east of Leeds.

In February 1801 Francis Shield bought a cottage and maltkiln in Seacroft and converted the latter into a pottery.[71] In December

1802 he advertised the pottery for sale or to let, and in October 1803 it was bought by William Ripley and John Schofield, workmen from the Castleford Pottery.

They traded as 'Ripley & Schofield' until Ripley's death in the mid-1820s. In 1831 Ripley's son, William jr, sold his half share to Schofield's widow Sarah, who ran the pottery with her son, Edward, and Timothy Penny.

The pottery was worked by the Schofield family until about 1868, when J. T. Schofield moved to the York Road Pottery, Leeds. Henry Foster took over the Seacroft Pottery around 1870. In 1872 H. Pick is listed as the occupant, and by 1878 the pottery had closed.

All occupants are given as earthenware manufacturers. There are no known marks or pieces.

SWILLINGTON BRIDGE POTTERY
Location: SE 373294

Built on the west bank of the River Aire, south of the road at Swillington Bridge, on land now occupied by Leeds University Boat Club.

The pottery was built in 1791[72] almost certainly by the same William Taylor as had worked the Rothwell and Castleford potteries. Taylor went bankrupt in 1795, and the pottery was taken over by William Butterill and Richard Rhodes, the former managing the works, which traded as 'Butterill & Co'. In March 1807 a notice appeared in the *Leeds Mercury* announcing that 'James Clarkson & Co' had taken over the Swillington Pottery and intended carrying on 'in all Branches', flattering 'themselves that their articles will be found as good in Quality, and as reasonable in Price as at any Manufactory in the Country'.

By 1810 'John Hindle & Co' were the occupants, but by 1814, when William Wilks, the owner, transferred the property to his son, William jr, the deed states that the pottery was then occupied by 'Hordhirst, Greasbath (?) & Co'. (The name Greasbath is questionable, since the deed is hard to read.) The property then comprised a dwelling house, pottery, limekilns, a wharf, eight cottages and five acres of land.

Two early employees of interest are Samuel Rainforth, who worked at Swillington Bridge from 1797 to 1799, before establishing the Hunslet Hall Pottery; and Joseph Garrett, who worked here from 1797 to 1800, having previously worked in Hunslet and later establishing a pottery in Castleford. In 1799 Garrett was bound over to keep the peace with Rainforth, both described as potters, and William Butterill of Swillington Pottery, dealer in pots, stood surety.

In 1815 William Wilks jr was running the pottery, but by 1817 had let it to William Wildblood, trading as 'Wildblood & Co'. The Wildbloods stayed for many years, but very little is known about them.

By 1833 James Reed and Benjamin Taylor had taken over. They were also proprietors of the Rock Pottery at Mexborough and the Ferrybridge Pottery. An entry in a bargee's account book, 1837, refers to 50 tons of blue clay to be delivered to Swillington Bridge Pottery, the account to be sent to Reed & Taylor at the Ferrybridge Pottery.

Wilks sold the pottery in December 1838 to Sir John Lowther of Swillington Hall, across the river from the pottery. Tradition has it that the smoke from the kilns blew across the Lowther estate and Sir John bought the pottery to close it down. He certainly did not close it immediately, for there is evidence that it continued for some years.

The partnership of Reed & Taylor was dissolved in the early 1840s, Taylor continuing at Swillington Bridge and Ferrybridge, and being joined by his son Samuel; they traded at Swillington Bridge as 'Messrs Taylor'. The pottery is mentioned in a deed dated December 1842, but in the following year the cottages were occupied by men working for Messrs Wildblood, who then ran the Woodlesford Pottery. In an estate survey, 1845, the premises are described as 'house and site of pottery', implying that it was no longer operational.[73]

Wares

Excavations have established that a very wide range of wares were made. Creamware, with a pale sea-green glaze and often painted with enamel colours, was produced, the commonest design being a yellow and green sprig pattern with brown twig motif; there were also a blue clover design, an overall pattern of brown arrow marks and various designs of tulips, Maltese crosses and multi-coloured floral sprays. Leaf terminal handles and double-twist handles were found, too.

Large quantities of pearlware, especially that with the blue 'grass' edging, were found. Transfer patterns in blue and brown include Chinese landscapes, pastoral scenes and Gothic ruins with borders of beehives, dragon combats, exotic flowers and rococo compositions. Kitchen ware decorated with slip banding and mocha designs in varying colours were made, and after 1827 ironstone china and opaque granite china became popular. 'Willow Pattern', 'Fibre', and all-over formal patterns were common. White earthenware with bands of narrow ribbing painted blue was popular, as was green glazed ribbed ware; and mugs with horizontal rouletting, their handles often decorated with crude leaf terminals, were made. Some slipware and black glazed earthenware was also found.[74]

The Yorkshire Museum has a circular pearlware plaque with low relief figures, decorated in enamel colours and inscribed on the back 'John Wildblood Swillington Bridge Pottery, July 12 1831'. The five known examples of a very large two-handled mug dated 1829 and decorated with a verse about the nearby Eshald-well Brewery were probably made here.

Marks

All the marks (nos 36–45) shown on pp 245–6, except nos 43 and 44, were found on the site of the pottery, where they had remained undisturbed since the demolition of the works. Marks nos 38, 39,

41 and 42 have since been found on complete willow pattern pieces; they all probably date from about 1820.

Pieces bearing marks of 'Reed & Taylor' or 'Reed, Taylor & Co' (nos 122–9, p 253) may have been made here, at Ferrybridge or at Mexborough.

WOODLESFORD POTTERY
Location: SE 367294

Situated on the south bank of the River Aire on the Farthings-worth, north of the turnpike road and west of Pottery Lane, Woodlesford, about 4½ miles south-east of Leeds.

The date of foundation is uncertain. Several potters lived in Woodlesford in the late eighteenth century, but they probably worked at the nearby Swillington Bridge Pottery. The first documentary evidence relating to the Woodlesford Pottery is dated 1819, when Charles Collins became insolvent and relinquished his lease of the pottery to Joseph Wilks.[75] Wilks then ran it himself, mortgaging it for £300 in 1821 and trading as 'Wilks & Co' by 1823. The premises were equipped for the manufacture of coarse earthenware, with kilns, sheds, stoves, drying houses, drying ground, workshops and wharf, etc.

In 1830 John Clark was the tenant. In 1831 reference is made to the new blackware pottery at Woodlesford, and as it was hardly new at this date, it seems likely that the premises had been extended. The property was sold to Thomas Hall, butcher, in 1832, following Wilks's death, Clark still being in occupation.

Thomas Wildblood and his son Thomas had taken over the pottery by 1837, trading as 'Wildblood & Co'. Thomas jr continued, under the same style, for some time after his father's death in 1842. 'Brunt & Co' followed until bankruptcy in 1846.

By 1849 James Shackleton, Benjamin Taylor and William Gibson were working the pottery, and they shortly bought the premises, described again as a coarse earthenware manufactory. They also ran the Leathley Lane Pottery, Hunslet. Taylor ran the Woodlesford Pottery, but they traded at both as 'Shackleton,

Taylor & Co' until about 1861, when Taylor is listed alone at Woodlesford, where he remained until the late 1870s.[76]

In 1881 Horn Brothers, who were also at the Australian Pottery, Ferrybridge, in the 1880s, were running the works, but in 1888 Hewitt & Jenkinson took over for a few years. In 1892 or 1893 the pottery was acquired by James W. Senior and a few workmen from the Leeds Art Pottery, and reopened as the 'Woodlesford Art Pottery'. About 3 years later the pottery finally closed.

Wares

Coarse and black earthenware were the staple product in the early days. The Wildbloods and Shackleton, Taylor & Co made utilitarian white domestic earthenware, transfer-printed or crudely painted, but it is indistinguishable in the absence of marks from products of other urban potteries. Several pieces attributed to Woodlesford are known. A loving cup inscribed 'R. RAPER OULTON 1856' was probably made here (see plate, p 141).

Examination of the site produced a wide variety of sherds, ranging from pieces of pancheons to printed willow pattern, Eton College, Asiatic pheasants and some unidentified patterns, plus banded kitchen ware in blue and white, and sponge decorated ware. Other discoveries included pieces of thick heavy moulded art pottery glazed in deep green, mustard yellow and turquoise.

The Woodlesford Art Pottery, like the other Yorkshire art potteries, made highly coloured and glazed ornamental pieces—some with beautifully merging glazes, others with multi-coloured flowers and/or cut reliefs. Unmarked pieces are indistinguishable from the products of the Leeds Art Pottery and Burmantofts, since many of the same patterns and designs were used at all three.

Marks

No factory marks were used by the earlier proprietors, although some pieces bear the name of the pattern. The Woodlesford Art Pottery sometimes used its name, impressed (see no 21, p 243).

LITTLE or WEST MANSTON FARM, WHITKIRK

Whitkirk is situated due east of Leeds and north of Temple Newsam.

In 1782 advertisements in the Leeds newspapers were offering a freehold estate, lately belonging to the bankrupt Thomas Medhurst, for sale. Included in the sale were 'four cottages, Pot Ovens and other suitable erections for carrying on the business of a Pottery . . . under lease for 21 years commencing February 2nd 1776 to Mary Vevers and Lancelot Vevers'.[77]

Nothing further is known of the pottery.

BARWICK

Documentary evidence suggests there was a pottery at Barwick in Elmet in the second half of the eighteenth century. Potters named in the parish registers for Barwick include William Gough, 1745 and 1770, Brown Moor; Godfrey Gough, 1764 and 1771, Barwick; Thomas Parker, 1764 and 1766, Barwick; Samuel Mawkin, 1764, Barwick; and Thomas Bennet, 1763, Barwick. Jonathan Roper, potseller, is mentioned in 1762. Cornelius Toft the younger, potter of Barwick, was charged with assault in 1771.

POTTERTON
Location: SE 403387

Situated in what is now the front garden of Potterton Grange Farm, Potterton, near Barwick in Elmet, south of Wetherby.

The pottery was probably operative around 1500. Excavations have revealed three main types of pottery—coarseware, Cistercian ware and reversed Cistercian ware. Decorations on the Cistercian ware two-handled cups consisted of applied circular or oval pads of white clay, and variations included faces, leaves and wheel patterns. Most of the pottery was made in white clay covered with a clear glaze, but some green glazed ware was found as well. Bowls and pitchers were also made.[78]

FOLLIFOOT
Location: SE 345524

A sixteenth-century pottery kiln situated south of Follifoot, between Harrogate and Wetherby.

Pottery excavated was all undecorated, most vessels being partially covered with dark brown glaze. Jugs, bowls, large pitchers with broad striated handles and bung holes were found.[79]

ROBINSON & RHODES

'Robinson & Rhodes' was an important firm of enamellers in Briggate, Leeds, advertising in the *Leeds Intelligencer*, 28 October 1760, as follows:

> Robinson and Rhodes, opposite the George, in Briggate, Leeds, Enamel and Burn in Gold and Colour, Foreign and English China, and match broken setts of Enamel'd or Burnt-in China and Tea Ware and make them complete to any pattern required—either Indian or Dresden. They also enamel Coats of Arms, etc; and sell a good assortment of Foreign China and a great variety of useful English China of the newest improvement, which they will engage to wear as well as Foreign, and will change gratis if broke with hot water. They likewise enamel Stoneware which they sell as cheap as in Staffordshire. The best prices for Broken Flint Glass.

A similar advertisement appeared in May 1761.

Jasper Robinson retired from the partnership in 1763, becoming an employee in the firm, which then became 'D. Rhodes & Co'. The senior partner, David Rhodes, left Leeds in 1768 and settled in London, working as an enameller for Wedgwood until his death in 1777.

The firm was taken over by Leonard Hobson, who advertised himself in June 1779 as 'Leonard Hobson Glass and China-Man, at the Golden-Jarr in Briggate, Leeds (Successor to Mr D. Rhodes) . . . continues to mend broken Foreign China by Burning, in the neatest and strongest manner.' He died in April 1799.

In the early 1760s Rhodes worked for Wedgwood and supplied him with material. He also decorated creamware from Derbyshire potteries, but whether he did so for the proprietors of those potteries or on his own account is not known. He is considered responsible for the red and black painting, often with cottages, clouds, smoking chimneys, and double stemmed trees (see plate, p 33).

It was once thought that some early Leeds Pottery creamware was decorated by Rhodes, but recent research has cast doubt on whether the pieces in question were made at Leeds or not.

2

SOUTH YORKSHIRE

SWINTON POTTERY, ROCKINGHAM WORKS
Location: SK 441988

Situated north of Wath Road and west of Pottery Lane at Swinton, 4 miles north of Rotherham, in the parish of Wath-on-Dearne, the Swinton Pottery was established in 1745 by Edward Butler, the date being confirmed by a bill heading later used by the Bramelds. By 1759 Butler was paying £11 a year rental to the Marquis of Rockingham, on whose land the pothouse was built;[1] and in that year the Marquis paid Elizabeth Butler 2s 6d 'by Pots'. Butler died in 1763 and William Malpass took over the works, where he was joined by William Fenney, dissolving partner of John Platt at the Rotherham Pottery, in 1767 or 1768. Malpass and Fenney continued together until 1777, and Malpass worked alone until 1778, when the works were taken over by Thomas Bingley and Willoughby Wood, who traded as 'Bingley, Wood & Co'.[2] The Bingleys were landowners and farmers, and Wood, a working partner in the firm, had been the local schoolmaster.

In 1783, in a case before Pontefract Quarter Sessions, reference is made to the day book and ledger belonging to 'Messrs Willoughby Wood & Co' of Swinton Pottery being stolen by Joseph Barker, a Swinton potter; Thomas Amery of Rawmarsh and Thomas Hawley of Kilnhurst, potters, stood surety for him. At the Rotherham Quarter Sessions of 1784 reference is made to 'Mr Bingley & Co'. The partnership was obviously known by various names. Grabham says a man named Sharpe was a partner, and there may have been others.[3] John Brameld worked at the pottery, but at what date he became a partner is not known.

81

Jewitt attributes a posset pot, dated 1759, with a label inscribed 'Swinton Pottery' attached, as having been made either by or for John Brameld.

In 1785 the Swinton Pottery was amalgamated with Hartley,

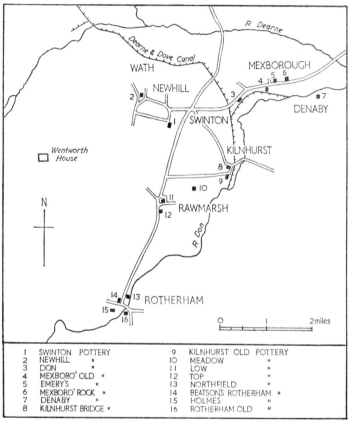

I	SWINTON POTTERY	9	KILNHURST OLD POTTERY
2	NEWHILL "	IO	MEADOW "
3	DON "	11	LOW "
4	MEXBORO' OLD "	12	TOP "
5	EMERY'S "	13	NORTHFIELD "
6	MEXBORO' ROCK "	14	BEATSON'S ROTHERHAM "
7	DENABY "	15	HOLMES "
8	KILNHURST BRIDGE "	16	ROTHERHAM OLD "

FIG 8   Location of pottery sites in the Rotherham area

Greens & Co of the Leeds Pottery, a thriving concern with widespread markets. The Green family originally came from the Swinton area and had connections in the neighbourhood (see p 21). For the next twenty-one years the Swinton works were controlled by the Leeds partners, trading throughout the period as

'Greens, Bingley & Co' at Swinton and 'Hartley, Greens & Co' at Leeds.

John Brameld's eldest son, William, started work at the pottery in 1786, and his second son, Thomas, 9 years later.

The pottery expanded greatly under the Leeds partners' guidance. In the 1795 Land Tax assessment it was rated at £3 17s 4d. John Green of the Leeds Pottery appears to have been the force behind the organisation, and greatly respected, but the fortunes of the pottery industry generally declined, and friction occurred between the Swinton and Leeds partners. As the latter had the controlling interest at the Swinton Pottery, however, there was little the Swinton partners could do. Several of the original Leeds partners died, and their successors do not seem to have had the enthusiasm of their predecessors. John Green ran into serious financial trouble, sold his shares in the Leeds Pottery, and by 1800 was bankrupt. He moved to Newhill, near Swinton, and in 1801 established the Don Pottery at Swinton with John and William Brameld and Richard Clark of Leeds.

The lease of the Swinton Pottery became due for renewal in 1806, and the Bramelds became worried about the way they were being treated by their Leeds partners who, it was clear, were trying to run down Swinton in favour of Leeds. At this stage all was not well at the Leeds Pottery, for there had been many changes of partnership, trade was poor, and the Leeds partners probably found running the two works beyond their means.

The Bramelds offered to buy the Leeds partners' shares in the Swinton works, but work had almost come to a standstill before agreement was reached. In desperation the Bramelds considered taking the Mexborough Pottery (see p 114), but this proved unnecessary when the Leeds partners finally withdrew from Swinton and the partnership was dissolved. The lease of the pottery was then renewed by the Bramelds alone.[4]

Production restarted on a limited scale, sales being confined to the home market. The Earl was an obliging landlord and, after appeals for help, built a flint mill and cottages. Workmen from the Leeds Pottery, which had temporarily closed, were enticed to Swinton.

William Brameld, the eldest son, died in 1813, and the running of the works passed to Thomas. Two other sons, George Frederick and John Wager, were also employed at the pottery. John Brameld died in 1819. The works were then employing about 300 hands, a large percentage of the local population.

George Frederick Brameld went to Russia as a salesman, and John Wager Brameld travelled throughout Britain, obtaining orders from as far afield as Scotland, and Lowestoft, where Robert Allen, the decorator, ordered undecorated wares from Swinton to paint.

Exports to Russia grew, but bills remained unpaid. The economic climate at home deteriorated, the Bramelds fell heavily into debt, and in 1826 became bankrupt. Assignees ran the works while bankruptcy proceedings went forward, and the pottery was advertised to let. There were two biscuit ovens, five glazing ovens, hardening kilns for six printers, three enamelling kilns, seven throwing wheels, large green rooms, and a sliphouse room for up to 50 tons of clay per week '. . . for the manufacture of china and earthenware on a very extensive scale'. The flint mill, warehouses, and a farm of over 150 acres were all offered, as was the stock in trade—china and earthenware, moulds and copper plates.[5]

Appeals to Earl Fitzwilliam eventually saved the day, and he became mortgagee, the Brameld brothers having to comply with certain stipulations, including the restriction of their sales to the home market.

The works were renamed the Rockingham Works and thereafter the griffin, the crest of Earl Fitzwilliam, was included in the trademark. A showroom was opened in Coney Street, York, in 1827,[6] but closed in 1833 through lack of support.[7]

The 1830s were difficult years for the Bramelds. They were ambitious regarding production, but poor businessmen, and by 1842 were bankrupt again. The 2nd Earl had died and could no longer help, the 3rd Earl did not wish to do so, and so the works were closed.

A large auction was held in May 1843, at which vast quantities of china earthenware and biscuit ware was sold.[8] In June the pottery was advertised to let.[9]

Wares

No pottery attributed to the Swinton Pottery earlier than Brameld's occupation is identifiable, but it is assumed Butler made coarseware from local clay. Bills of sale from Malpass & Fenney and subsequent proprietors to the Marquis of Rockingham and Earl Fitzwilliam are housed in the Sheffield Reference Library.

There are a few bills dating from the late 1760s, for black dishes, pudding pots, and rose, lard and garden pots, indicating the type of wares then made. It should be remembered, however, that Fenney had been at the Rotherham Old Pottery where fineware was made, so it is likely that production of fineware commenced at Swinton in the late 1760s.

In the early 1770s creamware, pierced and enamelled, was the chief product together with tortoiseshell ware, marbled ware, blue bowls and enamelled purple teapots, sugar bowls and cups. Baskets with stands, chamber pots and general tableware was all sent to the big house.

'Bingley, Wood & Co' continued making similar wares: cream and purple bowls at 8d each, cream-coloured teapots at 5d each, cream-coloured chamber pots at 8d and coarseware ones at 2d, cream table plates at 2½d each, Queen blue bowls, cups and saucers, galley pots, and coarseware items. 'Greens, Bingley & Co' extended the range to include printed wares: pressed Tuscan teapots with festooned middles, enamelled table plates, green edged plates, Egyptian teapots, Red China teapots, Devonshire Brown festooned sugar cups, Queen blue sprigged dishes and plates and purple teapots in varying sizes, together with coarseware and chimney pipes.

A price list headed 'Greens, Bingley & Co', Swinton Pottery, was issued, and it was an exact copy of the Leeds list. A late eighteenth-century catalogue was headed: 'Swinton Pottery, 1st

February, 1796 Greens, Hartley & Co, Swinton Pottery make, sell, and export wholesale all sorts of Earthenware, Cream, Coloured or Queens, Nankeen Blue, Tortoise Shell, Fine Egyptian Black, Brown China, etc., etc. All the above shapes enamelled, printed or ornamented with gold and silver.' A further list covered a wide range of shapes produced—the usual products of fineware potteries of the day and possibly identical with those then made at the Leeds factory.

A speciality of the Swinton Pottery was creamware dipped in a brown manganese oxide stained glaze, subsequently known as 'Rockingham Ware', which was produced from about 1785 to the closure of the works. Other factories tried to copy this brown glaze with varying degrees of success, and several even advertised their own 'Rockingham Ware'; but none achieved the standard and beauty of the genuine article.

After 1806, when the Bramelds took control, the pottery was often marked; in consequence it is collected and better documented. The same price list was used, 'Brameld & Co' being substituted for 'Greens, Bingley'.

Perhaps the most distinctive pieces produced were the Cadogan teapots, usually glazed in brown, sometimes green, but rarely in other colours. Other brown glazed ware included Toby jugs, shoewarmers, teapots and jugs, but marked pieces are rare, and without marks attribution cannot be considered certain. Later pieces, after 1826, include impressed Rockingham teapots, cream jugs and coffee pots.

Creamware continued to be made, some enamel-painted and some transfer-printed. The plates illustrated on p 69 are two of a

---

Don Pottery: Pierced creamware basket and stand; 1801–10; mark no 83; see p 100. 'Daisy Jug'; mark no 89; see p 103. Creamware plate overglaze painted in brown; mark no 83.

Don Pottery plaque; pearlware, painted in pink, orange, green and blue with black border; incised mark no 88; 1829; see p 103.

set of four all with differing animal scenes, transfer-printed in black. They are of comparatively poor quality, the glaze being full of impurities. All are impressed BRAMELD, and two have +o in addition. Pierced creamware plates and baskets are known, and a beautifully decorated jug with cricketing scenes and a castle, printed underneath 'Brameld & Co Swinton Pottery', is illustrated by Rice.[10]

The commonest products were the transfer-printed table and toilet wares; the majority were printed in blue, but green, beige and black examples are known. Patterns include 'Castle of Rochefort', scenes from Don Quixote, 'Returning Woodman', 'Willow', 'Twisted Tree', 'Blackberry', 'Rocking Horse', 'Horse & Hounds', 'Boys Fishing', 'Sweet Peas', 'Sprays of Flowers', 'Parroquet', 'Indian Flowers', 'Burns' Cotter', 'Paris Stripe', 'Bo-Peep', 'Steamer Forfarshire', 'Girl with a Bird', 'Dromedary', 'Chinese Temple' and 'The Packhorse', several of which are illustrated on pp 52 and 70. Occasionally transfer-printed pieces were painted in colour over the glaze, most commonly the 'Twisted Tree' pattern.

Experiments resulted in a strikingly white bodied earthenware called chalk body. Known examples tend to show distortion, and

———

Don and Newhill blue transfer-printed plates: (*top row*) 'Wild Horse' pattern; unmarked, but marked specimen recorded by Little, no 85; Don Pottery. 'Castello St Angelo' pattern in the Landscape series; Don Pottery; mark nos 83 and 85. 'Sun and Fountain' pattern; Don Pottery; mark no 85; see p 102. (*Bottom row*) 'Italian Scenery' series: 'View in Palma'; mark nos 83 and 85; Don Pottery. 'Obelisk at Catania', mark no 85; Don Pottery. 'Alicata'; mark no 102; Newhill Pottery; this pattern was formerly used by the Don Pottery. 'Terrace of the Naval Amphitheatre of Taorminum'; mark no 85; Don Pottery; for list of others in the series see p 101.

Green glazed plates: (*top*) 'Thistle Pattern', with roses and shamrocks; Don Pottery; mark no 83; see p 100. (*Bottom row*) Swinton Pottery; mark no 50; note identical moulding in middle bottom row, p 52. 'Thistle Pattern'; Newhill Pottery; mark no 101; see p 100. Swinton pottery; mark no 50.

it was not a commercial success. The plate illustrated on p 52 in chalk body is of the same mould as the green glazed plate illustrated on p 88.

Green glazed ware was made (see plate, p 88). Leaf plates and dishes in three designs, a moulded jug with daisies and cauliflower leaves, a model of Conisburgh Castle and the lotus vase

FIG 9 (1) Cadogan pot, (2) Caneware jug, (3) earthenware transfer-printed teapot, all pre-1826 Swinton Pottery shapes; (4), (5) and (6) brown glazed earthenware coffee and teapot shapes of the Rockingham period, after 1826

are recorded; the moulds of the last two passed to James Reed at the Mexborough Pottery, and then to Bowman Heald at the Kilnhurst Pottery.

Cane coloured ware was produced in teawares, and coffee cans, often with applied figures or motifs in a contrasting colour such as pale or deep blue, brown or 'off white'. The jug handles are sometimes shaped like a horse's hoof at the base and a tail at the top.

Yellow glazed ware was made, but is rare, only one marked piece being known. That is a lidded jug in the Smithsonian

Institution, Washington, DC, which has pineapple moulding, painted with blue lines and red stars. Black basalt was also made, and pieces have been unearthed on the site, but it is extremely rare.

As at most contemporary factories, experiments were carried out to produce whiter, more durable pottery; and Swinton marketed granite china and stone china, many pieces of which bear not only the factory mark, but a transfer mark that includes the name of the body and pattern.

Porcelain made at the Swinton works and known as Rockingham has been collected and studied in great detail in recent years (see Bibliography, p 283). It has been found that a great deal of porcelain is mistakenly attributed to Rockingham, despite the literature available. For instance, there is no evidence that pieces depicting poodles, sheep or cottages were made, though such pieces are often described as Rockingham.

Serious production of porcelain began in 1826, though, judging from the advertisement of the sale of stock that year, some porcelain was already being marketed. Artists from Derby and Staffordshire were engaged. At first the quality was extremely high, the decoration being skilfully executed, often gilded. The wares were often flamboyant, in the revived rococo style, particularly the ornamental pieces.

Teawares were usually marked under the saucer only, a practice that continued until the factory's latter years, when standards deteriorated. Other teaware items were rarely marked, but most bear a pattern number within the range 400–1565 or in a range where a number below 100 is preceded by 2/, eg 2/25. Anything outside these ranges is unlikely to be Rockingham. The numbers were usually painted in red or gold, but blue, green and black examples are recorded.

Another help in the recognition of teawares is the shape of the cup handles in Fig 10 which, with the exception of no 8, appear to have been made at the Rockingham Works only. A double-twisted handle and a horse's-hoof handle were also made.

The dinner and dessert services were also numbered, but in a different range to the teawares. In existing pattern books the numbers range from 450 to 875, but lower numbers were also used, the lowest known being 417.

Certain motifs appear frequently, though they are not exclusive to Swinton. Moulded shell edges, scallops and gadroons are commonly found, together with vine leaves and grapes, and a seaweed pattern decoration. Useful but highly decorative items

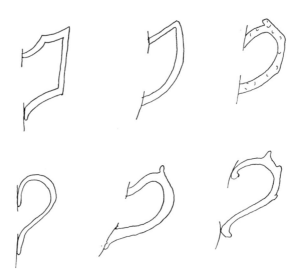

FIG 10   Drawings of some typical teacup-handle shapes found on Rockingham porcelain

made include comports, vases, jugs, baskets, urns, inkwells and trinket sets; and unusual items to be found in porcelain are thimbles, collar-studs, brooches, scent bottles, boxes, toy teasets, animals, and other unusual objects ranging from bedposts to lampstands.

Some of the figures made were left in the biscuit state, while others were glazed and coloured. They are fairly rare and were probably only manufactured for a few years. Many of the subjects, both people and animals, bear the factory mark plus an incised number on the base in the range 1–136. Eighty are listed by Rice.

A series of busts of famous personalities are listed, most of them factory-marked but without the incised number. The figures generally have a solid base with a small circular hold. Sometimes the pattern numbers are accompanied by a letter or letters and numbers (see below).[11]

Marks

With the possible exception of no 49 (see p 245) there are no recorded marks earlier than 1806; it is possible that during the partnership with Leeds the Leeds Pottery marks were used. On pottery thereafter there were two basic marks consisting of 'Brameld' or 'Rockingham' in varying forms, though not all pottery was marked. The former appears either alone or with a + sign followed by a number; numbers 0, 1, 2, 4, 5, 6, 7, 8, 10, 11, 12, and 16 are known. Sometimes there is a second + sign and/or a symbol. The Brameld marks were generally impressed, but occasionally painted, and were used from 1806 to 1842; though most of these marks are probably earlier than 1826. The Rockingham mark used after 1826, on pottery, is generally impressed.

After 1826 the griffin was incorporated in the mark used on porcelain. Up to 1830 it was painted in red, and from 1831 to 1842 in puce, when it was generally accompanied by the words 'Manufacturer to the King' or, rarely, 'Royal Rockingham Works'. On blue decorated items the mark was printed in blue. On biscuit and some coloured figures the mark was impressed (see p 248).

In addition to the factory marks, there were the pattern marks and incised numerals already mentioned. Several painted letters and numerals are also found, including the letters S, T, H, X, and Cl followed by a number up to 17. Their meaning, which is uncertain, is discussed by J. G. and M. I. N. Evans in 'Some Views on Rockingham Pattern Marks':[12] they suggest that the letter S when found on tea, dinner and dessert ware was used when the decoration is devoid of gilding; and that the letter X may apply to substandard items in teaware, either misshapen or showing firing faults, and is generally found on late pieces that may even have been bought from other factories. No explanation has yet been found for the letters T and H. The letters C or Cl followed by a number, found on figures and ornamental porcelain, and occasionally on pottery, are painted over the glaze in various colours. The Evans' suggest that these are not gilder's marks as previously thought, as they are sometimes found on pieces with no gilding, but may be quality control marks.

The Baguleys, who continued decorating porcelain at the Rockingham Works after the closure, used similar factory marks, and the collector should beware of confusing their pieces with 'Rockingham'.

See nos 49–80, p 245.

LATER ROCKINGHAM WORKS, AND THE BAGULEYS

After the collapse of the Rockingham Works, part of the pottery was taken over by Isaac Baguley, formerly manager of the gilding department. He decorated and gilded wares from other potteries until his death in 1855. His son Alfred remained at the Rockingham Works until 1865, when he moved to Mexborough and opened a shop in Bank Street, on the corner of Dolcliffe Road. Here he decorated and gilded the local white ware, and also ware from Staffordshire, and sold it. He had an enamelling kiln behind the shop. His signboard 'A Baguley, Rockingham Works' was a familiar sight in Mexborough, until his death in March 1891. He and his father were solely decorators. They used the brown glaze from the old Rockingham Works (under the Bramelds) extensively. It eventually passed to Bowman Heald of the Kilnhurst Pottery. The wares were generally marked (see nos 81–2, p 249).

Another part of the old Rockingham Works was taken over about 1850 by Peter Hobson and his son William, who remained until at least 1857. Peter Hobson had previously partnered William Earnshaw in Rotherham.

The flint mill was run successively by Thomas Brameld, his widow Jane, and James Parker, a former workman, until 1887. After that it passed to I. & I. Walker for about a year and then closed.

SWINTON BRIDGE

George Hampshire and Thomas Newton are listed in 1837–9 as earthenware manufacturers of Swinton Bridge, which is ½ mile east of Swinton village.

DON POTTERY, SWINTON
Location: SK 466995

Built in 1801 on the north-west bank of the Don Canal, near the junction of the Don and Dearne & Dove canals at Swinton.

John Green had left the Leeds and Swinton Potteries when he went bankrupt in 1800, but by 1801 he had moved to Newhill, near Swinton, and had once again ventured into the pottery industry. Joined by Richard Clark, rope manufacturer of Leeds, and John and William Brameld of the Swinton Pottery, he bought Stork Close and Hewell Dyke and erected the Don Pottery on the former.[13] At the date of purchase there were quick kilns, limekilns and a warehouse on Hewell Dyke, together with cottages housing workmen of 'Greens, Bingley & Co' of the Swinton Pottery. These cottages were later converted into two houses and occupied by John Green's son William and Septimus Frost.

By November 1803 there were four further partners—John Green's son John; William Clark, a Leeds merchant; John Milner, of Swinton; and John Wade, a surgeon and apothecary of Swinton, who was John Brameld's son-in-law. They traded as 'Greens, Clark & Co', and William Green, John's second son was employed as clerk.[14]

John Green sr died in 1805, aged sixty-two, and William Green became a partner. The pottery was run by John jr and William Green, and possibly John Milner, who is listed in the 1807 Poll Book as a potter. There is no record of any of the Brameld family working at the Don Pottery, and it seems strange that they had an interest in what has always been assumed to be their biggest rival. It must be remembered that the relationship between the Bramelds and their Leeds partners in the Swinton Pottery was deteriorating at this time, and they may have thought that investment in the Don Pottery would give them an excellent opportunity of continuing should the Swinton Pottery collapse. There are many unanswered questions, however. For instance, why did Earl Fitzwilliam's agent specify that the Swinton Pottery must not be let to a company of which some of the partners were interested in different commitments in the same trade, referring to the Leeds partners,[15] when he must surely have known of the Bramelds' connections with the Don Pottery. Perhaps further research may throw light on the situation.

As the original partners died, other members of their families appear in the list of partners, the business being kept very much a family concern. By 1817 they included John Brameld; William Clark, now of Swinton; Richard Clark; Elizabeth Green, John sr's widow; Sarah Green; John and William Green (the last four all of the Don Pottery); Joseph Green, late of Rio de Janeiro but then of London, merchant; John Birks, gentleman; Thomas and George Frederick Brameld of Swinton, potters; Charles Milner, a London barrister; and Samuel Thompson Lunn, potter of Swinton. Lunn entered into partnership about 1816, when the style of the firm changed to 'John & William Green & Co' or 'Greens & Co'. Lunn sold his share to John and William Green in December 1822, and settled in Mexico City.

The pottery was extensive, built in circular form with large entrance gates and situated on the canal, which facilitated transport of both raw materials and finished products. Coal was easily accessible, and the railway was later built on the far side of the canal, with Swinton station nearby. Don Pottery House, occupied by John Green from c 1824, is described as a mansion with pleasure grounds, shrubberies, lawns, gardens, plantation, coach house and stables.

The fortunes of the Don Pottery fluctuated. There is evidence that throughout the Greens' occupation finances were strained.

By 1823 the partners had changed yet again. William Clark had died and they included John Greaves Clark, his son, John Wager

Brameld, and Marianne Milner. Joseph Green had settled in Swinton (by 1826 he had moved to Liverpool), and Charles Green lived in Rio de Janeiro. Joseph Green had previously lived in Rio, so it is possible that Joseph and Charles acted as agents for the pottery there. After 1823 there is no record of other than the Green family having any interest in the pottery.

Fortunes deteriorated in the early 1830s, and on 22 January 1834 John and William Green were declared bankrupt.[16] A meeting of creditors was held in order to 'assent to or dissent from the Assignees working up, finishing, and completing all or any of the earthenware and unfinished stock . . . also to determine whether the Assignees should relinquish premises lately held by the Bankrupts at Sprotbrough, near Doncaster . . . under lease from Sir John Copley.' This referred to a flint mill. The farm and equipment and almost 20 acres of land, lately occupied by the Green brothers, was advertised.

In July 1834 William Green wrote to Earl Fitzwilliam pleading for assistance, pointing out that the family had been tenants both in agriculture and industry for upwards of a century. He wrote of the 'grievous failure of Messrs Bramelds and the liquidation of responsibilities for them, to the serious amount of Four to Five Thousand Pounds . . .' and stated that 'Trade had been in an unprecedented state of disorganisation'. John Green was a sick man, and writing to the Earl in August 1834 he said: 'During the last fifteen years I have been totally unable to attend personally to active business, and incapable of moving even without assistance. My sons, who are numerous, are now arriving at an age to assist me . . .'[17] But his appeals were unavailing. Lord Milton had succeeded his father in 1833, and the new Earl did not show the same personal interest in the local potteries as his father had shown.

Bankruptcy proceedings went ahead: in September the household effects were auctioned, and in January 1835 the Don Pottery was advertised for sale.[18] The advertisement spoke of the pottery's establishment in 1801, its work force of over 600 persons at its peak, its extensive and valuable connections in England and on the continent, and the reputation and excellence of its wares. In the following June the stock of original and working moulds, copper plates and engravings was advertised.[19] The sale was expected to take several days.

Subsequent events are confused, owing to contradictory contemporary evidence. *White's Directory* of 1837 states that Samuel Barker was at the Don Pottery, but the Land Tax assessments for 1836–9 list the assignees (who included Edward Wright, earthenware manufacturer, of Chesterfield) and William Green as occupants, and those for 1839–41 list John, William and Charles Green as owners and occupiers. In a deed John Green is recorded as being at the Don Pottery in September 1836, but of Sprotbrough Mills, dealer in ground flint, with Joseph William Green in December 1837; and William Green, who died in August 1841, aged sixty-five, is described in the parish register as 'of Don Pottery'.

Samuel Barker of the Mexborough Old Pottery bought the Don Pottery from the assignees in July 1839, and worked the two potteries for several years.[20] About 1847 a flint mill was built at the Don works. Samuel Barker's three sons joined him, the firm trading in 1851 as 'Samuel Barker & Son'. Barker died on 15 July 1856, aged fifty-three, and the pottery was worked by his sons Henry, Edward, and Peter Jesse, who continued trading as 'Samuel Barker & Son'. Henry Barker died in 1876, and Peter Jesse became 'of unsound mind', his third share passing to Edward in 1879. The pottery was managed by Thomas Williams.

Edward Barker lived at Swinton Hall until his retirement in 1882. The works closed for several weeks but at the end of 1882 were taken on lease by John Adamson, John Wilkinson, Edward T. Smith and Charles Scorah, still trading as 'Samuel Barker & Son'. Many old hands had left to work in Staffordshire during the closure, but by the mid-1880s the work force had risen to nearly 500. After about 4 years Wilkinson and Scorah retired, leaving Smith and Adamson, who employed John Long as manager.

All was not well financially, but the works continued until August 1893, when the stock was auctioned to pay the rent.[21]

Estimated to be worth £2,000, the stock included about $2\frac{1}{2}$ tons of copper plate engravings, flint, ground stone, ball clay, china clay, 4,000 saggars, moulds, printing presses, sixty casks of finished and unfinished stock, etc. Bowman Heald of the Kilnhurst Pottery bought some of it.

The premises were partially demolished and shops and houses erected. Messrs D. & J. S. Wilson, former apprentices of E. T. Smith, took over the remaining buildings as wholesale china and earthenware dealers and decorators. They had wholesale and retail shops in Rotherham and Mexborough.

Today a single kiln remains, but in a sorry state. The site is used as a builder's yard.

Wares

The early products of the Don Pottery closely resemble those of Leeds. Jewitt describes a pattern book issued by the firm in the same style as the latest edition of the Leeds Pottery pattern book.[22] The Don book described has been lost without trace, but Jewitt says that 292 patterns were given, many of them obviously traced from the Leeds book. Designs included all types of table, toilet, and ornamental ware.

Specifically mentioned as being identical with Leeds designs are perforated, open-work and embossed baskets and stands, some of which had covers; a perforated chestnut tureen; a melon-bowl; and an asparagus holder. At the end of the book was a series of plates, numbered 1–54 and lettered A–K, devoted to tea equipage, comprising a remarkable and very striking variety of teapots, coffee-pots and milk jugs. Jewitt says that 'such as were adapted for the colour were made in green glazed ware'; and also says, speaking of teapots, that 'many patterns, with raised groups, trophies &c and others for loose metal "kettle handles" are also engraved'.

Dessert services in creamware and fine white earthenware were painted with flowers having 'a truth to nature that has seldom been equalled'. Jewitt also describes plates with the underside left white, and the rest tinted deep buff, with a black line on the edge and inner side of the rim and a landscape painted in the centre of the plate, 'which has all the beauty and effect of a well-executed Indian ink drawing'.

Very little creamware attributed to the Don Pottery is known today; possibly very little was marked, and a large percentage was exported. The creamware basket and stand, and the creamware plate painted under the glaze in brown illustrated on p 87 are examples from the early period.

Green glazed ware was obviously produced in quantity, but known pieces are rare, with the exception of the moulded plates with a thistle, rose, and shamrock design (see plate, p 88). The same design was made by the Twiggs, probably at Newhill, they having bought the moulds on the Greens' bankruptcy; and it was also later made by the Hawleys, possibly using the same moulds. Flower vases and root pots were made in green glazed ware.

The famous Orange Jumper Jugs (see plate, p 69) were made in 1807 on the occasion of an election at which Lord Milton, son of Earl Fitzwilliam, was a candidate; the name Milton appears on the hat band of Orange Jumper, who is depicted on the jug. The verse under the spout reads:

> The Figure there is no mistaking,
> It is the famous Man for—breaking,
> Oh! that instead of Horse & Mares
> He had but broken Crockery Ware,
> Each grateful Potter in a Bumper
> Might drink the Health,
> of Orange Jumper!

These jugs are comparatively common, varying in size and design of handle. Some have 'Don Pottery' painted underneath in red. The jugs are in pearlware and are printed and painted, with a reddish-brown rim and handle edge.

'Grass' edged borders were made at Don, as at so many other contemporary factories. One interesting example is in brown, with an underglaze painted pagoda scene, similar to work done at Leeds, Castleford, Swansea and elsewhere.

Cane-coloured ware, teapots, jugs and sugar basins were made and ornamented with figures, borders and other designs in relief. Jewitt illustrates a sugar box, with relief figures and trophies in black, marked 'Green's Don Pottery'. He does not say whether the mark is printed or impressed, but if impressed, it is the only recorded example of the mark. Egyptian blackware and redware was made, but there are no known examples. Brown glazed pottery, probably an attempt to emulate the Rockingham brown glaze, was also made in varying qualities throughout the years.

Transfer-printed white earthenware is perhaps the commonest ware found today. Scenes printed in black, often with a black line on the plate edge, without border designs, are known, sometimes overpainted in enamel colours (see plate, p 70). The plate illustrated on p 69 is of similar design to one used by Sewell & Donkin, except that the Don engraving is finer and the Sewell & Donkin scene omits the cottage and beehive. Other designs are known, generally depicting rustic scenes. The bluish glaze is sometimes pitted with impurities; the standard of workmanship appears to have deteriorated by the late 1820s.

The pearlware teapot illustrated on p 69 is impressed DON POTTERY and painted over the glaze in green, pink, orange, blue and yellow with a reddish-brown line edge. A plate and saucer painted in the same style have the lion rampant impressed mark (see no 86, p 249).

Perhaps the best-known Don Pottery pieces are the blue transfer-printed wares, particularly the series of Italian views, which have a floral border with two cherubs at the top left-hand side and an urn centre bottom. Twenty-one differently named views are recorded to date, and several unnamed views known:

1 Tomb of Theron Aggrigentum
2 Ancient Cistern near Catania
3 Monastery at Tri Castagne
4 Ruins near Aggrigentum
5 View in Palma
6 Residence of Solimenes near Vesuvius

7   Terrace of the Naval Amphitheatre of Taorminum
8   Obelisk at Catania
9   Cascade at Isola
10 Temple of Serapis at Pauzy
11 View of Alicata
12 View of Corigliano
13 Ruins of the Castle of Canna . . .
14 The Church of Resina at the Foot of Vesuvius
15 Rosalie near Palermo
16 Brunduim
17 . . . On the Poe
18 View near Taorminum
19 Port of Turenium
20 View in the Valley of Ortho near Palermo
21 Port of Ansetta

The Italian views are often but not always marked. They are of fine quality and beautifully glazed, and are found on dinner ware and foot baths, two examples of the latter being known. The marks employed included all those used by the firm during the Greens' occupation, with the exception of no 84 (see p 249). Sometimes two marks are found on one piece.

Several pieces impressed TWIGG NEWHILL, TWIGG or TWIGGS are known, with identical transfers from the above series, and these must have been bought at the sale in 1835. The Twigg pieces are heavier and the engravings not so crisp. Eight examples are known to the author, including three unnamed views which are not recorded in the list above.

The Greens produced a 'Landscape' series that had a panelled border with three types of flowers; patterns in the series include 'Castello St Angelo', 'Reading Woman' and 'Italian Fountain'. They also made 'Sleeping Babe', 'Chinese Pagodas', 'Willow Pattern', 'Broseley Pattern', 'Wild Horse', 'Girl Milking a Reindeer' and 'Milkmaid' (closely resembling a pattern produced at Hull and by Spode). The 'Sun and Fountain' pattern (see plate, p 88) has the printed lion mark, no 85. Coysh illustrates a plate[23] with this pattern impressed 'J Green & Sons', the name of a London retail firm at that time. There may have been some connection between the Swinton Greens and the London firm (see p 248).

Perhaps the most interesting known piece of Don Pottery is the moulded plaque (see plate, p 87), on whose back is incised 'Don. Pottery. July. th 21 1829'. In white earthenware with a blue glaze, painted over the glaze in pink, green, and brown, with red beading and a black border, it is the only known piece of non-utilitarian Don ware, and is extremely attractive.

It has been traditional to attribute to the Don Pottery a certain type of naively modelled pottery, usually painted in the 'Pratt' style, often with splashed or sponged bases, and comprising cow creamers, farmyard groups or cottages. There is no evidence to support this attribution. No known pieces are recorded and no sherds of this type of ware have been found on the site.

Lidded moulded jugs with an all-over daisy design are fairly common in creamware, white earthenware and drab-coloured earthenware. Made in a variety of sizes, they are sometimes picked out in colour. There is a distinctive incised line on the body of the jug, between the daisies, on Don examples, the same basic design without the lines being produced elsewhere. Most Don examples are marked, invariably with no 89, a raised pad with the word 'DON' impressed therein, but there are identically moulded jugs with the same pad but containing a number instead of 'DON'. Many other pieces of both pottery and porcelain of differing designs also bear the numbered pad mark. It is thought unlikely that these pieces were made at the Don Pottery but that Don copied whoever made them, using a similar looking mark.

Experiments in manufacturing porcelain were made about 1810, but none were produced commercially. No authenticated pieces exist in museum collections today, though Jewitt records three pieces.

During the Barker family's occupation the quality of the products declined. Most known examples are thickly potted transfer-printed pieces in a variety of colours. Patterns included 'Wild

Rose', 'Willow', 'Gem', 'Delhi', 'York', 'Manilla', 'Turin''
'Persian', 'Syrian', 'Asiatic Pheasant' and 'Royal Exchange''
Fragments bearing these names have all been unearthed on the
site, many also bearing the factory mark. Two 'Royal Exchange'
plates have the names of the wholesalers 'Lidner & Co' or 'J. M.
Eskenazi' on the back. Marked plates were often found, but it
was noted that cups and saucers never were. Large quantities of
white earthenware boldly painted in red, green and black were
found.

John Tomlinson, having visited the pottery, wrote in 1879 that
the spacious yards and the wharf had heaps of flint from the
south coast, stone from Guernsey and clay from Cornwall, all
brought by boat.[24] He was surprised that the lathes were not
power-driven, as at many other potteries, but were worked
manually by decent looking girls. He noted with what rapidity
rings or string courses of colour were blown on to circular
articles, the turner using a tin teapot-shaped article that had at
one side a short blowpipe and at the other a shorter spout perforated with the required number of holes; he blew down the
tube, squirting thin streams of pigment on to the revolving pot
and producing finer lines than any pencil could have drawn.
Tomlinson understood that none of the ware was hand-painted,
though printing was common, invariably in only one colour at a
time. Saggars were made from fireclay from Leeds.

D. & J. S. Wilson were not manufacturers; they imported both
pottery and porcelain, in the white, from Staffordshire, and
decorated it, specialising in gilding and lustre. Collections of Don
Pottery can be seen at the Doncaster Museum, The Yorkshire
Museum, York, and Weston Park Museum, Sheffield.[25]

Marks

See nos 83–100, p 249.

Saltglazed jug painted in pink, iron red, blue, green and yellow with
black outlines, inscribed 'John Platt 1767'. Rotherham Old Pottery;
see p 120.

BEATSON'S ROTHERHAM POTTERY, EFFINGHAM WORKS
Location: SK 427933

William and Robert Beatson took over the glassworks on the north side of the River Don at Masbrough, Rotherham, in 1783. William married Martha Close, whose father Henry joined the firm, which traded as 'Henry Close & Co', in 1810. Close supplied bricks to the Rotherham churchwardens in 1813. In 1817, when William Beatson and his brother-in-law William Close entered partnership, they are described as glass and bottle manufacturers and potters, trading as 'Beatson & Close'. In 1822 Close left and the firm became 'Beatson & Co'.

William Beatson died in 1825, aged sixty-five, and his widow Martha continued the business, with the help of her father and brother. Primarily glass manufacturers, they advertised the pottery to let in 1826.[40] 'The Rotherham Pottery, was capable of making three ovens a week, having two glazing and one biscuit kiln and every convenience for hardening and enamelling. The pottery was not let, but continued to be run by Martha Beatson. George Taylor and William Shackleton, probably employees, are both described as potters of Rotherham at this time.

In 1828 John Greaves Clark, only son of William Clark, an original partner in the Don Pottery, married Martha Beatson's daughter Ann. He entered partnership with his mother-in-law and

---

Castleford Pottery: White stoneware jug, glazed dark brown at the top; c 1795; mark no 172. White felspathic stoneware teapot; mark no 173; examples known in black basalt; see p 169. Creamware footed bowl overglaze painted in brown; mark no 173.

Castleford Pottery: Felspathic stoneware teapot; mark no 173, see p 169. NB: this and the teapot above are the only known designs of marked Castleford teapots.

her brother, William Close, trading as 'Close & Clark'. In 1836 the lease was renewed, with the Earl of Effingham, for the glasshouse, potteries, etc, occupied by 'Close & Clark' and their under tenants. At this time the pottery was sublet to Joseph Robert Taylor and his son Edwin, trading as 'J. R. Taylor & Son', but they went bankrupt in 1837, and the manufacturing implements and utensils, comprising printing presses, copper plates (many of them new), and a large assortment of blocks and moulds were offered for sale. The flint mill machinery 'of the most recent and approved construction' was also advertised.[41] However, the sale was cancelled and the pottery let to James Yates, an ironfounder. It was a sideline to him, but he ran it for several years before leasing it to Thomas Shenton, a glass manufacturer, who was in occupation in 1845, trading as 'Shenton & Co'. There is no further reference to the pottery. Yates rebuilt much of his foundry, and probably demolished the pottery in the process of expansion.[42]

Wares

There are no known early pieces, and the only clue to wares produced lies in the advertisements. In 1826 enamelling was done, indicating production of fineware. In 1837 printed ware was produced for the London market.

Guest says that Yates 'patented and manufactured a beautiful letter in china for sign boards, shop fronts and many other uses which being susceptive of every variety of elegant form and brilliant colour was for a considerable time in very extensive demand'. These were later made by Earnshaw & Greaves. A white earthenware spill vase in Rotherham Museum, reputedly from this pottery, is glazed and painted to look like marble.

There are no known marks.

NORTHFIELD POTTERY, ROTHERHAM
Location: SK 428936

Built on Cutside Close at Northfield, Rotherham, bounded on the west by the railway and on the east by the canal. The pottery was built by Joseph Lee, who leased the land from W. F. Hoyle in January 1852. In the deed there is no mention of a pottery, although the land is described in detail.[43]

Lee is described as a potter and glass cutter of Masbrough in 1842, and was at Bridgegate Pottery, Rotherham, in 1849. He traded first as 'Joseph Lee', and after taking Nathaniel Booth the younger into partnership in 1852, as 'Joseph Lee & Co'. In October 1853 Lee and Clement Kain are described as earthenware manufacturers and co-partners, with no mention of Booth.

The pottery comprised one biscuit and one glost kiln. According to C. Hawley's documents at Rotherham Library, 'Clement left for America doubtless as selling agent for the firm. The pottery's trade with America led to Joseph Lee & Co.s downfall owing to a financial crisis in that country resulting in bad debts to the firm.' The works were advertised for sale in 1854, and bought in October 1855 by the owner of the Low Pottery, Rawmarsh, George Hawley, who was in occupation.[44]

Hawley worked both Northfield Pottery and Low Pottery, appointing his son Charles as manager at Northfield. George Hawley died in October 1863, and in the following year Charles sold his share to his brothers William and George jr, who traded at both potteries as 'Hawley Brothers' or 'W. & G. Hawley'. William died in 1868 and his half share passed to his sons Matthew, Arthur George, and Walter, who entered into partnership with their uncle George. In 1873 the three brothers bought out their uncle's share in the Northfield Pottery, he taking the Low Pottery. Walter retired from the firm in 1875 but later returned to work at the pottery. Matthew Hawley became senior partner in the firm, and remained so until his death in 1888, aged forty-eight. Arthur George Hawley then took in his two nephews (Matthew's sons), Sidney and John William, into a partnership which lasted until Arthur's death in 1897. A limited liability company, 'Hawley Brothers Ltd', was then formed, the Northfield Pottery being run by Sidney Hawley.

The pottery boasted the largest kiln in Yorkshire for biscuit ware, two glost and two hardening kilns, and one enamelling kiln.

In 1903 the firm was taken over by a syndicate of Castleford and Ferrybridge potters, including E. L. Poulson, Joseph Horn and Thomas Gill, trading as 'The Northfield Hawley Pottery Co Ltd'; but the works had closed by November 1916, when the Co-operative Wholesale Society Ltd took over and modernised and re-equipped the pottery. It closed in 1929.

Wares

Joseph Lee made domestic white earthenware, mainly transfer-printed, and furniture cream bottles, but is best known for his shop letter signs, which were made of fireclay and enamelled in white.

The Hawleys made a great variety of table and toilet wares, usually transfer-printed, and marine blue linings for Sheffield Plate mustard and salt cellars. In 1885 they advertised in the *Rotherham & Masbrough Advertiser* as follows:

It is in fact perhaps not generally known that at the Northfield Pottery, Rotherham, the Public can have the opportunity of inspecting a collection of all descriptions of earthenware, of a class and extent seldom to be met with in a provincial town. The showrooms of Messrs Hawley Bros. is replete with every kind of service that can be required by any family, no matter in what station of life they may be placed. The sets of toilet, table and tea and breakfast ware vary in style and quality as they do in price, but all are of excellent workmanship, and the better sorts are really excellent designs. Glass, cut and moulded, and black and brown ware is also largely shown; whilst the stock of garden pots, comprising all sizes, of excellent quality cannot fail to be of great convenience to the neighbourhood gentry and gardeners. The trade and householders cannot do better than pay this place a visit before making their purchase. Wholesale and Retail . . . Also glass and china merchants. Have the largest showrooms (in the trade) in the county . . .

In the late 1880s experiments were carried out in the manufacture of porcelain and leadless glaze. Several pieces of beautifully decorated porcelain remain in the hands of the Hawley family today. These include a cup, saucer and plate painted in blue, red and gold in Imari type patterns, the cup completely gilded on the inside. Some earthenware of the same period was similarly decorated. A black basalt cameo of a classical head made by Sidney Hawley, and an earthenware fern pot with open wickerwork pattern and grey leadless glaze, are in the same collection.

John Hawley's daughter has some green glazed plates of the 'Thistle' design, as made by the Don and Newhill Potteries, from Northfield, and an octagonal white earthenware child's plate with a coloured printed scene of two children and a beehive.[45]

Advertising in 1913 the firm claimed to manufacture every description of leadless glazed earthenware in 'Dipt, cream coloured, sponged, Pheasant, Willow etc Potted meat and shrimp pots', and to specialise in slip and underglaze painting on vases, flower pots, toilet jugs, mugs and also in lithographed and gilt dinner and tea ware. They also produced souvenir and commemorative items.

Marks

There are no known marks used by Joseph Lee. Marked pieces of Northfield Pottery are fairly rare, suggesting that only a small proportion was marked.

See nos 140–4 and 146–9A, p255.

HOLMES POTTERY, ROTHERHAM
Location: SK 412925

Situated in Psalter Lane, Holmes, Rotherham, adjoining the railway and near the station, the Holmes Pottery was built by Thomas Jarvis, builder, about 1850, and leased to William Earnshaw and Jervis Greaves. Earnshaw had previously partnered Peter Hobson at a pottery in College Road, Rotherham. Hobson later took over the Rockingham Works. 'Earnshaw & Greaves' exhibited 'painted biura and Yates's patent porcelain letters' at the 1851 Exhibition. There is no further mention of Earnshaw at the Holmes Pottery, but Greaves was joined by Thomas Dickinson, John Jackson and George Shaw, the firm trading in 1854 as 'Dickinson & Jackson' and in 1860 as 'John Jackson & Co'.

The firm bought land in New York, Rotherham, where it built a flint mill and warehouses. (A map dated 1896 shows extensive premises on the Holmes site, with six kilns, and large premises in New York.)[46]

Greaves died c 1866–8, Dickinson left the concern shortly after, and the remaining partners, Jackson and Shaw, bought the pottery in 1875. T. S. Goodwin was manager until 1871, when he left to manage the Newhill Pottery. John Jackson died c 1881 and George Shaw assumed sole charge, trading under the old style until about 1887, when the firm became 'George Shaw & Sons'. After Shaw's death in 1892 the pottery was continued by his sons Thomas and Charles; in 1909 it became a limited company and traded as 'George Shaw & Sons Ltd'. The Holmes Pottery is listed in directories until 1931.

Wares

All the occupants of the Holmes Pottery are described as earthenware manufacturers. John Jackson was apprenticed at the Swinton Pottery and, as his grand-daughter put it, 'appreciated fine things'. There is no record, however, of fine things being produced, only domestic ware—pudding basins, kitchen items and white transfer-printed pottery in the popular patterns of the day, such as 'Wild Rose' and 'Willow Pattern'. Jewitt records that 'an attempt at china manufacture was made here, but was abandoned'.

Marks

See nos 150–1, p 257. Very little was marked and such pieces are rarely seen.

BRIDGEGATE POTTERY, ROTHERHAM

Joseph Lee is listed in a directory of 1849 as being at Bridgegate Pottery, Rotherham, and Joseph Lee of 'The Pottery, Rotherham' exhibited a sign board with porcelain letters at the 1851 Exhibition. He later founded the Northfield Pottery.

COLLEGE ROAD POTTERY, ROTHERHAM

In 1848-9 William Earnshaw and Peter Hobson worked a small pottery in College Road, Rotherham. Earnshaw later went to the Holmes Pottery and Hobson to the Swinton Pottery.

LOW POTTERY, RAWMARSH
Location: SK 438963

Situated between the High Street and Dale Road, north of Stocks Lane (originally Stork Lane), Rawmarsh, the pottery was probably established by the Hallam family in the early eighteenth century. The first reference to it appears in a conveyance of January 1790: 'three tenements or dwellinghouses with the pottery and other premises . . . in Rawmarsh now in the several tenures of Robert Hallam, John Naylor and Thomas Amory . . .'. Five other dwellings were conveyed, some of them occupied by known potters.[47]

In the early eighteenth century the Hallam family are strongly represented as 'potters' in the parish registers, and Robert Hallam, potter, inherited three cottages in Stork Lane from his father, also Robert Hallam, who is described in his will, registered 1747, as a potter. The Marquis of Rockingham paid Robert Hallam jr £3 17s 9d for pots in 1759, and a bill of 1766 headed 'Hallam & Co' for garden pots is also preserved.[48] Robert Hallam jr died in the early 1790s and his widow Mary let the pottery to John Wainwright and Peter Barker, trading as 'Barker & Co'.[49]

Wainwright bought the pottery and three cottages in 1810.

About 1812 Peter Barker joined his brother at Mexborough and Wainwright continued alone until his death *c* 1830. John Broughton, an innkeeper and Wainwright's nephew, inherited the pottery and ran it until *c* 1833, when he let it to 'T. Taylor & Co'.

In 1836 the firm was 'Taylor, Ask & Co', and the principals were Thomas Taylor, his son Elisha, and Robert Ask, who also worked the Meadow Pottery, Rawmarsh. In January 1838 the partnership was dissolved, the Taylors taking the Low Pottery and trading as 'Thomas Taylor & Son'.[50] In 1840 they went bankrupt.

George Hawley, son of the William Hawley who founded the Top Pottery, Rawmarsh, took over the works, buying the premises in July 1859. He lived in the Pottery House, which was in Dale Road, adjoining the entrance gates, and later became the Horse & Jockey Inn.[51] He also owned the Northfield Pottery.

After George Hawley's death in 1863, aged sixty-eight, the two potteries passed to George's widow and sons William, George and Charles, the last-named selling out to his brothers in 1864, after which William and George jr ran both works as 'W. & G. Hawley'. Four years later, in 1868, William died and his three sons Matthew, Arthur George and Walter took their father's place in partnership with their uncle George. George ran the Low Pottery, trading as 'G. Hawley', and in 1873 bought the half share of the Low Pottery owned by his nephews. However, he ran into financial difficulties and closed the pottery. The *Rotherham & Masbrough Advertiser* of 30 December 1882 comments that the Low Pottery had 'been got into working order again', having been taken by 'Messrs Leyland, Walker & Hornsey', then 'Walker & Hornsey', before being bought back into the Hawley family again by Matthew and Arthur George in 1884. Being now the only pottery of any consequence in Rawmarsh, the Low Pottery became known simply as 'The Rawmarsh Pottery'. Matthew Hawley died in 1888 and his sons Sidney and John entered into partnership with their uncle Arthur George until the latter's death in 1897 at the age of forty-eight. The firm became

'Hawley Bros Ltd', and the Low Pottery was run by John Hawley.

On 5 August 1903 the firm was taken over by a syndicate of Castleford and Ferrybridge potters, including E. L. Poulson and Joseph Horn as directors and Thomas Gill as secretary, trading as 'The Northfield Hawley Pottery Co'.

The premises 'recently used as and for the purpose of carrying on a Pottery known by the name of the Low Pottery' were sold in 1904.[52] The demolition of the buildings in 1905 meant the demise of the oldest pottery in the district.[45]

Wares

Apart from the fact that the Hallam family made garden pots, nothing is known of the products of the early years.

'Barker & Co' are described as earthenware manufacturers and probably made the better quality domestic wares. Several pieces impressed 'BARKER' are known, but it cannot be said whether they were made here, at the Mexborough Pottery or in Staffordshire. Two examples can be seen at the Victoria & Albert Museum —a black basalt creamer and a 'Pratt' type teapot.

John Broughton made domestic earthenware. A man appeared in court in 1833 charged with stealing from Broughton 'shaving pots, teacups and saucers, some printed meat dishes and baking dishes the last two of Willow Pattern design'.

'Taylor, Ask & Co' and 'Thomas Taylor & Son' continued making domestic white earthenware at the Low Pottery, and making firebricks and allied wares at their other works.

The Hawleys also made domestic earthenware, including tea and toilet sets, paste pots, earthenware toys and miniature tea and toilet sets, in sponged, printed and underglaze painted ware. Two inscribed examples exist depicting cottages with blue painted roofs and splashes of pink, yellow and green, with cheeky children's faces peering from the windows. Articles made by the first George Hawley were continued up to 1880, when the German felspar china toys finally captured the trade and perhaps caused the second

George Hawley's financial troubles in the 1880s. A blue printed plate with a vine creeper border and a lake scene with a castle beyond has 'Geo. Hawley', the registration mark for 1849 and 'WINDSOR' printed on the back. It is also known in sepia. Another blue printed plate (mark no 141, p 255) with a lacy border design, a formal garden scene with a fountain, swans on a lake and an eastern building, was also made by George Hawley.

Hawley Brothers made a wide range of domestic earthenware and garden pots (see advertisement, p 128).

A jug and bowl set with mark no 145 is the only known piece made by 'Leyland, Walker & Hornsey'. It is in white earthenware transfer-printed in deep blue with butterflies, fans and a bee with a very human face.

The Rotherham and Yorkshire Museums have examples of Rawmarsh pottery.

Marks

The mark BARKER may have been used here (see p 116). No other marks are known until the pottery was occupied by the George Hawleys. Thereafter only a small portion of the products was marked and known pieces are rare.

See nos 121, 140–2, 145, pp 253, 255.

TOP POTTERY, RAWMARSH
Location: SK 437961

Situated on the east side of the town street, Rawmarsh, about 300yd south of the Low Pottery, it was founded in 1790 by William Hawley, who had previously partnered Samuel Walker at the Rotherham Old Pottery. In 1796 Hawley bought the land, homestead and outbuildings, 'which premises are now in the occupation of William Hawley and used as a pottery'.[53] He traded as 'Hawley & Co' until his death in 1818. His widow Elizabeth, known locally as 'Dame Hawley', carried on, assisted by her numerous sons, two of whom—George, an earthenware printer, and Abraham, a turner—managed the works after their mother's death in 1844. George Hawley took over the Rawmarsh Low Pottery and later bought the Northfield Pottery, leaving the running of the Top Pottery to his brother Abraham. However, Abraham ran into financial difficulties, and in January 1855 sold his third share in the Top Pottery. On 3 July 1858 it was advertised for sale:

> All that Pottery or Earthenware Manufactory, with the Warehouses, Glost Kilns, Biscuit Kilns, Hovels, Dipping House, Slip Houses, Throwing and Turning Shops, Printing and other shops, stable, cow house, cart shed, yard and vacant ground thereto belonging, situate in and fronting the Town Street of Rawmarsh adjoining the Earl Grey Inn, late in the occupation of Mr Abraham Hawley, the site thereof containing two roods and thirty perches or thereabouts. Further particulars may be had on application to Mr George Hawley of Rawmarsh Pottery.[54]

The premises were sold to a local blacksmith and converted into a house and blacksmith's shop.

Wares

William Hawley worked at the Rotherham Old Pottery where fineware was made, and would have had the knowledge and skill necessary for manufacturing high quality wares. Several known pieces of 'Prattware', judged to have been made in the early nineteenth century and impressed 'HAWLEY', were made at the Top Pottery or at the Kilnhurst Old Pottery. These include Toby jugs and teapots (see plate, p 69), and a jug with the head of Nelson in a panel on one side and the heads of a man, woman and child in a panel on the other. Other potters named Hawley worked in Staffordshire later in the century, but the historical attribution of some of the pieces establishes that this mark was used by the Yorkshire Hawleys. Other early pieces with historical attribution, but unmarked, include a loving cup painted overglaze with flowers in colour on a white ground, inscribed 'Isaac Walton, 1805'; an earthenware jug with a light green wash ground and the head of satyr or Bacchus decorated in green and brown; a jug painted on a white ground in orange, green and yellow underglaze, with applied ornamentation of foliage and foxhounds, and the top of the handle in the shape of a dog; and a loving cup painted overglaze with flowers in colour on a white ground, inscribed 'James Best 1806'.

'Dame' Hawley is reputed to have made good domestic ware, buff ware and hearth tiles. She exported to Australia. George Hawley's recipe book, dated 1816, shows formulae for blue jasper and blue turquoise under dates for 1842–3. Later products comprised general domestic white earthenware, much of it printed after the fashion of the day.[55]

THOMAS AMORY'S POTTERY, RAWMARSH
Location unknown

Documents relating to a late eighteenth-century pottery in Rawmarsh have recently come to light. On 1 October 1786 Thomas Amory's pottery, stock and utensils were assigned to creditors who intended carrying on the business for 4 years; but profits proved insufficient to pay off the creditors, and in September 1790 the pottery was advertised for sale. There was no buyer. The pottery was valued by Thomas Newton of the Kilnhurst Pottery, and an appraiser, at £737 18s 1½d; and agreement was reached with Thomas Button, a workman from the Rotherham Old Pottery, and Peter Barker, a potter of Rawmarsh and also the landlord, to take over the pottery.[56]

Thomas Amory is listed as a potter of Rawmarsh in 1783 (p 81), which suggests that his pottery was then in existence. He worked for Robert Hallam at the Low Pottery, Rawmarsh, in 1790.

MEADOW POTTERY, RAWMARSH
Location: SK 446965

Built near Roundwood Brook, to the east of Clay Pit Lane and south of Kilnhurst Road, Rawmarsh.

The first known occupants were 'Messrs Goldsbrough & Co', mentioned as occupants previous to 'Thomas Taylor & Co', who bought the land in 1836. In July 1835 two closes were advertised for sale, and on one of them, Brickyard Close, it was stated that 'a firebrick yard has been advantageously carried on for some years which has sheds, kilns . . . the estate contains beds of excellent coal and firebrick clay'.

Thomas Taylor, his son Elisha and Robert Ask, who were the partners in 'Thomas Taylor & Co', also worked the Low Pottery, Rawmarsh. In January 1838 the partnership was dissolved, Robert Ask remaining at the Meadow Pottery until his death, c 1840. His widow, Lydia, ran the pottery until the mid-1840s, when she sold it to John Edwards and others. Edwards took Henry Howard into partnership, c 1858, and traded as 'Edwards & Howard', but in 1863 sold the 'Meadow Works' to George Beeley. In 1872 the 'Meadow Pottery Works', which had three small kilns, passed to Thomas W. Roome, and he ran it until he went bankrupt in 1904. He was then described as a brickmaker.[57]

Wares and Marks

The early occupants were potters, earthenware makers and brickmakers. In 1840 a pottery and brickyard existed on the site. 'Edwards & Howard' discontinued the manufacture of earthenware in favour of firebricks, pipes and tiles, and the name was changed from 'The Meadow Pottery' to 'The Meadow Works' or 'Meadow Pottery Works'.

There are no known pieces or marks.

GEORGE TAYLOR'S POTTERY, RAWMARSH

George Taylor bought Ings Head Close, Rawmarsh, in 1826, and built a small pottery. The land abutted a brook dividing Rawmarsh from Greasebrough on the west and a road leading to a colliery on the north. Taylor died in 1843 and the works were sold.[58]

George Taylor is recorded as a brickmaker in Masbrough in 1823, as a potter of Masbrough when he bought the above land in 1826, and as an earthenware manufacturer at Newbiggin and Rawmarsh in 1830.

DALE POTTERY, RAWMARSH

In 1802 John Mangham bought two cottages in The Dale, Rawmarsh, the area north of the Low Pottery. In 1805 the cottages and 'all that new erected pottery with the smoke house, drying kilns . . . situate in Rawmarsh . . . now in the occupation of Frederick Flower . . .' were sold.[59] In 1807 Frederick Flower was still in occupation.

WARREN VALE, RAWMARSH
Location: SK 435975

Two pottery kilns were recently discovered in the house wall of a cottage at 9 Warren Vale, Rawmarsh. The kilns contained an almost complete black glazed bottle waster, sherds of creamware and silver resist. Some coarseware plaster moulds for casting ink bottles were also found, together with several inkwells made from the moulds in a smooth red fabric with brown glazed interior and mouth. The finds are in Rotherham Museum.[60]

ATTERCLIFFE OLD POTTERY
Location: SK 384983

Attercliffe is 2 miles north-east of the centre of Sheffield. The Old Pottery was built on a 6 acre site north of Bradley Nook Road, later called Pot House Lane, south of the Sheffield—Tinsley road, on land owned by the Duke of Norfolk. Potters are recorded in Attercliffe from 1790.

John Smelter bought the land, 'buildings and erections', in 1815, and sold them in 1819 to James Hill and his son George, cornmillers. James Hill died in 1836; and 2 years later George

Hill is described as a cornmiller and earthenware manufacturer. In 1844 George Hill, in the *Leeds Mercury*, advertised the pottery to let: '. . . It is in complete working order, with a twelve month's stock of clay, prepared ready for use. The clay is got on the premises. The Oven holds 350 Dozen ware; is the only Coarse Ware Pottery (except one) within twelve miles of Sheffield.'

In 1849 George Hill sold the pottery, the deeds stating that it had been 'for many years then past called the Attercliffe Old Pottery', though this is the first mention of the fact. Richard Bedford was in occupation in 1849 until his death *c* 1866, when his widow Hannah, and sons William and Richard, carried on the pottery. A third son, John, worked as a potter at Strensall, near York. Richard Bedford bought the Kilnhurst Bridge Pottery in 1854.

The pottery changed hands several times in the late 1860s, coming into the possession of Thomas Stead, an ironfounder, in 1867. He reputedly worked the pottery until 1872.

Wares and Marks

There are no known pieces or marks. George Hill is given as earthenware manufacturer, and the Bedfords as common earthenware and blackware manufacturers. Local clay was used.[61]

DARNALL ROAD POTTERY OR ATTERCLIFFE NEW POTTERY
Location: SK 386887

Situated about 200yd south of the Sheffield canal, south of Doctor Lane and east of the Worksop Road, on land owned by the Sheffield Church Burgesses. The pottery was occupied by John Fearnley during the years 1823–33. John and William Walkland were tenants from 1838 to 1845, followed by John Cooper in 1849 until his death in 1884; John's widow Emily Cooper, who remarried and became Emily Jackson, continued the pottery until 1889. After that, there is no further reference.

Wares and Marks

There are no known pieces or marks. John Fearnley is listed as a pot-maker, the Walklands as manufacturers of red and black earthenware, and John Cooper as a black earthenware manufacturer. Local clay was used.[62]

SHEFFIELD

A pottery kiln was built at Sheffield Manor in the early eighteenth century. Brown mottled glazed earthenware was made.[63]

In 1861 J. Parker was working as a potter in Hermitage Street, Sheffield; in 1864 he was dealing in drainpipes, tiles and chimney-pots.

Thomas Marshall and William Crapper, potters, worked at Storrs Bridge, Ecclesfield, north of Sheffield in 1867. They later became firebrick manufacturers and clay merchants.

BRAMPTON BIERLOW, WEST MELTON

In 1837–8 John Booker, formerly a brickmaker, made brown earthenware.

MILTON POTTERY, SKIERS SPRING

This pottery was built on land owned by Earl Fitzwilliam, and named after Lord Milton, at Skiers Spring, Hoyland, south of

---

Castleford Pottery: Blue printed 'Castle and Fisherman' pattern plate; 1800–20; mark no 172. Blue printed 'Riverside Cottage' pattern plate; 1800–20; mark no 172.

Blue printed loving cup 'R. Raper, Oulton, 1858'; unmarked; attributed to Woodlesford Pottery. White felspathic stoneware teapot; mark nos 119 and 6. White felspathic stoneware sucrier, impressed '22'; note almost identical moulding to above. White felspathic stoneware teapot; mark nos 119 and 1; see p 115.

Barnsley, in 1902. Managed by David Kier, a potter from Cumberland, it had one large kiln capable of firing 250 dozen pieces, a large throwing shed and a drying shed. Eight men were employed, and local clay was used. The pottery closed in 1937.

Wares and Marks

Traditional country ware, chiefly breadpans, mugs, stewpots, flowerpots and peggy pots. Some novelties were made to order, including chests of drawers and money-boxes.

No marks were used.

GRANGE, SADDLEWORTH
Location: SD 987091

Grange is situated on the Yorkshire–Lancashire border 1 mile north-west of Delph. Pottery Hill is shown on the 1906 Ordnance Survey map north of the crossroads at the centre of the village.

Earthenware manufacturers listed in directories include John Marland, Grange Bank, 1853; James Taylor, The Grange, 1853; and Robert Whitehead, Ship, near Waterhead Mill.

TODMORDEN

Reuben Haigh worked as an earthenware manufacturer at Weatherhill, Todmorden, in 1837.

Red-bodied bottle glazed in very dark brown; inscribed 'RB 1779'; Silkstone Pottery; see p 144.

Puzzle jug in red body with dark brown glaze. Inscribed 'Gentlemen. now. try. your. Skill Ile. hold. your. sixpence. If. you. Will. That. you. don't. drink. unless. you. Spill. W. E. Green. Ingleton.' and '1825' on the top of the handle. Attributed to Burton in Lonsdale.

DODWORTH

In 1879 George Senior owned the Albion Earthenware Works at Dodworth, west of Barnsley. He also had a pottery at Whittington, Derbyshire.

SILKSTONE POTTERY
Location: SE 293058

Situated south of the A628 Barnsley to Woodhead road, east of the river and Pot House Bridge, at Silkstone, 3 miles west of Barnsley.

A pottery is first mentioned in deeds dated 1754, when potovens, a house and cornmill occupied by John Bailey, Ralph Taylor, Joseph Goldthorpe and Michael Taylor are recorded as belonging to James Scott.[64] The estate was bought by Richard Fenton in 1775 when the occupants, except for Michael Taylor, were those listed above.

In 1767 John Taylor, potter of Silkstone, was married. The Land Tax assessments give him as tenant from 1781 (the earliest record available) to 1812; he died in 1815, aged seventy-two. William Taylor, who is recorded as a potter in the 1780s, and as renting premises in 1781, then ran the works until 1821.

The 1802 militia list for Silkstone gives Edward Taylor, aged twenty-five, and William Taylor, aged thirty-four, as potters. There must have been two William Taylors (see previous paragraph).

A picture of the pottery is reproduced in *The English Country Pottery* by P. C. D. Brears. The site is now used as a market garden.

Wares

Two pieces only appear in museum collections. Cawthorne Museum has a large, dark red earthenware flagon, with a dark brown lead glaze and a white slip-trailed inscription 'PE 1777'; and the British Museum has a cylindrical bottle of similar fabric, 'RB 1779', which was made for Richard Bailey and bought from his grand-daughter in 1898 (see plate, p 142). Broken wasters found on the site are made of coarse thick earthenware, some with an interesting striped dark brown and buff glaze.

MIDDOPSTONES POTTERY
Location: SK 238997

Situated at Midhopestones in the parish of Ecclesfield, bounded north and east by the River Don, and west by the Midhopestones–Penistone road, and now covered by Underbank reservoir.

In 1720 George Walker and Robert Blackburn took a 99 year lease of Nether Mill Green, Midhope 'on which to build a Pot-House and other conveniences thereunto'. Robert Blackburn, who also worked the glasshouse at Bate Green, died in 1727, and his widow Mary assigned the lease to William Gough. Tenants of the pothouse include Thomas Dyson in 1747 and John Kay in 1750.

In 1762 Gough assigned the lease to John Taylor, but he shortly became indebted to John Whiteley, who took over the lease in 1765. Whiteley's widow sold the lease to Edward Appleyard of Sheffield Park in 1793. Joshua Lindley occupied the pothouse from the late 1780s until his death in 1801. Appleyard then advertised in the *Sheffield Advertiser* 'that an old established Pot House' was for sale or to let, stating that there was a very good bed of clay for common and brown earthenware or good firebrick, and excellent coal in the neighbourhood. The works were not let, however, and Elizabeth Lindley continued as tenant. A further advertisement appeared in July 1803, after which Thomas Fawley took the pothouse. In 1816 William Appleyard inherited the lease of the pottery, but this expired 3 years later and was not renewed.

Matthew Thickett is listed as earthenware manufacturer of Midhope in 1822, but in 1828, when John Haigh bought the pottery, William Stead was in occupation. The 1833 directory gives Thickett & Co again, but when Haigh wrote his will in 1835, the pottery was occupied by James Barraclough. Competition from the growing number of factory potteries in south Yorkshire proved too great and the Middopstones Pottery closed some time before 1845, when the premises, described as 'formerly used as a pottery', were sold to Luke Moorhouse.

Wares

Traditional red-bodied earthenware was made from local clay. The inside and part of the outside was given a dark brown to black glaze, known locally as meeas glaze, which reputedly never crazed. Products included porringers, bottles, basins, pancheons, cups and saucers, jars, plates and chimneypots. Plates and dishes were sometimes ornately decorated in contrasting slip on the upper surface only, in combed or marbled designs, and occasionally with figures and birds. Some dated and initialled pieces are known.

There is a collection of wasters at Weston Park Museum, Sheffield.[65]

BATE GREEN POT HOUSE, STOCKSBRIDGE
Location: SK 266980

Joseph Kenworthy (see Bibliography) says that the glasshouse at Bate Green was converted into a pothouse in 1778 and tenanted by Joshua Lindley, who worked it concurrently with the Middopstones Pottery. Later maps show two distinct buildings some distance apart, one named the Glasshouse and the other the Pot House.

Recent excavations by D. Ashurst have revealed red fabric dishes and bowls decorated in yellow and brown slip, with flower patterns and combing.[66]

UPPER DON VALLEY

Kenworthy records two other potteries in the Upper Don Valley. One was at Unsliven Bridge at the eastern end of Underbank reservoir, reputedly worked by Matthew Thickett before he went to Middopstones Pottery, and in the mid-nineteenth century by a Mr Barraclough. The other, at the Hand Bank Brickworks, between the river and the main road north-west of Midhopestones, was built by Halstead & Sellers in the mid-nineteenth century to make firebricks and allied wares. The works were taken over by Mr Hill who made brown and saltglazed earthenware, and lustre decorated and transfer-printed wares. The property was demolished about 1870.

DONCASTER

There was a pottery in Hallgate, Doncaster, in the late thirteenth and early fourteenth centuries. Main products comprised face jugs, jugs with tubular spouts, baluster and globular shaped pipkins, pancheons and some roof tiles. Wasters may be seen in Doncaster Museum.

FERRYBRIDGE, PONTEFRACT AND CASTLEFORD

FERRYBRIDGE OR KNOTTINGLEY POTTERY
Location: SE 489242

Built on the southern bank of the River Aire, almost a mile downstream from the bridge at Ferrybridge.

It has been suggested that the Knottingley Pottery, as it was originally called, was built on a site used by a Mr Clifton, who reputedly copied the work of Francis Place of York, but this suggestion is incorrect. Timothy Smith, coal proprietor, bought the land in 1773, and no pottery was in existence then, nor had one ever existed there. In January 1793 Smith, William Tomlinson, grocer of Pontefract, and John Seaton, banker of Pontefract, obtained permission to erect a flint mill on the northern bank of the River Aire.[1] In May of that year and in the following February John Foster, shipowner of Selby, John Thompson, gentleman of Selby, and Robert Smith, on behalf of his father Timothy, joined Tomlinson and Seaton in buying about 30 acres of land, where they 'erected a pottery and diverse other buildings and jointly carried on the business of a pottery there', trading as 'Tomlinson Foster & Company'. There were twelve shares, John Seaton and William Tomlinson each having three and the others two each. John Thompson died in July 1798 and his son, also John, took his father's shares.

In June 1798 Ralph Wedgwood, nephew of Josiah Wedgwood and previously owner of a pottery in Burslem, joined the partnership, when two additional shares were created for him. The

Ferrybridge partners welcomed this talented inventive new-comer, and it was arranged that Wedgwood was to receive an extra £200 a year in consideration of the secrets he was to communicate to the firm. The partnership, intended to last 10 years, was styled 'Tomlinson, Foster, Wedgwood & Company'.

Ralph Wedgwood's experiments proved expensive, the partnership was not a success, and 18 months later the agreement was dissolved. In January 1801 Wedgwood was paid £1,025 'to quit the concern at Knottingley Pottery and relinquish to Tomlinson, Foster & Company all their engagements with him . . . and shall quit the Knottingley premises and remove therefrom entirely on or before the first day of January 1801 . . .' This stipulation was followed by an inventory which included a drawing book and three boxes of samples of earthenware.[2] A drawing book dating from this period is owned by Josiah Wedgwood & Sons Ltd today, and is probably the one mentioned above.

The firm then traded as 'William Tomlinson & Company'. Finances were low and the pottery was mortgaged. In August 1802 it was advertised for sale, but was not sold.

Timothy Smith died in 1803 and his shares passed to his son Charles. On 1 July 1804 the partnership of 'William Tomlinson & Company' was dissolved by mutual consent, 'the pottery concern having proved a disadvantageous one' and 'having contracted debts which then remained unpaid to a considerable amount'. John Foster retired and John Foster jr, Thomas Foster and John Plowes jr (son of John Plowes, late partner of David Dunderdale of the Castleford Pottery), joined the firm, which became 'Tomlinson, Plowes & Company'. The name of the works was changed to 'The Ferrybridge Pottery'.

John Plowes was to be paid travelling expenses which suggests that he became a representative for the firm. Of the others there is no indication that any except William Tomlinson took an active part in running the pottery; he lived in the pottery house and was in charge of the works.

John Plowes sr joined the firm in April 1805, when its fortunes were improving. The price of a share had risen considerably from

£1,008 6s 8d in 1804 to £1,618 12s 8d in 1805. In the following year John Fox Seaton, banker of Pontefract, joined the firm.

The partnership was not a stable one: John Seaton and John Fox Seaton went bankrupt in connection with their other businesses; John Plowes sr died in 1812; John Plowes jr, living in London, left the firm in 1817; and both the Fosters went bankrupt in 1819. William Tomlinson acquired their shares, eventually owning nine, compared with Charles Smith's two and John Thompson's one.

The fortunes of the firm declined again. In fact the Ferrybridge Pottery was for ever plagued by one financial crisis after another. The firm was still in debt when John Thompson (third generation in the firm) died in 1826. William Tomlinson bought his share and in 1828 bought out Charles Smith, becoming sole owner of the pottery. By this time, however, he was becoming an old man, and although his son Edward helped on the business side, he was not interested in running the pottery. They advertised the works for sale or to let in the *Leeds Intelligencer* in 1828, stating that they carried on an extensive foreign trade, but there were no offers. The pottery was now situated on the bank of the canal completed 2 years earlier between the river and the pottery buildings, and for a considerable time it had been managed by Thomas Braim, manager of the Castleford Pottery in its early days.

In 1830 William Tomlinson transferred ownership to his son Edward, dying 3 years later, aged eighty-seven. With him died the artistic merits of the Ferrybridge Pottery.

In 1830–1 the works were divided, a large portion being let to Mr Wigglesworth, and the remainder to Mr Lindley. In 1832 James Reed and Benjamin Taylor took over Wigglesworth's part, the remainder standing empty.[3] Reed & Taylor were proprietors of the Mexborough Rock Pottery, and later took over the Swillington Bridge Pottery. Taylor ran the Ferrybridge and Swillington Potteries, whilst Reed ran the Mexborough works, trading at all three first as 'Reed & Taylor' then as 'Reed, Taylor & Co'. In 1841 the Ferrybridge firm is listed as 'The Ferrybridge Pottery Company'. In the following year the pottery was again advertised for sale or to let, to be taken in the November,[4] but again there were no takers, and Reed & Taylor remained in occupation. Shortly afterwards the partners split up, Reed remaining at Mexborough, and Benjamin Taylor retaining the Ferrybridge Pottery, assisted by his son, and trading by 1848 as 'Benjamin Taylor & Son'. The son would probably be Samuel, who witnessed Benjamin's signature on several occasions, and is described as a potter of Swillington in 1842 and as an earthenware manufacturer of Ferrybridge in 1847.

Benjamin Taylor retired to Brotherton nearby, and in February 1850 Edward Tomlinson once again advertised the pottery to let; there were now six biscuit and gloss kilns, three hardening on kilns, one enamelling kiln and other workshops.

Walden Poulson and Edward Shaw took over the works for a time. A note written by Shaw states:

> I do hereby agree to give up my share in the Pottery with all profits which as been gained since I have been in business with Mr Poulson on the following conditions Viz, that is for Mr Woolf to give me employment for the term of 15 months at the rate of Thirty shillings per week and rent free and coals—these terms I do hereby agree to providing Mr Tomlinson and Mr Woolf comes to terms about the rent. (signed) Edward Shaw. Witness: W. Poulson this day 15th May 1851.[5]

What became of Shaw is not known, but Walden Poulson became pottery manager in 1858 and remained until his death in 1861.

On 20 May 1851 Lewis Woolf, china merchant of London, leased the pottery for 5 years at £200 a year, Edward Tomlinson contracting to keep certain premises 'as is necessary for the safe and proper keeping of the moulds, copper plates . . . now upon the premises'. It appears that Lewis Woolf introduced new designs and patterns. The premises included the following: cane baker workshop, printing shop, throwing house, glaze shop, painting shop, black sliphouse, cane sliphouse, modellers' shop, lead house, laboratory, dipping house, and clay mill.[6] Ground flint was obtained from the mills of Joseph Horn at Castleford.

In 1856 Lewis Woolf bought the pottery for £4,400 and brought his sons Sydney and Henry into the business. They built another pottery on adjoining land to the west, which they named 'The Australian Pottery', trading as 'Lewis Woolf & Sons'. Thomas, son of Walden Poulson, managed one of the potteries, and Thomas Walker, previously book-keeper, the other. In 1877 Enoch Turner was manager.

In January 1884 the pottery was let to Philip Ernest Woolf, earthenware manufacturer of London, for a few months. It was then leased by Thomas Poulson and his brother Edward Llewellyn at £125 a year. They owned the 'West Riding Pottery' and leased 'The Calder Pottery', trading as 'Poulson Brothers' at all three. The lease is witnessed by Thomas Brown, pottery overlooker. Thomas Poulson, who lived at Dresden House, died in 1893, following which, in 1895, Edward Llewellyn Poulson gave up the Ferrybridge Pottery but continued at the West Riding Pottery. The Ferrybridge Pottery was then leased by Thomas Brown and Charles Sefton, a farmer, who bought it in 1902. They traded as 'Sefton & Brown' until 1919, when Thomas Brown bought out his partner and the firm became 'Thomas Brown & Sons Ltd'. The pottery has remained in the hands of the same family ever since, the present owner, T. G. Brown, being the third generation. The firm now employs about seventy hands and has a flourishing trade, mainly in domestic earthenware; some of it is exported.[7]

Wares

Little is known of the first products and no marked pieces are known. A 'Shape & Pattern Book' with 'W & Co Ferrybridge' on the spine, in use at the pottery during Ralph Wedgwood's time (probably his personal copy), contains 171 pages of drawings, border patterns, shapes, descriptions, transfers and several designs cut from Wedgwood's first pattern book.[8] A wide variety of wares were made, including creamware, pearlware printed in blue and olive, marbled ware, stoneware, blackware, buff-bodied ware, and jasper ware in dark and light blue. Designs included

Queens, Royal and Paris patterned plates, feather edge, pierced, basket work, scalloped shell, stone jugs, marbled and chocolate rib, chintz, buff-bodied flowerpots with chocolate dip and blue bands, and black octagon teapots, filling many pages. Some descriptions are in French, and a note 'Mr Foster New York via Liverpool' suggests an export trade to France and America at that time. A note on a drawing of a teapot—'March 30th/99 The Newest Pattern in the Pottery'—nicely dates the book to 1799.

There are sketches of jug, teapot and coffee jug shapes, with details of some knobs and handles, and one of a double twisted handle with flower and leaf terminals similar but not identical to that used at Leeds. Several tracings from the book are shown in Figs 11, 12 and 13. A large portion of the book consists of border patterns probably used on creamware, several of which are very similar to those used at other potteries—notably the grape and vineleaf design used at Wedgwood and Castleford. The transfer prints in the book are 'Willow', 'Elephant', 'Cottage', 'Temple', 'Shield' and several Etruscan figure patterns. There are some beautiful flower paintings.

Marked pieces from this period are to be found, but it is impossible to tell whether a piece originated from Ferrybridge or Ralph Wedgwood's pottery in Burslem, which he ran before coming to Ferrybridge, unless it is dated or identifiable stylistically. Known pieces include creamware teapots with cauliflower spouts as used by Wedgwood and loop handles with overlapping scales only slightly different from Wedgwood's; there are several examples at the Yorkshire Museum, some enamel-decorated and some transfer-printed in black. The glaze on creamware is usually a very pale green. The potting varies, but it is generally not as light as Leeds ware and is sometimes flecked with impurities. A sepia brown painted line, which tended to flake, was popular on edges and rims (see creamware plate illustrated on p 123).

Cane-coloured ware (termed buff-bodied in the drawing book) was made, examples being the Yorkshire Museum's teapot and sugar bowl with a blue medallion on each side, a profile of a head

FIG 11   Tracings of teapots from the Ferrybridge Pottery Shape and
Pattern Book, 1799

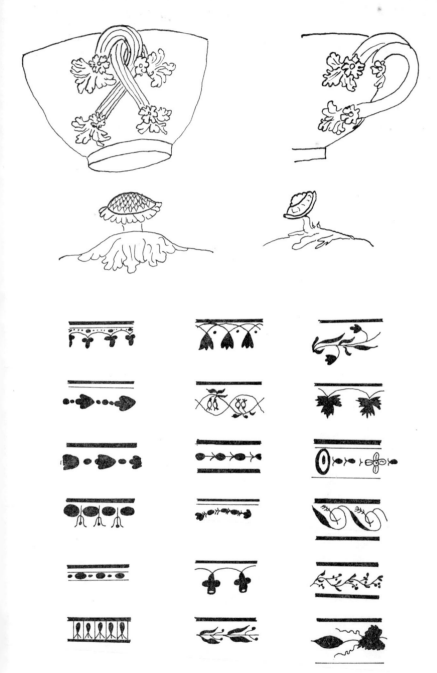

FIG 12 Tracings of handles and knobs and simple painted designs for plate edges from the Ferrybridge Pottery Shape and Pattern Book, *c* 1799

FIG 13   Tracings of teapots and jugs from the Ferrybridge Pottery
Shape and Pattern Book, *c* 1799

in black and the impression 'WEDGWOOD & Co'. Black basalt teaware, moulded and engine-turned, was also made, one example being a cream jug impressed 'Wedgwood & Co', which is highly glazed inside, has two spouts, and swans on the sides, their necks acting as handles. Two pieces impressed 'W. T. & Co' are known, and they may have been made here (see p 166).

Pieces marked 'FERRYBRIDGE' are not uncommon. The same designs and transfers continued in use for some time. The glaze is of a very high quality, and the blue printed wares are generally in a lighter shade than that on many other contemporary wares.

After William Tomlinson's retirement the quality of the products declined. Several pieces made by Reed & Taylor are known, but it is impossible to say whether they were made here, at Swillington Bridge or at Mexborough. Transfer-printed wares were the main product in white earthenware, stone china, ironstone china and opaque china. Patterns included 'Albion', 'Wild Rose', 'Landscape and Castle', 'Genevese', 'Chinese Figure', and 'Indian Bird'. Jewitt says that porcelain was manufactured at this time, but no pieces are now known.

Examples bearing the marks of the Woolf family are not common, possibly because the generally blue printed utilitarian earthenware they made was not considered worth preserving. Common patterns found are 'Albion' and 'Rhein'. A loving cup at Castleford Museum is inscribed 'Joseph Radley', and a man of this name lived at Knottingley in 1839. Porcelain was certainly made by the Woolfs. A cup and saucer inscribed 'Walden Poulson 1858' is still in the hands of descendants.

Succeeding occupants made utilitarian domestic earthenware, only identifiable if it is marked.

Marks

Jewitt gives the impressed mark 'TOMLINSON & CO', but it appears that no writer since has seen this mark. 'WEDGWOOD & CO' and 'Wedgwood & Co', both impressed, were both used from mid-1798 to 1800 inclusive. It was thought that one of these marks might have been used by Ralph Wedgwood at Burslem and the other at Ferrybridge, but a study of marked pieces confirms that both these marks were used concurrently at Ferrybridge. See nos 152–71, p 257.

AUSTRALIAN POTTERY, FERRYBRIDGE
Location: SE 487242

Built by Lewis Woolf and his sons Sydney and Henry in the late 1850s, to the west of and adjoining the Ferrybridge Pottery. The Australian Pottery was reputedly so called because the majority of the products were exported to Australia. Sydney Woolf was given the pottery to run and became its owner in 1877. In 1873 he bought the Mexborough Pottery and once again the two potteries came under one owner. In 1880 Sydney Woolf mortgaged the Australian Pottery for £13,000, but the mortgage was not redeemed.[9] Verbal agreement was made with Horn Brothers, the next occupants, that they should buy the works, but the transaction was not completed until 1899.[10] The original partners in 'Horn Brothers' were Joseph Stringer Horn, William Horn and

---

Middlesbrough Pottery: (*top*) Brown printed plate 'Devon' pattern; 1852–87; mark nos 207, 199 and 216. (*Bottom*) Green printed plate 'Caledonian' pattern; 1834–44; mark no 203. Black printed 'Hop Pickers' pattern plate with moulded floral border; 1834–52; mark nos 198 and 208. Black printed plate 'Cyprian Bower' pattern; 1834–44; mark nos 200 and 202.

(*Top row*) Black printed 'Dancing Dog' pattern plate; Don Pottery; *c* 1820–34; mark no 86. Brown printed plate 'May', crudely painted in red, yellow, blue and green; *c* 1860–70; mark no 113; Kilnhurst Pottery. (*Bottom row*) Black printed plate with moulded floral border painted in green, yellow, pink and blue; 'Der blinde Wilhelme'; *c* 1840; mark no 235; William Smith & Co, Stockton. Green printed plate 'Feeding the Hens'; *c* 1840; mark nos 230 and 247; William Smith & Co, Stockton. Black printed 'The Dog' pattern; moulded floral border painted in maroon and green; *c* 1860; mark no 103; Kilnhurst Pottery.

John Henry Warwick Horn. 'Horn Brothers' worked the pottery until 1920, when it was sold to the Co-operative Wholesale Society Ltd, which in turn sold it to T. H. Newsome & Company Ltd in 1947.

Wares and Marks

Ordinary domestic earthenware, often transfer-printed. For marks, see nos 158–62, p 257. No marks are known for 'Horn Brothers'.

WEST RIDING POTTERY, FERRYBRIDGE
Location: SE 486243

Situated to the west of and adjoining the Australian Pottery at Ferrybridge. Thomas Poulson and Edward Llewellyn Poulson, tenants of the Calder Pottery at Whitwood Mere, Castleford, bought the land at Ferrybridge in 1882 and built the West Riding Pottery.[11] In the following year they leased the Ferrybridge Pottery, trading at all three as 'Poulson Brothers' and then 'Poulson Brothers Ltd'. Following Thomas's death, E. L. Poulson retained the West Riding Pottery, the only one he owned, and ran it until his death in 1925. The pottery was closed in the following year.

Belle Vue Pottery, Hull: Sucrier with lid; blue printed 'Vermicelli' pattern; unmarked; found on the site during excavations. Cup printed in green, 'Fruit Basket' pattern; unmarked. Coffee pot printed in blue in 'Milkmaid' pattern; unmarked; see p 222. Cup and saucer printed in blue in 'Swan' pattern; unmarked; all 1826–42.

Belle Vue Pottery, Hull: Teapot and cup painted in blue, green, pinkish-red; unmarked; of several hundred pieces of painted ware excavated on the site, only six bore marks; mark no 260. Mocha ware bowl with blue slip ground; unmarked. Cup and saucer decorated in puce lustre with brick red flowers; mark no 260. Jug with broad band of coffee-coloured slip with trailed whirl of dark brown, white and blue mixed slips; green ribbed border; unmarked. No marked examples of this ware were found.

Wares and Marks

Mainly domestic ware, much of which was transfer-printed. A large trade was done in commemorative and souvenir pieces. 'Fryston Ware', glazed in black and yellow was popular in the 1920s.

Marks are as used at the Ferrybridge Pottery (see nos 165–9, p 257).

POTTERY HOLES, KNOTTINGLEY
Location: SE 493240

The Masterman family were potters at Pottery Holes, Knottingley, for many years. Little is known of the products except for a crudely made white earthenware figure of Red Riding Hood, reputedly made by J. Masterman, in the Yorkshire Museum. Wares were sold in Pontefract market. Directories list Thomas Masterman in 1838, Hannah Alcasterman (Masterman) in 1841, and James Masterman in 1854–81.

There were other small potworks in the neighbourhood of Ferrybridge and Knottingley, including Richard S. Blackburn making blackware, South Pottery, Knottingley, in 1887; Thomas Paver making black earthenware, 1857 and 1861, and described as an earthenware dealer in 1866; Richard Crossley making blackware at The Common, Knottingley, in 1877; and William Crossley being described as earthenware manufacturer in the same year.

In the Yorkshire Museum are two large watch stands in yellow glazed earthenware in the form of castles, incised 'B. Watts Ferrybridge 1839'. There is no trace of a potter of this name, but a James Watts, potter of Knottingley, is recorded in 1808. In 1812 he is described as late of Knottingley, now of Pontefract, potter.

PONTEFRACT

The following advertisement appeared in the *Leeds Mercury* on 28 December 1799:

POTTERY. To Be Let and Entered to Immediately All that Extensive and well accustomed EARTHENWARE POTTERY situated at Pontefract, in the County of York, with a Dwelling house, Warehouse and other ancillary outbuildings, for carrying on the Trade of a Pottery to a great extent. For further particulars, enquire of Mrs Button on the premises.

No further reference to this pottery can be found, but subsequent references to potters suggests that the pottery continued for some time. In 1805 George Balgey, in 1808 William Wildblood, in 1812 James Watts, in 1822 William Firth and Paul Dawson, are described as potters of Pontefract.

THE OLD VICARAGE POTTERY, PONTEFRACT

A second, and entirely different, pottery was worked by James Cawthorne at the Old Vicarage House in Low Baileygate, Pontefract, 1829–48. Cawthorne is described as an earthenware manufacturer.

CASTLEFORD POTTERY
Location: SE 419259

The fineware pottery known today as the Castleford Pottery was situated north of the Methley Road and south of the River Calder, and lay east of a disused arc of the river at Whitwood Mere, west of Castleford, where the Rivers Aire and Calder merge. A coarseware pottery was situated immediately south of the Methley Road.

John Clay, brickmaker, bought land at Whitwood Mere in 1724 and subsequent years, and built brick and tile kilns. They were bought by Thomas Brough early in the 1770s, and he must have built a small pottery, for when he sold the property in 1783, for £170 to Nathaniel English of Allerton Bywater and William Thompson, a Leeds merchant, there were 'workshops warehouses and brick or tyle kilns and also a hovel for burning pots'.[12]

The pottery, known as the Castleford Mere Pottery in 1783, was situated south of the Methley Road.

Early in 1784 English informed the Aire & Calder Navigation Company that he proposed erecting a pottery for which a flint mill

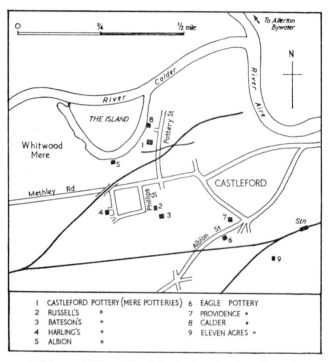

1	CASTLEFORD POTTERY (MERE POTTERIES)	6	EAGLE POTTERY
2	RUSSELL'S "	7	PROVIDENCE "
3	BATESON'S "	8	CALDER "
4	HARLING'S "	9	ELEVEN ACRES "
5	ALBION "		

Fig 14 Whitwood Mere, Castleford, showing location of potteries

was necessary, and in the following year Thompson requested permission to erect an oven on the island to burn flint.[13] It is clear that English and Thompson intended manufacturing a finer type of ware than had previously been made. This new fineware pottery was built north of the Methley Road on land rented from the Hippon family.

In August 1785 Thompson bought English's half share in the concern,[14] and he was joined by William Taylor from the Rothwell Pottery, trading as 'William Taylor & Co'.[15] Thompson and

Taylor bought the land on which the fineware pottery was built in 1786, and in 1790 both the potteries and brick and tile kilns were sold to their best-known owners, David Dunderdale and John Plowes.[16] William Taylor established a pottery at Swillington Bridge in the following year.

David Dunderdale, born in 1772, was reputedly apprenticed at the Leeds Pottery, which would have given him valuable knowledge and expertise, and was only eighteen years old when he took over at Castleford. He married Miss Bramley in 1794, and lived at Dunford House, north of the river. His manager was Thomas Braim, who later became manager of the Ferrybridge Pottery. John Plowes was a merchant in Leeds and was considerably older than David Dunderdale. They traded as 'D. Dunderdale & Co' and called the concern simply the 'Castleford Pottery'. They continued working the brick kilns for some time, and extant bills show that they supplied the bricks for building Warren House in Wakefield.[17]

The fineware pottery expanded rapidly, wares were exported, and a pattern book was issued in 1796. Money was constantly being raised by mortgage and loan, and in 1793 the saleable value was estimated at £3,000. The partners bought a large additional estate from Edward Hippon in 1802, and almost 17 acres of land were allotted to them under the Whitwood Inclosure Award, 1807.

In May 1803, however, John Plowes was declared bankrupt in connection with his merchanting business. His half share in the pottery was eventually sold for £4,313. After recovering from his bankruptcy Plowes became a partner in the Ferrybridge Pottery in 1805, his son John being already a partner there. John Plowes sr died in 1812.

Eight shares were created in the firm, David Dunderdale retaining half of them, Thomas Russell of Leeds taking two, and John Bramley and Thomas Everard Upton, both of Leeds, and Dunderdale's brothers-in-law, taking one each.

The firm still traded as 'D. Dunderdale & Co' or 'David Dunderdale & Co' and continued to be run by Dunderdale.

There is nothing to suggest that his partners had any active interest in the concern, although Russell's son, Thomas Stephen, managed the coarseware pottery. Money still had to be raised and gradually the firm became heavily indebted. In January 1818 Thomas Russell retired from the partnership and in 1820 the other three dissolved it. David Dunderdale was indebted to the concern for much more than his share and left the business. His debts were finally paid, but he died in May 1824, aged fifty-two, a broken man.[18]

In 1821 the fineware riverside pottery was advertised for sale or to let.[19] It was split into two working units, one being taken over by former workmen trading as 'Asquith & Co', and the other by George Bateson. T. S. Russell continued at the coarseware pottery. The 1823 directory refers to Whitwood as being 'remarkable on account of its very extensive pottery, usually called Castleford Pottery, but now goes under the name of the Mere Pottery, on account of one being recently established at Castleford'. This probably refers to Joseph Garrett's pottery.

The potteries remained in the ownership of the Upton and Bramley families until 1853.

Wares

Nothing is known of the first products, but they probably consisted of coarse country ware made from local clay. After 1784 and the erection of the fineware pottery and flint mill, a finer type of ware would be made. William Taylor came from the Rothwell Pottery and, judging by contemporary pieces from there, good quality creamware was probably made. Three pieces—two earthenware mugs, each with a royal portrait and the initials 'GR' on the front, and a blue printed pearlware mug—are impressed 'W. T. & Co', and could possibly have been made here (1785–90) or by William Tomlinson & Co, Ferrybridge (1801–4).

The products of 'D. Dunderdale & Co' are far better documented. The French title of a pattern book of creamware designs issued in 1796 in French and Spanish is *'Desseins des pièces de Fayence fabriquées à CASTLEFORD POTTERY près de LEEDS, par Dᵈ Dunderdale & Co.*', followed by a translation in Spanish, and the date '1796'. The book contains an index, and fifty-seven pages of designs illustrating 259 pieces. The designs are very similar in character, and in a few cases identical, to drawings in the Leeds Pottery pattern book. The products were probably intended to pass as Leeds, and many probably do today. The pattern book has now been reprinted.

Marked examples of Castleford creamware are extremely rare, probably because much was exported, and very little was marked. Tracings from the pattern book are shown in Figs 15 and 16. The bowl illustrated on p 124 is not in the pattern book, but is interest-

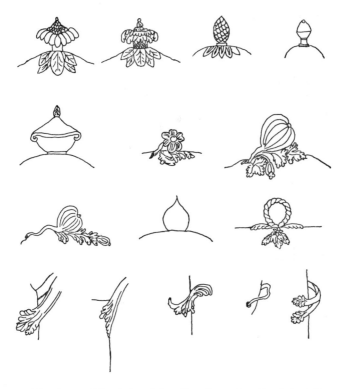

FIG 15   Tracings of knobs and handles from the Castleford Pottery
Pattern Book, 1796

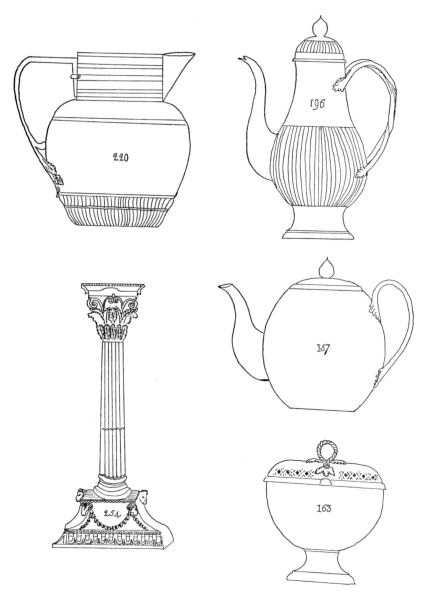

Fig 16   Tracings of creamware shapes from the Castleford Pottery
Pattern Book, 1796

ing in that the brown painted border pattern is a Wedgwood design, and if it was not marked, the piece would certainly be attributed to Wedgwood.

A small excavation on the site revealed fragments of underglaze blue painted ware in pagoda designs, double twist handles with leaf terminals, flower knobs, grass edging in blue and green, fluting, check patterns on a plain blue or buff yellow body, and granite ware in brown and pale blue.

Probably the best known ware made at Castleford, and so often incorrectly attributed, is the felspathic stoneware known generically today as 'Castleford'. Marked examples of moulded mugs, jugs, bowls, sucriers and teapots are known. The mugs and jugs known to the author all have the top third of the pot glazed in dark brown on the outside and the handle similarly glazed to the same level (see plate, p 124); the jugs also have a 'grass' like decoration on the shoulder and applied moulded scenes of cherubs, goats and foliage. The interiors only are glazed. Similar jugs were made by Adams of Tunstall.

The so-called Castleford stoneware teapots pose many problems. Only two basic designs are marked and can conclusively be attributed to the Castleford Pottery, and they were used on sucriers, bowls and lidded jugs (see p 182n). The first (plate, p 124) has the same sort of handle as the jugs described above, and is very elaborately moulded, with a symmetrical floral pattern on the spout, a lift-out lid with a flat-topped knob, and two concave panels on each side. They were often decorated with blue lines, occasionally with brick red, and sometimes the whole would be painted in several colours. Moulded scenes are applied to the side panels and known Castleford motifs include a seated female with a lion on her right, a man in chariot in clouds with cherubs, a hatted female with cornsheaf and basket, another in feathered top hat, a draped female with bird in her raised left hand, a man with bunch of grapes, a half clad female with hawk on her raised left hand, one playing a harp with pillar and urn, a man in chariot drawn through clouds by two goats, and a seated female holding bunch of flowers, her right hand on her hip.

This basic design was also made in black basalt, and a brown glazed lidded jug is known. Several of the applied reliefs described are to be found on stoneware from other factories.

The second design consists of sixteen panels alternately flat and concave, with swags and garlands of flowers at the top of the panels. The spout is straight and panelled, and the handle resembles a wavy number seven. Teapots to this design again are often picked out with blue lines, and they were also made in black basalt. Glazed and enamel painted examples are known (see plate, p 124). Not all examples are marked.

These two designs are the only known marked designs of Castleford stoneware. Most unmarked pieces of this ware are attributed to Castleford, probably in error, as far more marked designs are known from other factories. A group of pots with impressed numbers, the most common being '22', are generally attributed to Castleford, but again this is probably in error. The '22' pots bear far more resemblance to a group made by an unknown firm using the mark 'S. & Co' (see Mexborough Old Pottery, p 115, and plate, p 141).

Other Castleford products included dip-decorated, engine-turned, and transfer-printed earthenware in blue and brown. The commonest pattern is the 'Buffalo and Ruins' (see p 52). The pottery also made 'Willow' pattern, with two men on the bridge, a man in a boat at the bottom and no birds. Other patterns are rare, but known examples include pastoral scenes and all-over floral designs (see plate, p 141).

Marks

See nos 172–6, p 259.

MERE POTTERY, CASTLEFORD—PART ONE
Location: 419259

The fineware riverside pottery was divided and part taken by 'Asquith & Co', and shortly became 'Asquith, Wood & Co', when John Wood joined the firm. Thomas Nicholson had joined by 1837, when the firm was styled 'Wood & Co' or 'Wood & Nicholson' until Wood's death c 1855. Thomas Nicholson then took Richard Nicholson and Thomas Hartley into partnership, trading as 'Thomas Nicholson & Co'. They leased the pottery for 14 years in January 1854 at £55 a year. A new co-partnership deed, signed in 1855, states that the partnership had been carried on for some time past.

In 1864 Richard Nicholson died, and on 1 January 1865, when the partnership of 'Nicholson & Co' was dissolved, Garnett Thompson is given as a partner. Thomas Hartley carried on alone until John Masterman joined him in the following June, and in February 1868 Hugh McDowall became a third partner. On his death in the following November Hugh McDowall Clokie took McDowall's share. A few weeks later Thomas Hartley died, leaving the firm in the hands of 'Clokie & Masterman'. This partnership lasted for many years, and took over the nearby Albion Pottery and the other part of the old Dunderdale premises.

John Masterman died in 1885, and Hugh McDowall Clokie bought his share, the firm trading thereafter as 'Clokie & Co'. Clokie died in 1903 and was succeeded by his son James Thompson Clokie, who died in 1911. The firm continued in the hands of descendants, becoming a limited company in 1940, until its closure in 1961. The last owner was Mrs Pike.[20]

Wares and Marks

Domestic white earthenware was made during the nineteenth century. Marked pieces are extremely rare. The last order book records ' "Ideal" Semi-Porcelain, All kinds of Mugs and Beakers, Litho, Hand-painted, Pudding Bowls and all Utility Lines'. They supplied hospitals and institutions. Fancy wares made included Tyke mugs, ashtrays with London views or old crocks. Only pieces made for export were marked at that time.

No marks are known for the early partnerships, and marked pieces of later firms are rare (see nos 177–82, p 259).

MERE POTTERY, CASTLEFORD—PART TWO
Location: SE 419259

The northern end of Dunderdale's old pottery, fronting on Pottery Street, was occupied by 'Taylor & Co' or 'Taylor & Harrison' from at least 1835. The partners were George Taylor, William Harrison, William Dibb and Paul Hurdus. In 1841 the partnership was dissolved, Taylor and Harrison retaining the Mere Pottery, at which they are recorded until 1867, and Dibb and Hurdus removing to the Allerton Bywater Pottery.[21]

In 1854 the firm possessed a turning house, hothouse, biscuit kiln, plate and dish makers' rooms, sheds, seggar house, printing shop, two muff kilns, a glossing kiln, warehouse and yard.

The premises were bought by Masterman and Clokie in 1883, but were unoccupied in 1885. The pottery as originally owned by Dunderdale was again complete.

Wares and Marks

The staple product was white and printed earthenware. No known pieces.

No marks are definitely known to have been used here. The printed mark 'Taylor & Co' is recorded, but there is no evidence it was used by this firm. Godden records a mark 'T. H. & Co', which he suggests could relate to this firm and could have been used before 1841.

MERE POTTERY, CASTLEFORD—PART THREE
Location: SE 419258

The southern end of the old Dunderdale pottery, fronting on Pottery Street, was occupied by 'Asquith, Ford & Co' in 1848, having been vacant in 1841.

There were five partners—John Asquith, Edward Ford, Arthur Blackmoore, Richard Gill and George Dibb. The partnerships 'Asquith & Co' at the Castleford Mere Pottery and 'Asquith, Gill & Co' at the Allerton Bywater Pottery were dissolved in February 1853, the partners in both firms being those named above. Asquith, Ford and Blackmoore remained at the Mere Pottery, whose stock was valued at £559 9s 4d.

In 1854 the firm occupied a glossing kiln, biscuit kiln, hothouse, throwing house, dish and plate makers' rooms, printing shop, turning shop, sliphouse, seggar house and warehouses.

In 1853 the three remaining partners built the Eagle Pottery. By 1857 and until at least 1868 the Mere Pottery was occupied by 'Hurdus & Asquith', the premises having been bought by Hartley, Masterman and McDowall, who later occupied the works themselves.[22]

Wares and Marks

Domestic white earthenware, much of it printed. Edward Ford is described as a painter in the 1850s. There are no known pieces and no known marks.

RUSSELL'S POTTERY, WHITWOOD MERE
Location: SE 419256

Situated south of the Methley Road and east of Phillips Street, this pottery was the earliest in the district (see p 163), being the forerunner of the Castleford Pottery. After the dissolution of 'D. Dunderdale & Co', Thomas Stephen Russell remained at the coarseware works until the late 1830s, to be succeeded by 'John Bateson & Co', who had built another coarseware pottery nearby. The Batesons remained until at least 1841.

The property was sold in 1853 when Thomas Wilson and James Harling, trading as 'Wilson, Harling & Co', were in occupation. They had also built another pottery nearby. Charles Phillips became a partner and the two works were run together as 'C. Phillips & Co' until 1863, when the partnership was dissolved. Phillips then took over the pottery, trading firstly under his own name, and by 1877 as 'C. Phillips & Co'; and James Harling took over the other works formerly in the partnership.

Phillips was joined by his son in 1878 and the firm became 'C. Phillips & Son'.[23]

Wares and Marks

There are no known pieces or marks. Coarseware pottery was made throughout. Russell is described as a stoneware manufacturer, and Bateson's as earthenware or brown earthenware manufacturers. Phillips' were principally stoneware bottle manufacturers, but in the early days made blackware and by the end of the century were making bricks.

ALLERTON BYWATER POTTERY, CASTLEFORD
Location: SE 417276

Situated on the east bank of the River Aire at Allerton Bywater, just under a mile from where the Aire joins the Calder at Castleford, on land owned by Thomas Davison Bland, Lord of the Manor of Kippax.

The pottery was occupied by Thomas Jeffries and Samuel Sugden before 1838, when it was bought by Thomas Dobson.[24] The pottery, for manufacturing stoneware, was advertised for sale by auction in February 1839, but was not sold, Dobson remaining until his bankruptcy in September 1840, when James Wells took over. In the following January a further advertisement appeared in the *Leeds Mercury* offering the stone and black ware pottery to let. Coal was available a quarter of a mile distant and transported to the works for 4½d per ton. Boats 'passing from all parts of the coast . . . come alongside to load', which implies that products were shipped considerable distances.

The pottery was taken over by William Dibb and Paul Hurdus, dissolving partners in 'Taylor & Harrison' at Castleford Mere Pottery, who traded as 'Dibb & Hurdus' until August 1848, when notice of their assignment appeared in the *Leeds Mercury*. The next occupants were 'Asquith, Gill & Co'—John Asquith, George Dibb, Edward Ford, Arthur Blackmoore and Richard Gill—of the Castleford Mere pottery. This partnership was dissolved in 1853, when the stocks at Allerton Bywater were valued at £485 10s 8d. 'Gill & Dibb' worked the pottery until going bankrupt in June 1859, when William Gill took over the pottery, remaining for at least 10 years. Hugh McDowall appears to have had some interest, being described as of Allerton Bywater in 1859 and 1863.

Thomas Robinson was in occupation in 1877, and bought the premises in 1886.[25] He bequeathed the pottery to his sons John and Thomas, who later worked the Eleven Acres Pottery in Castleford, trading at both as 'Robinson Brothers Castleford & Allerton Potteries'. Thomas Robinson managed the Allerton Bywater works. In July 1903 the 'large building formerly used as a Pottery and sundry other buildings' were sold.

Wares and Marks

There are no known pieces attributable to the early occupants. Stoneware and blackware were made in the early days and by the Robinsons. 'Dibb & Hurdus', 'Asquith & Co' and William Gill are listed as potters and earthenware manufacturers; all had had connections with other potteries producing white and printed earthenware and may have continued this trade at Allerton Bywater.

No known marks used by the early occupants. See nos 183 and 188, p 259.

BATESON'S POTTERY, CASTLEFORD
Location: SE 422255

Situated north of the level-crossing where the railway crosses the Wakefield Road, just inside the Castleford boundary, bordering Whitwood Mere.

In 1823 George Bateson of the Castleford Mere Pottery bought land in the West Field of Castleford and built a pottery. He was succeeded by John, Cuthbert, Christopher and William Bateson until January 1843, when John retired. The firm was styled

'Bateson & Bros' and later 'Christopher Bateson & Son'. The property was mortgaged and passed to Thomas Wilson in 1855, when it was still occupied by 'Christopher Bateson & Son'.

There are no known pieces or marks. It is likely that coarse-ware only was made.

CALDER POTTERY, WHITWOOD MERE
Location: SE 419260

Situated north of the old Castleford Pottery, east of the disused arc of the River Calder and south of the Calder itself.

John and Thomas Clegg and James Wilson, earthenware manufacturers of Castleford, built the pottery, which was occupied by 'Lowther, Gill & Co' in 1857, and by Henry Lowther and John Ford, trading as 'Lowther & Ford', by the early 1860s. Following Lowther's death in 1875, John Ford ran the pottery alone.

By 1877 the pottery had been let to Thomas Poulson and Edward Llewellyn Poulson, who were in occupation until at least 1893. In 1882 they built the West Riding Pottery at Ferrybridge and in 1884 leased the Ferrybridge Pottery.

John Ford, the owner, died in 1891 and his son Frank mortgaged the pottery, which was sold to Hunt Brothers, chemical manufacturers, in 1896. There is no mention of a pottery in this deed.

Wares and Marks

No known pieces and no known marks. It is likely that domestic white earthenware was made, the occupants all being listed as earthenware manufacturers.

EAGLE POTTERY, CASTLEFORD
Location: assessed as SE 425256

Situated in Castleford, south of Albion Street and north of the railway on the North Railway Close.

In July 1853 John Asquith, Arthur Blackmoore and Edward

Ford, dissolving partners of 'Asquith, Ford & Co' of the Castleford Mere Pottery, bought 1,460 sq yd of land and erected a pottery. Ford intended running the pottery, but by 1855 James Pratt, earthenware manufacturer of Castleford, and Charles Abson, lockkeeper of Allerton Bywater, had taken over the works.[26]

Early in 1856 Pratt and Abson went bankrupt and Hugh McDowall, tea merchant of Pontefract, bought the pottery, then known as the Eagle Pottery, and traded as 'Hugh McDowall & Co' until at least 1861. Directories of 1864 list both 'McDowall & Roberts' and 'John Roberts & Co'.

Hugh McDowall was something of a tycoon in the pottery trade. In 1859 he is described as an earthenware manufacturer of Allerton Bywater; he acquired a financial interest in Isaac Fletcher's old pottery; and in 1868, in partnership with Richard Nicholson and Thomas Hartley, he bought the Flint Mill at Whitwood Mere and joined them at the Castleford Mere Pottery, a few months before his death. It is not known whether he continued at the Eagle Pottery after he entered the Mere Pottery.

By 1878 the buildings of the Eagle Pottery had been converted into a glassworks.

Wares

Recent excavations east of Welbeck Street have revealed wasters that include glazed and unglazed white earthenware, printed and painted. Printed patterns included 'Albion', 'Willow', 'Wild Rose', 'Fibre', 'Asiatic Pheasant' and 'Eton College'—patterns made at many other potteries. Several pieces with applied moulded flowers were found, together with blue and white banded kitchen ware, and blue 'grass' edging.[27]

Marks

Several fragments bearing a printed mark used by 'H. McDowall & Co' were unearthed during the excavations (see nos 186–7, p 259).

ELEVEN ACRES POTTERY, CASTLEFORD
Location: SE 423251

Situated in central Castleford, bounded by Regent Street, Bean-croftfield Road, Nicholson Street and Bond Street.

The pottery was occupied by 'Robinson Brothers' of the Allerton Bywater Pottery in 1892 and run by John Robinson. In the early 1900s he traded as 'John Robinson', and about 1905 as 'John Robinson & Son'. After he died in 1915 the pottery was run by Harry E. Robinson until the early 1930s.

Arthur Rudge is recorded as being at Nicholson Street in 1927.[28]

Wares and Marks

Robinson's advertised themselves in 1904 as makers of black-ware, stoneware, garden pots, wash bowls, milk bowls, cream-pots, stewpots, etc, and later as simply makers of black and common earthenware.

See nos 188–9, p 259.

GARRETT & FLETCHER'S 'CASTLEFORD POTTERY'
Location: SE 433257

Situated east of Ferrybridge Road, between Healdfield Road and Eastfield Lane, in Castleford.

The pottery was probably built by Joseph Garrett early in the nineteenth century. In 1787 and 1795 Garrett was a potter in Hunslet, Leeds, owning property in Jack Lane. In 1797 and 1800 he worked at Swillington Bridge Pottery, but by 1804 was resident in Castleford. By 1822 the pottery was occupied by Isaac Fletcher, whose wife Ann was Garrett's devisee.[29]

Fletcher carried on in a small way for many years but by the early 1840s was in financial trouble and suffering ill health. In February 1844 the pottery was advertised to let, at which time it comprised 'two large kilns for making Black and Stone Wares,

Fire Bricks etc., with warehouse, storerooms . . . Good Beds of Clay for Bottles and Firebricks on the premises . . .' The advertisement was headed 'Castleford Pottery'.[30]

In the early 1850s the works were let to George Turner Taylor and Joshua Hartley, trading as 'Taylor & Hartley', for £100 a year. They changed the name to the Castleford Clayworks. Fletcher died in 1852, and ownership passed to his widow and son Isaac, a potter who worked in Leeds. The property was mortgaged several times and in 1857 Hugh McDowall obtained an interest.[31] In 1862 Pope, Pearson & Woodhouse are given as occupants.

Wares and Marks

No known pieces. Fletcher is listed as black pot-maker in the early years, as brick and tile manufacturer in 1837, and as potter and earthenware manufacturer in 1841. In 1844 blackware, stoneware and firebricks were made. Taylor & Hartley made similar wares. There are no known marks.

HARLING'S POTTERY, WHITWOOD MERE
Location: SE 417256

Situated in Harling Street, south of the Methley Road, where the Whitwood branch railway crosses the road.

It was built in 1852 by Thomas Wilson, Thomas Nicholson and James Harling. Nicholson left in the following year. Harling & Wilson were also occupants of the old pottery formerly occupied by T. S. Russell, then Bateson's, and traded as 'Harling, Wilson & Co'. Wilson retired in 1861 and Harling took Charles Phillips into partnership, trading here as 'Harling & Co' and at the old Russell's Pottery as 'C. Phillips & Co' until 1863, when the partnership was dissolved. Harling kept this pottery and Phillips Russell's Pottery.

James Harling and his son Job traded as 'Harling & Son' until James's death in 1878. Job retained the old designation, but in one reference the firm is called 'Job Harling & Co Ltd'.

The pottery was bought in 1915 by Walter Mottishaw and Henry Bradshaw, who remained partners until 1921, when Mottishaw retired and Bradshaw was joined by his son Henry. They traded as 'Henry Bradshaw & Son'. In 1936 the firm became 'Henry Bradshaw, Son & Co', and in 1943 a limited company.[32]

Wares and Marks

In the early days blackware and stoneware were made, particularly stoneware bottles. Job Harling is listed as an earthenware manufacturer, and all other occupants as stoneware manufacturers. There are no known examples and no known marks.

ALBION POTTERY, WHITWOOD MERE
Location: SE 417257

Situated south of the southernmost point of the arc of the old River Calder, north of the Methley Road, near the old Castleford Pottery of Dunderdale & Co, Whitwood Mere.

Established by George Gill, who bought the land and buildings in 1867, the pottery passed to 'Clokie & Masterman' in August 1882.

PROVIDENCE POTTERY, CASTLEFORD
Location: SE 423255

Situated in the triangle formed by Wood Street, Albion Street and Chain Street, Castleford, well back from the road.

In February 1858 George Gill, earthenware manufacturer of Castleford, and William Farquhar, stonemason, bought land in the West Field on which they had recently erected 'sheds, kilns and other buildings used as an earthenware manufactory'.[33] However, creditors took over in April 1862, and William Gill, earthenware manufacturer of Castleford, bought the property in August 1863. George Gill remained in occupation until the mid-1870s, when he moved to the Albion Pottery, Whitwood Mere. William

Gill then ran the pottery, trading as 'William Gill' and then, with his son Thomas, as 'William Gill & Sons'. William Gill died in 1883 and Thomas ran the works, using the same style, until his death in 1928 when the firm became 'William Gill & Sons (Potters) Ltd'. It was then run by William Reginald Gill until 1929.

Wares and Marks

Domestic white and printed earthenware. See nos 183–4, p 259.

VICTORIA CLAYWORKS, CASTLEFORD CLAYWORKS
Location: SE 420256

George Turner Taylor and Joshua Hartley had moved from Fletcher's Pottery by 1862 to a site south of the Methley Road and north of the railway at Whitwood Mere. Taylor died in the late 1860s leaving Hartley, who was trading in 1874 as 'Joshua Hartley (late Taylor & Hartley)'. The firm was still working in the early 1970s, trading as 'Hartley (Castleford) Ltd'.

Wares and Marks

In the early days the firm made blackware and stoneware, firebricks and sanitary pipes. After the move to the Victoria Clayworks firebricks and allied wares were made. In the 1950s, some decorative pottery was produced.

See no 190, p 259.

MOUNT PLEASANT or NEW POTTERY, · CASTLEFORD
Location unknown

John and Thomas Clegg and James Wilson manufactured blue printed and white earthenware from c 1853. Wilson had left by 1857. In November 1860 the pottery was let to James Walton, potter of Castleford, and Thomas Walton, potter, formerly of

Swinton. In 1861 they are listed as occupants of New Pottery, Castleford, and they worked until the late 1870s.

EXCELSIOR POTTERY, CASTLEFORD
Location unknown

'Garnett Thompson & Co', stoneware manufacturers occupied Excelsior Pottery in 1876 and 1877. In the following year Thompson, who had been a dissolving partner in the firm of 'Nicholson & Co' in 1865, was in the hands of his creditors.

VICTORIA POTTERY, WHITWOOD MERE
Location unknown

The pottery was occupied by Frank and Albert Ford, trading as 'Ford Brothers', 1887–93. There are no known pieces or marks.

Note
Recently, a third design has been found. It is a twelve-faceted oval teapot with typical applied motifs on side panels. It has a curved faceted spout with stylised leaves at the base, a castellated balcony and a square shaped handle, mark no 172.

4

HALIFAX, HUDDERSFIELD
AND BRADFORD

Several potteries were established north-west of Huddersfield and between Halifax and Bradford, where coal outcrops, fireclay and potclay abound. They were often run by several generations of the same family, notably the Mortons at Salendine Nook, the Catheralls at Keelham, Soil Hill and Denholme, and the Hallidays at Puel Hill, Bate Hayne and Howcans in Northowram. Several other small potteries were established by men who probably learnt their trade at one of the above potteries, and workmen moved from pottery to pottery with alarming rapidity. Three generations of Taylors are recorded, starting with Robert at Howcans in 1853, continuing with John Michael at Small Clues in 1870, and ending with Nicholas, who worked at most of the local potteries until finally settling at Ogden, Ovenden, in his own works, early in the twentieth century.

All the potteries used local clay, firing red brown, decorated at first simply with a rich black glaze but later slip-decorated with white clay found locally. This was used mainly on the insides of bowls and pancheons and for quill stringing in line and dot patterns; a clay pipe bowl was used to hold the slip, a practice that produced comparatively short lines of decoration. Lead glaze was almost invariably used, though some experiments in saltglazing were carried out at Soil Hill, and the Bradford potteries at Wibsey and Eccleshill made saltglazed brown stoneware as their staple product.

Other types of decoration employed resulted in rustic ware, in which the clay was scratched while still wet to give a bark-like appearance; and snailhorn ware, the local term for agate ware, a mixture of red and white clay. Sometimes a brown glazed pot would be covered in white slip and a pattern scratched through the white slip when it was partly dry to reveal the brown glaze beneath. Some wares were decorated by the application of stamped pads of white clay.

The majority of the wares were utilitarian, but ornamental wares were produced at all the potteries as novelties: they included money-boxes, pot cuckoos, frog mugs, miniature cradles, salt kits, puzzle jugs, knife boxes, candle holders and miniature chests of drawers. The majority of the products were thrown or slab-built. It is extremely difficult to attribute a piece to an individual pottery in the district.

PULE HILL, NORTHOWRAM, HALIFAX
Location: SE 092273

Situated at Pule Nick, a mile north of Halifax on the Bradford Old Road.

A pottery kiln was built here by the Halliday family, reputedly gypsies from Scotland, in the mid-seventeenth century. It was not very conveniently situated and by the end of the century the family had moved to Bate Hayne.[1]

Wares and Marks

Recent excavations have revealed internally glazed bowls, plates, eggcups, and platters, decorated with trailed and combed slip, and black glazed beakers, basket pots, porringers and malt-kiln tiles.[2]

No mark was used.

BATE HAYNE, NORTHOWRAM
Location: SE 087284

The Halliday family built a new pottery, in a more sheltered position, below Pule Hill in the late seventeenth century. They worked it until the late eighteenth century, four brothers—Richard, Isaac, George and Abraham—being the last of the family to do so.[3]

Wares and Marks

Domestic wares, similar to those made at Pule Hill.
No mark was used.

HOWCANS, NORTHOWRAM
Location: SE 085279

Situated at North Howcans on the west of the Bradford New Road.

In the late eighteenth century George and Abraham Halliday left Bate Hayne Pottery and established a pottery at Howcans. Like their predecessors, they ran the works very much as a family concern. They took their brother Isaac's son John as an apprentice in 1789, and he later married his cousin Ann, by whom he had nine children, including Isaac and John. Abraham's son John married George's daughter and after her death married her sister. Abraham and John Halliday are listed as occupants in the 1830s. John's sons George and William took over after their father's death, William continuing until his death in 1916, after which the works closed. Robert Taylor worked here as a thrower for 20 years from 1853.[4]

Wares and Marks

Pottery only was made until the mid-1840s, when the manufacture of firebricks and chimneypots was introduced. By the end of the century pottery production appears to have ceased. Examples can be seen at the Yorkshire Museum, York, and at the Halifax and Bradford Museums. The pottery made most of the items mentioned in the introduction to this chapter.

No marks are known.

KEELHAM POTTERY
Location: SE 088313

Situated at Keelham, near Thornton, on the north-east side of the Queensbury–Denholme road, opposite the old Raggalds Inn.

It was established by Jonathan Catherall, who came from Anglesey. While working as a navvy in Salterhebble, Catherall lodged with a potter named France, and married his daughter. He built the pottery at Keelham in the 1760s, but only worked it for a short time before moving to Soil Hill.

Wares and Marks

Fragments of coarse earthenware with a thick black glaze running unevenly down the sides were found on the site.[5] No marks are known.

SOIL HILL POTTERY, OVENDEN, HALIFAX
Location: SE 073315

Situated on the west side of Soil Hill, 300yd east of Long Causeway on the Halifax–Denholme road, at Ovenden, north of Halifax.

Jonathan Catherall moved from Keelham Pottery in the 1760s and established the Soil (or Swill) Hill Pottery, where he was joined by Stephen Catherall. Jonathan died in 1807, aged sixty-seven, and was succeeded by his sons John, Stephen and Thomas. Jonathan's fourth son, Samuel, founded the Denholme Pottery in 1784.

In 1857 John Catherall conveyed the premises to James Robinson, a potter of nearby Bradshaw Lane,[6] but remained at the pottery until his death c 1860. His widow and children worked it until the late 1860s.

Robinson died in 1861 and ownership passed to John Greenwood, potter of Bradshaw Lane. He sold the works in 1871 to George Wilcock, a local farmer, who installed Jonas and Ellis

Crabtree therein.[7] The Crabtrees were still in occupation in 1877. Tradition has it that Wilcock then tried his hand but, being unsuccessful, converted the buildings into a chicken farm.

In 1883 John Kitson reopened the pottery, working until his death in 1892, when his widow Hannah and their children took over. Hannah Kitson bought the property in 1894, and she in turn sold it to Isaac Button of the Fountain Pottery, Liversedge, in 1897 for £800.[8] Isaac Button erected new buildings lower down the hillside, and his sons Arthur, George and David ran the works while he divided his time between it and the Fountain Pottery.

Isaac Button died in October 1905 and his sons continued at Soil Hill until 1934, when David retired. George died in 1942, and Arthur in 1943, the works being taken over by Arthur's sons Arthur and Isaac.[9] Isaac became sole owner in 1947 and retired in 1965.

The pottery was closed for some time but was reopened by Donald Greenwood, who was still working there in 1973, manufacturing refractory wares.

Wares

Local clay from Swill Hill has been used throughout the life of the pottery, both red clay for the fabric and white for the slip decoration. Products comprised mainly domestic vessels, bowls, pancheons, stewpots, and garden pots. Fancy wares included knife boxes, candle holders, puzzle jugs, and cradles, both thrown and slab-built. Sgraffito wares were made by the Button family. Isaac Button is reputed to have thrown a ton of clay in a day into pots, the largest he made regularly being huge brine pots that took 70lb of clay.

Donald Greenwood makes garden pots and ornaments and some sanitary pipes.

Examples can be seen in the Halifax Museums and the Yorkshire Museum, York.

Marks

No marks were used in the early years, although several pieces with initials applied in slip can be attributed to Soil Hill Pottery, particularly from the mid-nineteenth century. Isaac Button jr occasionally marked his products (see no 192, p 259).

DENHOLME POTTERY
Location: SE 060354

Situated north of Milking Hot Beck, east of Pot Ovens Lane and south of the ancient boundary wall of Denholme Park, north-west of Denholme village. The pottery was established by Samuel Catherall, son of Jonathan Catherall of the Soil Hill Pottery, in 1784, and he worked there until his death in the middle of the nineteenth century. His widow and then his son John succeeded him.

A Samuel Catherall is listed in 1888 and 1892 as a pot-maker of Denholme. Samuel sr's other son, Jonathan, is listed in 1887 as an earthenware manufacturer of Wilsden, Bingley.

Farm buildings adjoined the pottery and succeeding occupants were also farmers.[10] John Catherall died on 1 August 1893, and the pottery passed to his son Ezra, a schoolmaster, who let the works to Nicholas Taylor. He had been in occupation since at least 1891, and remained until 1907, with a brief absence in 1898–9, when he built himself a small kiln in the old Wesleyan Chapel at Denholme. During the next few years Taylor is reported at potteries in Burton in Lonsdale, Littlethorpe, Castleford, Tunbridge Wells and finally Ogden, south of Denholme.

In 1918 a local farmer bought the Denholme Pottery for £500. It was then occupied by Arthur Knowles and George Garner.[11]

Wares

Local clay was used throughout. The pottery gave its name to a type of ware known as 'Denholme China', which described not china, but traditional country pottery with a deep red body and black or dark brown lead glaze. Tea services, salt kits, knife boxes, tobacco pots, bread crocks, mugs, puzzle jugs and domestic ware were made. Examples may be seen at the Yorkshire Museum, York, and at Keighley Museum. The latter possesses a salt kit, dated 1799, in red clay with deep brown glaze decorated with white slip, which is reputed to be the earliest known piece from Denholme.

Marks

Marks were used only by Nicholas Taylor, who sometimes incised his name on the underside of a piece. Unless the word 'Denholme' is present, however, the name is no guarantee of provenance, as Nicholas Taylor worked elsewhere.

SMALL CLUES POTTERY, BRADSHAW, HALIFAX
Location: SE 087306

Reputedly built by James Robinson in the early nineteenth century on land owned by the Spencer family, the pottery was situated north of Small Clues (Clough) Farm between Bradshaw Lane and Roper Lane, north-west of Halifax.[12]

The works were run by 'James Robinson & Co' until W. Wade entered the partnership, when it became 'Robinson & Wade'. Robinson died in 1861 and his widow Rachel ran the works, taking Mr Greenwood as a partner. Wade took over again until the pottery closed in the early 1870s.

Local clay was used, including white pipe clay found on the site.

Wares and Marks

Domestic and garden redwares, and plant pots and stands in decorated slipware were made. Examples may be seen at Yorkshire Museum and Bolling Hall, Bradford.

No marks were used.

ROSEMARY HALL, HILL TOP POTTERY, BRADSHAW, HALIFAX
Location: SE 074307

Situated 500yd east of the Halifax–Keighley road, south-east of Causeway Foot, north of Halifax.

In 1856 George and David Spencer bought clayworks, claypits, and a pottery at Bradshaw. It was called Rosemary Hall or Hill Top Pottery, and was then worked by Henry Spencer.[13]

There are no known examples, but it is obvious that local clay was used.

BRADSHAW ROW, BRADSHAW, HALIFAX
Location: SE 082307

A nineteenth-century pottery kiln was recently excavated at Bradshaw Row, 250yd north of Bradshaw Lane.[14] Tradition says that Samuel Catherall, grandson of Jonathan Catherall of the Soil Hill Pottery, worked a pottery in this area for about 2 years in the early 1830s. This was probably the site.

Wares

Domestic wares, baking bowls and stewpots.

NICHOLAS TAYLOR POTTERY, OGDEN, HALIFAX

Nicholas Taylor, one-time occupant of the Denholme Pottery' established a fineware pottery at Ogden, north of Halifax in the early twentieth century. He specialised in a painted type of pottery resembling 'Poole Pottery' and in marble decorated ware which he called 'Nicholas Ware'. He died shortly after starting the venture.

BARNS HILL AND PEPPER HILL POTTERIES, NORTHOWRAM
Locations: SE 110283 and SE 114289

Situated between Northowram and Queensbury, north-east of Halifax. Hartley Sunderland and his son John started a pottery at Barns Hill, Northowram, shortly after World War I, moving to Pepper Hill in 1920. John Sunderland died in 1925 and in the following year the pottery was bought by Samuel Bradley, who had been apprenticed to Arthur Button at Soil Hill.

John Bradley joined his father Samuel in 1934 and, except for the period of World War II, they worked the pottery until 1958. Up to seven hands were employed.

Wares

Domestic and horticultural lead-glazed red-bodied earthenware was made, including plant pots, bulb bowls, vases, jugs, candlesticks, dressing-table sets and puzzle jugs.[15]

FOUNTAIN POTTERY, LIVERSEDGE

Situated on Mortimer Ing, north of the Leeds–Elland turnpike road at Liversedge, between Halifax and Dewsbury.

In February 1866 Isaac Button, flowerpot manufacturer of Dewsbury Moor, bought the land and built a pottery,[16] remaining there until his death in 1905. In 1897 he bought the Soil Hill Pottery and worked the two concurrently.

The Fountain Pottery was sold to a firm of glass bottle makers in 1916.

Wares

Horticultural wares made from local clay.

CHURCHFIELD POTTERY, ROBERTOWN, LIVERSEDGE

From 1894 to 1901 George Brook, colliery owner, is given in directories as being at Churchfield Pottery, Robertown. A William Crossley was an earthenware manufacturer of Robertown in 1892.

LINDLEY MOOR POTTERIES, SALENDINE NOOK, HUDDERSFIELD
Location: SE 105181

Situated on the north-east side of Laund Road, Salendine Nook, Lindley-cum-Quarmby, Huddersfield.

The date of establishment is uncertain, though it is said that the pottery was built by members of the Morton family who fled from Scotland over 300 years ago. Mortons are in fact recorded in the parish registers from 1676. The pottery remained in the hands of the same family for generations, but in the mid-nineteenth century there was a family rift, and the pottery was split into two separate works, divided by a wall, and thereafter run as two distinct concerns.

The northern part belonged to Joseph Morton, the firm becoming 'Joseph Morton & Son's'. In the twentieth century it became 'Joseph Morton & Sons (Lindley) Ltd', and the works were called the 'Lindley Moor Potteries', until closure in 1945. The southern part belonged to Enos Morton, and became 'Enos Morton & Sons'.[17] It is still worked today by Harold Morton, and is known as the 'Lindley Moor Pottery'.

Wares and Marks

Both potteries made traditional country pottery from local clay. Joseph Morton & Son advertised in 1887 that they made bowls of all sizes, creampots, stewpots, pie dishes, plain and fancy tree pots, and rhubarb and seakale forcing pots. Pancheons, mugs, frog mugs, breadcrocks and a few fancy items were also made. Today Mr Morton specialises in plant pots, rim-culture pots, bulb bowls, milk coolers and bread pots.

The wares are rarely marked, only one mark being recorded (see no 193, p 259).

OLD LINDLEY, near HUDDERSFIELD
Location: SE 096188

Built on the Croft at Clough Head, north of Lindley Old Road, a small pottery occupied by Joseph Bolton was mortgaged by John Bolton in 1811.[18]

John Bolton is recorded as a pot-maker of Elland in 1790 and 1807, and of Blackley Top in 1811. Joseph Bolton worked the pottery until at least 1853.

WOODMAN HOUSE, BLACKLEY POTTERY
Location: SE 107199

Situated on the east side of South Lane, Blackley, south of Elland and north of Huddersfield.

A fineware pottery was built about 1720 by the Cartledge family, who lived in a cottage at Woodman House. Thomas Cartledge was a potter there in 1777 and James Cartledge was owner-occupier of a house and potovens, together with Woodmansfield copperas house and new potovens listed in the 1781 Land Tax assessments. James died in 1793, and it is likely that John Bolton sr, John jr, and Joseph Bolton, all three described as potters of Blackley Top, ran the pottery.

It fell out of use from about 1820 until 1866, when Titus and Edward Kitson took over the premises, buying the estate 2 years later. Titus built a blackware pottery which he worked with his family until 1896. The estate passed to his sons Oliver and Titus jr, and a Herbert Kitson Whitworth. They continued until the early twentieth century, when Samuel Wilkinson & Sons bought the premises, working the pottery for a few years before renting it back to Oliver Kitson and a Mr Bushell for a few years. Pottery production ceased about 1907, and the buildings were demolished about 1930.[19]

Wares and Marks

Fineware was made in the early days, a fact confirmed by quantities of unglazed white earthenware that have been found on the site. From Kitson's time, domestic brown earthenware, pancheons and stewpots, etc, were made.

There are no known marks.

AINLEY TOP POTTERY
Location: SE 114196

Situated north of a lane due west of the Huddersfield–Elland road at Ainley Top, now obliterated by the M62 motorway.

The pottery was reputedly established by Joseph Kitson about 1826. Joseph died in 1836 and was succeeded by his son Edward, who died in 1868. The stock and effects then passed to his son John. The pottery was run by the Kitsons until 1890 and then demolished.

Wares

Edward Kitson is listed as a brick and tile maker. In later years domestic and ornamental earthenware was made, including cradles, chests of drawers, and salt kits in a reddish fabric with applied white clay strips, and rouletted and zigzag indentations.

HAIGH'S POTTERY, BLACKLEY
Location: probably SE 107197

Another small pottery existed at Blackley; it was bought by John Haigh from Cartledge's assignees in 1836,[20] and included a 'farmhouse with the pottery, drying shed, barn and outbuildings . . . and several closes called The Ainleys'. The farm and pottery were sold in 1845 to John Sykes.

The exact location is uncertain, but local people still call a farm on the north side of Johns Lane, Blackley, 'John Haigh's house', which seems likely to be the farm in question. Unglazed sherds were found there but, as it is only 100yd from Woodman House Pottery, that is not conclusive evidence.

CINDERHILLS, SOUTHOWRAM, HALIFAX
Location: SE 103232

Situated at Cinderhills, Siddall, Southowram, 3 miles south of Halifax.

In 1781 John Gream owned potovens in Southowram. In the following year, when ownership had passed to Henry Gream, 'John Morton & Co' were in occupation, and by 1785 the Mortons had bought the works. They traded until the early 1790s as 'John Morton & Co' and from 1796 as 'John Morton & Son'.[21] In 1810 Joseph and his brother William Morton traded as 'Joseph Morton & Co'.

In 1818 there were two adjoining potteries, one known as the Smallware Potwork, run by Joseph, and the other, the Largeware Potwork, run by William.[22] By 1829 the brothers had split up— probably after quarrelling, for when Joseph mortgaged his works, walls had been built to separate his property from his brother's, including one down the centre of a warehouse![23] Joseph worked the Smallware Potwork until his death in c 1846, and was succeeded by his son Joseph, who is listed as a brickmaker, in contrast to his father, who was an earthenware maker.

William Morton continued at the Largeware Potworks until the 1840s. Isaac Halliday is described as a pot and firebrick maker at Cinderhills, Southowram, in 1845 and probably took over the works for a short time. In 1853 Joseph Morton jr bought back the Largeware Potworks, uniting the pottery once more. Thenceforth firebricks and allied wares were made, the firm continuing into the twentieth century, becoming a limited company, and trading as 'Joseph Morton Ltd', Cinderhills Fireclay Works.

There are no known pieces.

EXLEY POTOVENS, SOUTHOWRAM, HALIFAX

In 1774 John Morton is described as a yeoman of Exley Potovens, and in 1796 as a coalminer of the same place. The former deed is attested by Thomas Dowler of Exley, potter.[24]

John Morton was the father of Joseph Morton, who later worked the Cinderhills Pottery. Exley is only ½ mile south of Cinderhills, but sufficiently removed to suggest the possibility of another pottery there.

WIBSEY POTTERY, near BRADFORD
Location: SE 149297

Situated at the southern end of Pot House Road, overlooking the old road from Bradford to Halifax, at Wibsey, 2 miles south of Bradford.

The date of foundation is not known, but the earliest attributed piece is dated 1763. In 1770 the following advertisement appeared in the *Leeds Mercury*:

> To be sold or lett for a term of years, the well known and well accustomed potworks at Wibsey, near Bradford, with all utensils, etc., in very good repair. For further particulars enquire of Messrs William and John Tordoff, the owners, who will show the same.
>
> If the above are not sold or lett betwixt now and the 10th day of July next, very good wages will be given to two able and experienced workmen to carry on the said branch.

The pottery was neither sold nor let, but William Tordoff left and John took Joseph Bacon into partnership.

In December 1780 Edward Rookes Leeds, Lord of the Manor of Royds Hall, bought the potworks and leased them to William Shaw, who assigned the lease to Isaac North the elder and Isaac North the younger in the following November. The Low Moor Iron Works bought the pottery in the late eighteenth century, and it was worked until about 1840.

Wares and Marks

Brown saltglazed stoneware, similar to that made in Nottingham at the same period, and Eccleshill later, was made from local clay. The colour varied from light to dark brown and comprised mainly drinking and cooking utensils, some of which were crudely decorated with incised patterns. Lead glazed earthenware, reddish brown in colour, was also made. It was similar to wares made at Soil Hill, Denholme and Howcans. Several pieces attributed to Wibsey were illustrated by H. J. M. Maltby in an article in the *Connoisseur* in April 1929.

Drainpipes were made in the nineteenth century. There are no known marks.[25]

MORLEY CARR, NORTH BIERLY, BRADFORD

Edward Rookes Leeds built a glasshouse and potoven at Morley Carr in the eighteenth century. A neighbour objected to such buildings on the common land and authorised their demolition. Leeds therefore rebuilt the works on his own enclosed lands at Wibsey in 1780, near the Wibsey Pottery. The glasshouse, potoven, three cottages and a smithy were sold in 1784 for £105.[26]

MANOR HOUSE POTTERY, ECCLESHILL, BRADFORD
Location: SE 179356

Situated east of Stonehall Hill Road and north-east of the Leeds road, at Eccleshill, north of Bradford.

In September 1837 William Woodhead erected the Manor Pottery and a brickyard on common land at Eccleshill. He bought the land in 1854,[27] taking Davison and Cooper into partnership. Woodhead died in the early 1860s, and his widow, Hannah, took over. She was joined by her son-in-law William Marshall, a Bradford woolstapler, who worked there into the 1890s.

The works were bought by W. R. Bromet in 1879 and sold to Leathers Chemical Co Ltd in 1920.

Wares and Marks

William Woodhead made earthenware, stone bottles and brown saltglazed stoneware, similar to that made at Nottingham and Wibsey. Domestic articles, ornaments and garden vases, statuettes and busts of early nineteenth-century celebrities were also made. These busts, such as Nelson, Wellington, Burns, Byron and Scott, have a high sheen with a very granular 'orange peel' texture. Jugs, cradles, knife boxes, salt kits and puzzle jugs with raised figures round the belly were also made.

When William Marshall took over, pottery production ceased in favour of bricks, chimneypots, and allied wares.

Examples may be seen at Bolling Hall, Bradford, and the Yorkshire Museum, York, where a stoneware spirit flask bears mark 194A, the only recorded mark (see p 261).

BAILDON
Locations: SE 398139, SE 397141 and SE 396141

There is evidence of three medieval pottery kilns being worked on the northern slopes below Baildon Moor. Jugs, pancheons and bowls in a very light hard-gritted fabric, glazed in green of varying shades, were made. Jug shoulders were decorated with an incised looped line.

UPPER HEATON, near HUDDERSFIELD
Location: SE 180195

A late thirteenth- to fourteenth-century pottery kiln was situated at Upper Heaton, north-east of Huddersfield. Cooking pots, jugs and pancheons were made of grey fireclay, some of them being lead glazed. Decoration was confined to simple incised lines, applied strips and fingertip impressions. There are examples in the Tolson Museum, Huddersfield.[28]

5

WAKEFIELD AND DISTRICT

POTOVENS, WRENTHORPE
Location: SE 315226

About the middle of the fifteenth century several small potteries were built at Wrenthorpe, known then as Potovens, on the edge of the Wakefield Outwood, $1\frac{1}{2}$ miles north-west of Wakefield. A survey of the Outwood in 1608 records 'Certain clay-pits digged by ye Cuppers or Cupmakers inhabiting there, namely Ric. Andrews, Henry Glover, Henry Gill, Thomas Oliver and Ric. Eshall'.[1] A survey of the Manor, 1709, states that 'Amongst those who inhabit in the Cottages on The Outwood is a Manufactory of Earthen Ware, Potts of all sorts being made there w[hi]ch require noe more than Clay and Lead'.[2]

The potteries reached peak production in the late seventeenth century but had declined by the mid-eighteenth century. The small family concerns were unable to compete with the factory potteries in Leeds and Rothwell, and with the growing amount of imported Staffordshire pottery, and by 1785 production had ceased.

The most important family of potters was the Glovers, four generations having been traced. Their kiln was built at the rear of 155 Wrenthorpe Road. In 1699 Robert Glover supplied Viscount Irwin of Temple Newsam, Leeds, with four dozen 'potts' at 4d a dozen and three dozen at 3d per dozen.[3] Potovens pottery has been found at Sandal Castle, Thornhill Hall and Elland.

Other kilns were situated at No 7 Imperial Avenue, Wrenthorpe Road, worked by the Willans family; at the top and bottom of Bunker's Hill; in Wrenthorpe Road adjoining the Malt Shovel Hotel; and in the garden of No 7 Rodger Lane, Wrenthorpe.

Excavations show that at first each potter specialised in a certain type of ware, one making coarse traditional kitchen ware, another fine cups in Cistercian ware, and a third chamber pots; but from the late sixteenth century there was less specialisation. In the early years plain and decorated Cistercian ware was made, but by 1550 production of decorated ware had ceased. Plate making began in the late sixteenth century, and slipware plates were made from about 1640 until the closure of the potteries. Several distinctive slipware designs are illustrated by P. C. D. Brears in *Post-Medieval Archaeology*, Vol 1 (1967).[4]

SILCOATES
Location: SE 312221

Situated north-west of Wakefield, between Alverthorpe and Wrenthorpe on a site now covered by Silcoates School. Quite a large pottery existed here, probably in the late fifteenth and early sixteenth centuries.

Production consisted of Cistercian ware, posset pots, cups and beakers with an all-over dark brown glaze and applied decoration in white strip, spot or leaf designs; the colours were sometimes reversed, giving brown decoration on a white background.[5]

ROBIN HOOD FARM
Location: SE 319234

Situated just over $\frac{1}{2}$ mile north-east of Wrenthorpe. No kiln has been located, but quantities of pottery wasters and saggars unearthed recently indicate a pottery site. Finds also included a large number of trailed and feathered slipware pieces.[6] The pottery probably functioned from the early eighteenth century.

LINDLE LANE
Location: SE 306225

A late fifteenth-century kiln was situated ½ mile west of Wrenthorpe. Products were similar to those of Silcoates, ie posset pots and cups in Cistercian ware.[6]

WEST HALL POTTERY, STANLEY, WAKEFIELD
Location: SE 362250

Situated almost ¼ mile east of the Wakefield to Oulton road, ⅓ mile from the River Calder, just within the Wakefield boundary on what was the West Hall Estate.

The date of establishment is unknown, but a pottery was occupied by John Shaw in 1768.[7] Shaw was a tenant in 1758, but his trade then is not stated. A deed of 1788 describes the works as 'Pottery or building used for the making of potts and earthenware with the furnace, yard, garth and appurtenances . . . and all those five messuages . . . late in the occupation of John Shaw'. It was a small concern, but large enough to employ several potters.

On 14 July 1772 the whole estate was offered for sale in the *Leeds Intelligencer*, including 'a well established Pottery and several cottages adjoining, proper for the Lodging of Workmen employed therein'. On 22 September the estate was offered in lots, lot 4 including 'Messuage with good established Pottery and four closes . . .' In July 1788 a further advertisement appeared in the *Leeds Intelligencer* which can only refer to this pottery: 'A Pottery situated at Wakefield Outwood very near the navigation. With the pottery a tenant may be accommodated with a dwelling house and stable and a few acres of land'.

The pottery was working in 1790, but 2 years later it had been converted into a glasshouse, and used as such for a short period.[8]

Wares

No known pieces. Godden records a brown saltglaze earthenware mug with 'John Shaw 1742' under the handle, but as we do not know when John Shaw began working at West Hall, we have no certainty that the mug was made there.

Ploughing on the site reveals quantities of broken saggars and a vast range of pottery, suggesting that broken crockery from cottages may have become intermingled with pottery wasters. Pieces found have included brown saltglazed stoneware with incised decoration; slipware plate edges and pancheons of dark brown fabric, some glazed in cream-coloured slip with dark brown trailed decoration; and others in almost black slip with cream-coloured trailed decoration. Fine creamware, pearlware with underglaze painting, grass edging, green glazed earthenware and banded 'rouletted' mugs were all found. The presence also of a variety of unglazed white earthenware and unglazed coarseware wasters confirms that quite a range must have been made.

CRIGGLESTONE
Location: SE 313158

Situated on the Cliff House Estate, between Cliff House and Daw Green, at Crigglestone, some 4 miles south of Wakefield.

Fireclay and terracotta works were occupied by Ann Thompson Broughton in 1853 and 1861. The estate was advertised for sale in 1863. Products included firebricks and allied wares and terracotta ornaments.[9]

BRETTON POT HOUSE
Location: SE 282144

Situated south of Denby Dale Road and east of the roundabout at Bretton, 6 miles south-west of Wakefield. A small pottery was worked by William Harrison, who came from Stoke-on-Trent, from 1723 until his death in 1726.

6

BURTON IN LONSDALE

Burton in Lonsdale, or Blackburton, is 3 miles west of Ingleton in north-west Yorkshire, on an isolated coalfield. Local clay and coal were utilised for pottery-making from at least the mid-eighteenth century, when small family-run potworks with a single kiln were built for making blackware and brownware for the local communities.

About 1840 stoneware production was introduced and new larger potteries built, making bottles and jars and in latter years firebricks. Products were marketed in north Lancashire and bottles sent to the Irish whiskey distilleries. Earthenware bread bowls, dishes, plant pots and ornamental wares, including the 'Hen and Chicken' money-boxes, inkwells, knife boxes and puzzle jugs continued to be made. None of the potteries marked their products. Sometimes, however, inscriptions trailed on in white slip indicate the origin of the piece (see plate, p 142).

BAGGALEY'S POTTERY, BRIDGE END POTTERY
Location: SD 654720

Situated immediately north of the River Greta, on the east side of the road to Burton in Lonsdale at Burton Bridge.

In 1754 Thomas Lawson, potter, mortgaged a potter's work-house with two rooms over it, 'one smoakhouse, one dwelling-house, one warehouse and pot kiln' at Burton in Lonsdale Bridge End.[1] In 1785 the property was bought by John Brooksbank, John Baggaley being in occupation at the time.[2] Baggaley is described as a potter on his marriage in 1767. The pottery was

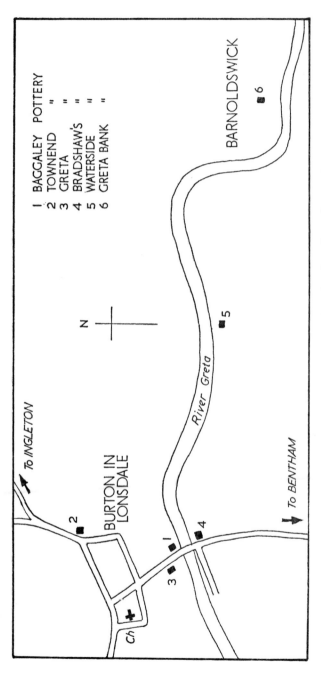

FIG 17   Burton in Lonsdale district showing location of potteries

worked by four generations of the Baggaley family—John I, John II, George and John III—until the mid-nineteenth century. Thomas Coates bought it in 1889, when he and his son Edward had been in occupation some time.[3] Richard Timperley Bateson, after occupying the pottery for several years, bought it in 1932.

Wares

The usual traditional country pottery was made here, black, brown and white glazed. A knife and fork box dated 1797, at the Yorkshire Museum, was reputedly made here. R. T. Bateson made horticultural pottery.

BRADSHAW'S POTTERY, BURTON BRIDGE END
Location: SD 654719

Situated at Burton Bridge End, south of the river, a pottery here was occupied by Joseph Bradshaw, master potter, in 1801,[4] and he remained until his death in 1812, aged seventy-six. Robert and Joseph Bradshaw succeeded to the pottery. Robert died c 1822 and Joseph was joined by Thomas Bradshaw. John Bradshaw bought the property in 1840 and was still in occupation when it was sold to Thomas Coates in 1886.[5] Shortly after that the property was converted into three cottages.

The Bradshaws were all pot or earthenware manufacturers.

BLAEBERRY POTTERY, WATERSIDE POTTERY
Location: SD 659719

Situated almost ½ mile east of Burton village on the southern bank of the River Greta, Blaeberry Pottery was established by John Bateson in the mid-nineteenth century. William Bateson followed, to be joined by his sons Henry, Frank and Robert, and traded as 'William Bateson & Sons'. They also worked the Greta Bank Pottery. On William's death in 1887 the pottery was renamed the Waterside Pottery. Robert left the partnership in 1902, but

Henry stayed on until his death in 1922, and Frank until his death in 1938. The pottery was sold in 1947 to Joseph Waggett.[6] Stoneware bottles, jars and cooking pots were the main products.

GRETA BANK POTTERY, BARNAWICK
Location: SD 665718

Situated north of the River Greta, south of Barnawick and just under a mile east of Burton village.

James Parker bequeathed his house 'Greta Bank' and pottery to his wife Jane in 1871. James Parker jr then worked the pottery until 1887, when it was bought by William Bateson of the Waterside Pottery, who ran it with his three sons Henry, Frank and Robert, trading as 'William Bateson & Sons'. After William's death, the sons continued under the same designation until 1902, when Robert left the concern. He later bought the Greta Pottery Company. After Henry died in 1922, Frank became sole proprietor.[7]

GRETA POTTERY
Location: SD 653720

Situated immediately north of the River Greta, on the west side of the road to Burton in Lonsdale at Burton Bridge.

The Greta Pottery was built by James Kilburn, potter, c 1860, when he mortgaged the property, described as newly erected. He also owned another newly erected pot kiln and premises on the opposite side of the road. Thomas Coates bought both potworks in 1879 following Kilburn's death, and in 1906 sold the Greta Pottery to Robert Bateson, late of the Greta Bank and Waterside Potteries. Robert Bateson died 2 years later and his brothers, Henry and Frank, bought the pottery, then controlled by the Greta Pottery Company, for £380. They ran the works until 1918, when the premises were sold to a general dealer who agreed neither to sell pottery nor produce it on the premises. The Batesons were allowed to remove bricks from the kiln, indicating that bricks

were then made, though the main product was stoneware bottles.
The second pottery mentioned above, bought by Thomas
Coates in 1879, was worked by him and his son Edward into the
twentieth century.[8]

TOWNEND POTTERY
Location: SD 654723

Situated on the east side of the road from Burton to Ingleton at
the north-eastern perimeter of the village, this pottery was worked
by four generations of another branch of the Bateson family—
Thomas, John, Thomas and Richard—until the middle of the
nineteenth century, when William Parker took over. It then remained in the hands of the Parker family until the twentieth
century.

POTTERS ARMS POTTERY

William Bateson, master potter, born 1748, had a small potworks
'on the east side of Burton in Lonsdale' in 1788. He died in 1811,
and his widow Mary and sons Thomas and Richard then ran the
works, as well as owning a public house called 'The Potters Arms'.
The sons worked in Blackburn for a period in the early 1820s, then
returned to Burton and ran the pottery until c 1860. James
Fothergill was in occupation in 1861.

The Batesons are described simply as pot-makers.[9]

Several other small potworks existed in Burton in Lonsdale,
including one 'facing the High Street', occupied by Gilbert
Yeats in 1766; one occupied by William Jennings in 1769 with
'Pott kiln, Smoakhouse, Workhouse and Warehouse'; one occupied by John Walmsley in 1774 (formerly by George Jennings);
and one occupied by John Bateson on the north-west side of
Higher Gate, near Lapish Fold, in 1786. In 1768 Thomas Bateson,
potter, bought land and premises, the pot kiln on the land occupied by John Baggaley being excluded from the sale. In 1788
John Lawson owned and occupied a pothouse which, in 1793,
was occupied by William Seward. It was worked well into the

nineteenth century, but its occupants are not named. A disused pottery consisting of three workhouses, a potkiln, pot hovel and potfold, situated on the south side of Higher Gate, Burton in Lonsdale, was bought by Edward Baines in 1826.

Many potters are mentioned in the Bentham Parish Registers, the earliest being John Swales in 1755. The names of Bateson, Baggaley, Walmsley, Seward are the most common (see Appendix I, p 267).

7

NORTH-EAST YORKSHIRE AND SCARBOROUGH

MIDDLESBROUGH POTTERY
Location: NZ 499211

Situated between Lower Commercial Street and Vulcan Street, immediately north of the gasworks in Middlesbrough, with easy access to the River Tees.

The pottery was built in 1834 by Richard Otley, Joseph Taylor, John Davison and Thomas Garbutt, who formed the 'Middlesbrough Pottery Company'.[1] In January 1835 the following advertisement appeared in the *Leeds Mercury*:

MIDDLESBRO' POTTERY, NEAR STOCKTON ON TEES. The Middlesbro' Pottery Company beg respectfully to announce to the Dealers in Earthenware, that they have completed their Manufactory, and are now prepared to receive orders to any Extent, for Ware of the following Descriptions, viz:— blue printed, and all other colours of Breakfast, Dinner, Dessert, Tea and Toilet Sets; Enamelled and Lustre Painted, Dipt and Cream Coloured Ware; Black and every Description of Brown Ware, Garden Pots, common and Fancy Chimney Pots &c &c.

The Company have been at considerable Expense in obtaining the most modern and elegant Shapes and Patterns, and beg to assure those who may favour them with their orders, that every Effort shall be used to execute them with Promptitude and Despatch, on the lowest possible terms.

From 1844 to 1852 the firm traded as the 'Middlesbrough Earthenware Company'. In 1852 the works were taken over by

Isaac Wilson, former manager, who traded as 'Isaac Wilson & Co' until the pottery's closure in 1887.

A thriving export business was established from the early days of the pottery, 250,000 pieces being exported in 1852. A warehouse was opened at Hamburg in Germany.

Wares

It is clear from the advertisement that the proprietors were ambitious men proposing to manufacture a complete range of pottery. They did, however, concentrate primarily on domestic white earthenware, using clay from the south-west of England. Most known examples are transfer-printed in a variety of colours —blue, red, brown, purple, green and black. Plates with German views were exported to that country. Sponged and gilded ware were made and a pink-purple lustre, as at so many other potteries in north-east England.

Marks

Several marks are known, generally comprising the name of the pottery or its initials (see nos 195–212, p 261). An impressed crown was also used, often in conjunction with other marks.

Several pieces of pottery bear the marks of 'Lloyd & Co', Wilson Street, Middlesbrough and 'John Wardle', North Street, Middlesbrough. Most of the items advertise local merchants, events or buildings. There is no evidence of manufacturers with these names, and it is likely that they were earthenware dealers. They probably date from the late 1860s.

LINTHORPE ART POTTERY, MIDDLESBROUGH

Built on the site of the Sun Brick Works at Linthorpe, Middlesbrough, bounded by Thornfield Road, Burlam Road, Roman Road and Oxford Road.

The pottery was built in August 1879 by John Harrison under the inspiration of Dr Christopher Dresser, the orientalist and designer. The works were soon enlarged and Henry Tooth, an artist, engaged as manager. The business flourished and by 1885 about 100 hands were employed. The Linthorpe Pottery was the first pottery in the country to use gas-fired kilns and was very up to date in both working conditions and the wares produced. Local red clay was used at first, but that was superseded by white clay shipped from south-west England.

Henry Tooth left Linthorpe in 1882 to join William Ault at the Bretby Pottery, and was succeeded by Richard W. Patey. Finished wares were sold by Lear & Sons of Darlington and at Harrison's London showroom, 19 Charterhouse Street.

The standard of production at Linthorpe was very high and the wares popular. Following the success of Linthorpe, other art potteries were established, possibly of a lower standard, and their products flooded the market. Competition, rising prices and possible mismanagement caused financial difficulties at Linthorpe; John Harrison went bankrupt and the pottery was closed in 1889. In the following year it was reopened for a short time, but closed for good after a few months. Several workpeople moved to Burmantofts, Leeds.

Wares

Linthorpe art ware was a new concept in English pottery but, reflecting the taste of the times and the desire for works of art as opposed to the traditional machine-made product, soon became very popular. It was strongly influenced by oriental and middle-eastern motifs. Almost all the wares were moulded. Highly coloured glazes typify Linthorpe art wares, whose speciality were running glazes, some of which show signs of crazing today. Some pieces were enamel painted over the glaze. Sgraffito and some red clay wares, left as terracotta, are also known. J. R. A. Le Vine recorded 474 patterns.

Marks

Mould numbers were generally impressed in the base, some incised, some raised or painted on under the glaze. Artists' monograms and signatures may be found. Numbers were also used, probably indicating the type of glaze.[2]

See nos 218–23, p 263.

STAFFORD POTTERY, THORNABY, STOCKTON-ON-TEES
Location: NZ 449178

Built between Thornaby Road and the River Tees at Thornaby, then known as South Stockton, the Stafford Pottery was established in July 1825 by William Smith, a Stockton builder. Smith took John Whalley, a Staffordshire potter, into partnership, and they were joined in 1826 by John Taylor, the firm trading as 'William Smith & Co'. There were difficulties almost from the start, but with timely assistance from George and William Skinner, sons of a Stockton banker, the firm found its feet; in 1829 the Skinner brothers were taken into partnership. The pottery expanded and export markets were established in Belgium, Holland and Germany.

The managers of the Stafford Pottery were go-ahead men: Smith carried out experiments with leadless glazes and George Skinner and Whalley patented new bodies. The pottery was noted for its extensive use of machinery at a time when throwing was usually manual.

For many years the firm copied Wedgwood wares, even using the marks 'Wedgwood' or 'Wedgewood'. In 1848, however, Josiah Wedgwood & Sons were granted an injunction against 'William Smith & Co' (William Smith, John Whalley, George Skinner and Henry Cowap were named as partners) restraining them from using the name 'Wedgwood' or 'Wedgewood' on the products of the Stafford Pottery.[3]

In 1855 George and William Skinner took over the firm, trading as 'George Skinner & Co'. The part of the works making brownware was rented to John Whalley, and he was followed by Thomas Harwood, who was in occupation in 1860. By 1872 the Brownware Pottery had reverted to 'Skinner & Walker' and was worked thenceforth in conjunction with the Whiteware Pottery. By 1860 the partnership comprised George Skinner, Robert Chilton and John Parrington. Ambrose Walker took Chilton's place, and the firm became 'Skinner, Parrington & Walker' until Parrington's death in 1875, when the style was changed to 'Skinner, Walker & Co'. In 1877 Ambrose Walker became sole owner, and traded as 'Ambrose Walker & Co'. He had about 300 employees, twice as many as there had been twenty-five years before.

In 1905 the firm became the 'Thornaby Pottery Co Ltd', but after a decline in production it closed. The buildings are now occupied by the Teesside Corporation Engineers' Department.

Jewitt says a branch of the Stafford Pottery was established at Genappes, near Mons, in Belgium, and workmen sent out there. The mark no 250 (p 265) probably refers to this 'branch'.

Wares

The first products were made from local clay, firing a red-brown colour, and continued to be made throughout the pottery's existence. Whiteware was made for domestic use—tableware and toilet sets. The pottery's pearlware and cream-coloured earthenware were generally transfer-printed in a variety of colours, and some were decorated with coloured slips or painted either under or over the glaze. Mocha ware and pink-purple lustre, bamboo ware, and feathered and trailed slipware were all made. Pottery cobbles (boats) were reputedly produced also. Small plates with moulded borders, the centre having a transfer print with a motto, are comparatively common, as are plates and saucers with a moulded daisy design. Many of the transfer patterns are to be found on wares from other potteries.

Marks

Much of the whiteware produced was marked. The pottery also used the marks 'Wedgwood' & 'Wedgewood', both of which have been noted in conjunction with other factory marks.[4] The brownware was not marked.

See nos 226–55, p 263.

COMMONDALE POTTERY
Location: NZ 664106

Situated north of Commondale in the Cleveland Hills, south-east of Middlesbrough.

In 1861 J. S. Pratt built the 'Cleveland Fire Brick & Pottery Co Ltd', but the firm closed in 1867. The works were reopened in 1872 by John Crossley and renamed the 'Commondale Brick, Pipe & Pottery Co Ltd'. Fine local clay was utilised for manufacturing terracotta of a warm buff colour. Workmen were brought from Staffordshire and Wales, but as the location was so isolated the men would not settle, and the works were closed about 1884. In 1893 Thomas Ness reopened them as the 'Commondale Brick & Pipe Co', and, following Ness's death, Messrs Crossley took over again.

Wares and Marks

The interesting period for the pottery collector is 1872–84, when art and domestic pottery were made. Some architectural terracotta ware, garden figures, ornaments and statuettes of former musicians were made later. A catalogue was published in 1881.

Fine art ware made at the 'Providence Works' covered a very wide range of domestic ware. There were 'Commondale Rockingham teapots', sometimes glazed on the interior, sometimes completely dipped in clear glaze; over thirty-two different shapes of other teapots, including 'Fine Rockingham', 'Malachite' (green), and 'Jet' (black); over twenty styles of water and cream jugs; candlesticks, spittoons, and all manner of bowls and jars; and over fifty types of vases, jardinières, plaques, and tea and toilet sets.

See nos 256–7, p 266.[5]

YARM POTTERY
Location: NZ 418133

Situated in a building at Wren's Vinegar Brewery, Yarm Bridge, Yarm, south of Stockton-on-Tees.

The pottery was established in 1927 by J. H. Clark, former manager of the Clarence Potteries Co Ltd at Stockton-on-Tees. The works closed in the late 1930s.

Wares and Marks

Local clay was used, firing to a reddish-brown colour. Bowls, crocks and containers were the chief products, some white glazed on the inside, though most were clear glazed, and some clear glazed all over. Unglazed flowerpots were also made. Examples of wares can be seen in Teesside museums.[6]

See no 258, p 266.

OSMOTHERLEY

Jewitt records a coarseware pottery here in the late eighteenth and early nineteenth centuries.

MIDDLEHAM, NEAR BEDALE

The only evidence of tin-glazed earthenware being made in Yorkshire is to be found in the Minutes of the General Meeting of the Society of Arts held on 19 December 1759, which reads:

A letter from Mr Francis Crossfield Dated Midleham near Bodale Yorkshire Decr: 11 1759 was read, wherein he mentions that he has attempted to make China, Flint Ware consolidated in its texture like such as come from Germany or Holland, and Borax; and would be glad to know what Encouragement the Society will give the Publication of his Art of making Flint Ware and burning Blue Tyles—He sends inclosed a small sample of the

Blue Tyles, which was produced to the Society. The Society replied that the sample was too small for judgement and Crossfield was invited to send further tiles for consideration, and to say what use they were.[7]

The County Record Office, Northallerton, lists a Francis Crossfield of Middleham between 1731–2 and 1776, who is described as 'Esq' or 'Mr' and was a man of some substance. By 1781 he had either died or left Middleham, though there is no record of his burial there. There is no reference at Northallerton to a pottery at Middleham.[8]

LITTLETHORPE POTTERY, PARK HILL POTTERIES, RIPON
Location: SE 325682

Situated east of the road from Littlethorpe to Bishop Monkton at Littlethorpe, south of Ripon.

James Foxton, a Ripon builder, erected brick and tile kilns here in the early 1820s. The works remained in the hands of the Foxton family, being occupied by Thomas and James Foxton in the 1850s. In 1904 James Foxton left for Canada, and Alfred Dougill and David Rhodes took over. In 1910 J. W. Hymas bought the premises, then known as the Park Hill Potteries, leasing them to J. Green for a few years. The pottery was bought by F. R. Richardson in 1915 and then by the Littlethorpe Potteries Ltd in 1919. Ownership passed through many hands until the Curtis family took charge in 1939.[9] George Curtis had come to Littlethorpe as a clayboy and worked his way up to become pottery manager, and finally owner. Potters of note who worked here early in the twentieth century include A. E. Kitson from the Soil Hill Pottery and Nicholas Taylor from the Denholme Pottery, who were employed as throwers.

The pottery is still working.

Wares and Marks

First products were bricks and tiles, brown earthenware being made by 1834 and throughout the nineteenth century. In the early twentieth century about twenty hands were employed in making traditional country pottery—pancheons, bread crocks and jars. The large tree pots at Newby Hall were thrown here by Albert Kitson. A 12in high pancheon made in 1966 by Mr Curtis is at the Yorkshire Museum; it has a red body with white slipped interior covered in lead glaze, typical of pancheons made in Yorkshire from the late eighteenth century.

In recent years the main products have been horticultural wares, plant pots and garden urns.

See no 259, p 266.

RIPON

The first edition of the Ordnance Survey, 1854, shows a pottery north of Ripon and north of the road just before it crosses the River Ure.

Baines's Directory of 1823 lists Ann Belle, firebrick maker, Mrs Ellen Smith and Thomas Lawson Hall and gives their address as 'Pottery'. J. W. Smith & Co were brick, tile and earthenware manufacturers at Millgate and Littlethorpe, Ripon, in 1867.

WINKSLEY, near RIPON
Location: SE 240716

Situated at Woodhouse Farm, Winksley, 4 miles west of Ripon.

Four thirteenth- to fourteenth-century pottery kilns producing roof tiles and pottery were recently excavated and thin, light buff bodied pottery was found, plus some pots in brick red or grey fabric. The glaze was thin, generally in green or greenish yellow but occasionally in rich brown or dark green.

Knight and zoomorphic jugs, bowls, pitchers and large

globular vessels were made, many decorated with complex wedge rouletting.[10]

SOURY HILL, YEARSLEY

Situated east of the road to Helmsley, about ½ mile south-west of High Warren Farm, Yearsley, near Easingwold in the North Riding.

Excavation of a late fifteenth- or early sixteenth-century pottery kiln revealed wasters of coarse Cistercian ware and some delicate wares with brilliant green glazing. Most of the pottery was left plain, but some was decorated with white slip. Bung hole pots, cups and basket pots with handles over the top were common. The finds can be seen at the Yorkshire Museum, York.

Pieces excavated at Byland and several other Yorkshire abbeys have been identified as originating here.[11]

WEDGWOOD'S POTTERY, YEARSLEY

John Wedgwood worked a pottery in Yearsley in the mid-seventeenth century. He was succeeded by three generations of Wedgwoods—John, William and another John—who transferred the business to Heworth, York (see p 226).

Northern reduced greenware, comprising large cisterns, plates, bowls and puzzle jugs, were made. A puzzle jug inscribed 'John Wedgwood 1691' in the Victoria & Albert Museum has a brown body with green lead glaze. Other examples may be seen in the Yorkshire Museum, York, and the Fitzwilliam Museum, Cambridge.

HELMSLEY
Location: SE 913598

A sixteenth-century pottery kiln was situated in a field behind Potter House, north-west of Helmsley.

Excavations revealed bung hole pots, dishes, small jugs, bowls and jars in a pinky-yellow or a sandy-coloured fabric with very sparse gritting; they were mostly glazed in a khaki colour, but ranged from a dark green towards orange. Examples are on show at the Ryedale Folk Museum, Hutton-le-Hole.[12]

STEARSBY
Location: SE 608715

Situated 4 miles south of Yearsley was a sixteenth-century kiln, recently excavated. Products, mainly buff and grey bodied ware, with a green-brown to yellow-green glaze at the top of the pot, included jugs, jars, bung hole cisterns, pipkins and bowls.[13]

CRAYKE, NEAR EASINGWOLD

Two sixteenth-century kilns were situated near the church at Crayke, 2 miles east of Easingwold. Products comprised local reduced greenwares.[14]

FALSGRAVE POTTERY, SCARBOROUGH
Location: TA 034881

Situated in Gallows Close, Falsgrave, 1 mile south-west of Scarborough.

The pottery was worked during the late eighteenth and early nineteenth centuries. The site has been occupied by a British Railways Goods Depot since 1902. Local clay was used.

Wares

The Scarborough Museum has six pieces of pottery attributed to Falsgrave. All are glazed domestic cottage-type wares, decorated in coloured slips. Three have mocha designs, and one jug has horizontal slip banding. All are similar to pottery made elsewhere in Yorkshire.[15]

CASTLE ROAD, SCARBOROUGH
Location: TA 044890

Situated on the south side of Castle Road, between Auborough Street and Tollergate.

Probably operative in the late thirteenth and early fourteenth centuries, the pottery produced mainly green glazed domestic ware, zoomorphic aquamaniles, bearded mask jugs, skillets, roof tiles, small jugs and shallow dishes. None of the cooking pots were glazed.[16]

NEWBY
Location: TA 015899

A fifteenth- to sixteenth-century kiln was situated here, 3 miles north-west of Scarborough. Products included deep bowls and large pitchers in grey fabric, often green glazed.[17]

STAXTON
Location: TA 015790

Several early thirteenth- to late fourteenth-century pottery kilns have been excavated at Staxton, 8 miles south of Scarborough, and quantities of sherds were found opposite the school. Products included cook-pots, bowls, large pans and shallow dishes. The unglazed pottery was characterised by hard sandy fabric.[18]

POTTER BROMPTON, NEAR GANTON
Location: SE 9877

Several early thirteenth- to late fourteenth-century kiln sites have been excavated at Potter Hill Farm. Products were similar to Staxton wares, by which name the type is now known.[19]

8

HULL AND DISTRICT

HUMBER BANK, BELLE VUE POTTERY
Location: TA 088277

Situated in west Hull, bounded on the north by English Street, on the west by Alfred Street, and due north of the River Humber, to which the pottery originally had access.

It was established in 1802 by James and Jeremiah Smith of Hull, potters, Joseph Hipwood of Hull, blockmaker, and Job Ridgway, the Staffordshire potter. Hipwood and Ridgway retired in 1804 and James Rose became a partner. The Smith brothers went bankrupt in 1806, and the proprietors assigned their interest to Job and George Ridgway, shortly after which the pottery closed.

In 1826 William Bell bought the premises, extended them and recommenced production on a large scale, calling the works the 'Belle Vue Pottery'. There were five kilns, warehousing, a flint mill, workshops, and a wharf on the river. Large quantities of pottery were exported, particularly to Holland and Germany, Bell's brother Edward acting as agent to the pottery in Hamburg. In his prospectus Bell offered earthenware 30 per cent cheaper than in Staffordshire; he also supplied potter's materials and colours to many Staffordshire firms.

In the late 1830s the Hull & Selby Railway Company built a line along the bank of the Humber, so cutting off the pottery from access to the river. Bell appealed to the law but failed to gain satisfaction, and in 1841 closed the pottery.

An advertisement, dated July 1841, offered the remainder of the stock for sale, including printing presses, sixty large copper plates, a kiln of unfinished ware, moulds, equipment and furniture.[1] The copper plates reputedly went to a pottery near Rotherham.

The site of the pottery has since been covered by engineering works.

Wares

Nothing is known of the products of the early Humber Bank Pottery, but it is probable that traditional country ware was made.

T. Sheppard writing in 1941, quotes recipes from the pottery recipe book, dated 1832, some of which apparently had been obtained from the Leeds and Don Potteries.[2] Recipes are given for Egyptian Black and stone bodies; white, yellow, green and cream coloured glazes; and various underglaze colours.

Part of the site was excavated in 1970, when wasters from the Belle Vue Pottery were found.[3] Transfer-printed earthenware in blue, pink, green, brown, black and puce was turned up, including many new patterns. A total of twenty-nine are now known, including 'Swan', 'Fruit Basket', 'Milkmaid' (also made by Spode and the Don Pottery), and 'Vermicelli' (see plate, p 160). The pottery also made 'Willow Pattern', one design with two men on

FIG 18   Shapes of teapots made at the Belle Vue Pottery

the bridge, another with three; 'Garden Scenery', a central panel of a landscape with a temple, fountain and bridge; 'The Proposal', a boy by a boat talking to a girl carrying a basket and pointing to a church; 'Pedestal and Bouquet', a bouquet of flowers alternating with an urn on a pedestal; 'Peacock Eye', reminiscent of peacock's feathers; 'Lightning', a jagged zigzag pattern with background of ragged branches; 'Rustic Cottage', a woman holding a basket by a cottage, mountains and trees; 'Man with a bundle of faggots', self-explanatory; 'The Shepherd', comprising shepherd, dog, sheep, girl and church; 'Hydrangea', a floral pattern with hydrangeas; and 'Chinese Marine', a Chinese pastoral scene. This last pattern was made at several potteries, but the wasters unearthed at Hull all had the letter 'G' in the cartouche on the reverse, and other potteries used different letters. None of the 'Chinese Marine' wasters bore the pottery mark, but it was found in such quantity that it was felt it must have been made there.

Another common product was earthenware dipped in coloured slip (pale blue or a light brown), with freely trailed bands of decoration piped on in contrasting coloured slip (most commonly white, blue and dark brown). These wares often had a green or white engine-turned ribbed border (see jug illustrated in plate on p 160). Combed decoration, with black upon a pale blue background was found, and mocha ware with a blue or brown background.

Much of the pottery was painted in blue, green, pinkish-red, two shades of yellow, orange, grey and pink. The designs were usually painted under the glaze, but some overglaze painting was noted (see plate, p 160).

Other products included banded and chequer patterns, puce lustre decoration, green glazed vine leaf dishes, pierced ware and jelly moulds, and souvenir plates with French or German inscriptions. Pottery with all-over yellow or green glazes, sometimes transfer-printed in black or painted in red or green, was also found. Examples may be seen at the Hull Museum.

Marks

Only a very small percentage of Belle Vue pottery was marked, and as vast quantities were exported, marked pieces are rarely found. No slipware was found bearing a mark.[4,5]
See nos 260–5, p 266.

OTHER HULL POTTERIES

There were several other small potteries, producing coarseware, on the outskirts of Hull in the late eighteenth century and first half of the nineteenth. Joseph and John Mayfield worked at 26 Church Street, Wincolmlee, and at Church Street and Stepney Lane, Sculcoates; Joseph and James Lapish at 57 Scott Street and 18 Church Street, Wincolmlee; William Askam at Wapping, Sculcoates, 1791; Richard Eggleston at Wincolmlee, 1791; Joseph and William Haigh at Sculcoates, 1807; John Wright & Co, 1818, John Wright, 1821, Mary Wright, 1851, and Charles H. King at Newland, Hull Bank or Stepney Bank; Turner & Rhodes at Stepney Lane, 1879; R. Young at Hull Bank, Cottingham, 1879; and John R. Young at Kingston Pottery, Green Lane, Newland.[6] None of their products are known.

A pottery is shown, on a map in *Greenwood's Picture of Hull*, 1835, in Sculcoates, on the west bank of Beverley and Barmston Drain.

NAFFERTON POTTERY

Nafferton is situated 2 miles north-east of Driffield, in the East Riding.

The pottery was built by Charles Longbottom, brickmaker, in 1848, and was worked first by Joseph Lagdon and later by Samuel Longbottom, and was operative until 1899.

Wares and Marks

They were chiefly horticultural wares—plant pots, ornaments, garden seats and chairs—and some unglazed white earthenware vases, pot-pourri vases, bowls and flower stands. The Long-bottoms also sold glazed domestic pottery bought from Stafford-shire.

Occasionally pieces were impressed 'SL' during Samuel Long-bottom's time, but they are rarely seen today.[7]

See no 266, p 266.

9

YORK AND SOUTH OF YORK

HEWORTH MOOR, LAYERTHORPE POTTERY

Situated on Heworth Moor on the York–Scarborough road, a mile from York.

Early in the eighteenth century John Wedgwood moved from his pottery at Yearsley to York, probably to Heworth Moor, and in 1763 a John Wedgwood, pot-maker, baptised his daughter. After Wedgwood's death his widow Alice ran the pottery. (These may have been two men of the same name.) In January 1790 John Bollans advertised in the *York Herald* that he had taken the pottery at Mr Ella's Brick and Tile Yard, Heworth Grange, near York. It had been '. . . (lately occupied by Mrs Wedgwood) where he intends making all kinds of Garden Pots, Chimney Pots and all kinds of Green Earthenware . . .' In 1846 John Webster took over the pottery, and it is last mentioned when he advertised it for sale in 1848.[1]

Wares and Marks

The Yorkshire Museum has a red-bodied milk churn covered in white slip over which is a lead glaze appearing green and brown, which is possibly a nineteenth-century product of Heworth Moor. It has distinctive horseshoe-shaped handles. Several other pieces with this characteristic are known.

There are no known marks.

YORK CHINA MANUFACTORY

In 1838 Haigh Hirstwood and his son-in-law William Leyland left the Rockingham Works at Swinton and established the York China Manufactory, assisted by Hirstwood's sons Joseph and William. They built a kiln and premises in Lowther Street, The Groves, and decorated and finished china bought from other potteries. The partnership was dissolved and Leyland moved to London, where he decorated and printed lamps. He died there in 1853, and Hirstwood died in York in 1854.

Wares

It must be remembered that no china was produced here, only decorated work. Jewitt writes that 'the goods principally produced were dinner, tea, dessert and other services, vases, figures etc.'[2] The decoration was so similar to that on Rockingham porcelain that it is hardly distinguishable from it. Grabham illustrates two beautifully painted plaques, one by Hirstwood and the other by Leyland. Rice points out that if porcelain was bought in the white and glazed at York, it is likely that Hirstwood used Rockingham recipes for his glazes, since he was familiar with them, and that would make identification even more difficult.[3]

FRANCIS PLACE OF YORK

Francis Place, a seventeenth-century gentleman, painter, mezzotinter and virtuoso, spent much of his time in York. Between 1678 and 1694 he experimented in producing porcelain. He was unsuccessful, but the resulting pottery, in very fine semi-translucent stoneware, has earned him a place in ceramic history. At the time Place was conducting his experiments he was probably living at Dinsdale, near Darlington, and possibly that was the site of his pottery. It was previously thought that he had a pottery on the site of the Kings Manor in York, but he did not come to live there until 1792, and there is no evidence that he made pottery after the early 1790s.

Wares

Four pieces of pottery are attributed to Francis Place. The first is a grey saltglazed stoneware bell-shaped cup with black spiral 'marbling', formerly owned by Horace Walpole and now in the Victoria & Albert Museum; and the other three are all globular mugs, in grey saltglazed stoneware with dark brown spiral 'marbling', which have passed by descent from Place to the Patrick Allen-Fraser Art College, Arbroath.[4]

COWICK, near SNAITH
Location: SE 647216

Cowick was a major pottery manufacturing centre from the late thirteenth century to the fifteenth. Excavations have revealed that at first plain pottery jugs and cooking pots having a brownish-green glaze were made in 'Humber-Basin ware'. Decorative ware was introduced later, and included jugs with 'blackberry' stamps and fleur-de-lys patterns. By the early fourteenth century highly decorative vessels were being made, principally bung hole jars and pancheons.[5]

CAWOOD, near SELBY
Location: SE 573377

Situated north-west of the village of Cawood and south-east of the brickworks.

John Fetherston is recorded as a potter here in 1823. In the mid-nineteenth century the works were owned by Thomas B. Fretwell, brick and tile manufacturer. George Ryder, pot manufacturer, was in occupation in the late 1860s, selling the pottery to William Ryder in 1882 when he left to work at Gilberdike in the East Riding.[6]

No products are known, but it is likely that coarseware was made from local clay.

RAWCLIFFE BRICK TILE & POTTERY, RAWCLIFFE, NEAR SELBY

In the mid-1880s rustic flowerpots and flower vases were made here.

HOWDEN
Location: SE 763274

Situated 1 mile south-east of Howden on the north side of the road to Kilpin. A pottery is shown on Greenwood's map of Yorkshire, surveyed during 1815–17, on Teesdale's reprint, which was corrected to 1828, and on Hobson's Map of Yorkshire, 1843.

NOTES AND SOURCES

Abbreviations:

WRRD—West Riding Registry of Deeds
WRQS—West Riding Quarter Sessions
Lds Merc—Leeds Mercury
Lds Int—Leeds Intelligencer

CHAPTER 1: Leeds and District

1 WRRD, 229 290
2 *Lds Int* (13 April 1826)
3 *Lds Int* (3 November 1849)
4 Guildhall MS 11936/202 293213 and 11936/208 302865. Extracted by Elizabeth Adams
5 *Lds Merc* (4 October 1774): 'On Wednesday died in childbed Mrs Green wife of Savile Green of the Pottery near this town'
6 *Lds Merc* (30 July 1776): 'Run away. Thomas Sykes apprentice to Humble, Hartley, Greens & Co. of the Leeds Pottery . . .'
7 *Lds Int* (20 February 1781)
8 Full text of this and other letters quoted by Towner. Originals pasted in Pattern Book, Victoria & Albert Museum
9 Parish Register of St Giles-in-the-Fields, London, baptisms, 1743: '18 December John of John and Frances Green (born) Dec. 4th'. Parish Register of Mexborough Parish Church, baptisms, 1743: 'Savile son of John Green of Swinton. July 7th'
10 Tombstone inscription, Leeds Parish Church: 'Samuel Rainforth, Pot Manufacturer, Hunslet Hall Pottery, near Leeds, died 20 Febry., 1817, aged 53.' *Thoresby Society*, Vol XXLV
11 Sheffield Reference Library
12 *The Connoisseur*, Vol 43 (September 1915), and *Lds Int* (2 October 1820)

13 WRRD, EC 179 289
14 *Lds Merc* (26 April 1800)
15 WRRD, BE 611 835
16 *Lds Merc* (17 June 1820)
17 WRRD, FU 713 793
18 WRRD, B 3
19 WRRD, EH 87 98
20 WRRD, HB 632 706
21 *Yorkshire Gazette* (24 May 1824)
22 WRRD, MF 463 488
23 *Lds Merc* (25 October 1834)
24 WRRD, FU 712 792
25 *Lds Merc* (10 May and 10 February 1816)
26 Eaglestone, A. A. & Lockett, T. A. *The Rockingham Pottery*, 11
27 Eaglestone & Lockett, 33
28 *Lds Int* (29 July 1830). I am indebted to Mrs E. Blatch for this information
29 WRRD, OL 682 566
30 I am indebted to John Goodchild for this information
31 *Lds Int* (19 January 1850)
32 WRRD, OZ 656
33 WRRD, 805 286
34 Towner, 148
35 Coysh, A. W. *Blue Printed Earthenware*, 43
36 Evans, J. G. & M. I. N. *The Antique Collectors Club Magazine*, Vol 3, No 11 (March 1969), 27
37 Kidson, J. R. & F. *Historical Notices of The Leeds Old Pottery* (reprinted 1970), 90–5
38 Thornton, David S. 'Some Trifles from Leeds', *Leeds Arts Calendar*, No 67 (1970), 13–15
39 Much of this information comes from notes of an interview with Mr Morton. Leeds Art Library
40 I am indebted to John Goodchild for making this information available. South Yorkshire Industrial Museum
41 Leeds Reference Library
42 South Yorkshire Industrial Museum
43 As No 42
44 Kiddell, A. J. B. 'John Platt of Rotherham', *English Ceramic Circle Transactions*, Vol 5, part 3, 174

45 British Museum, Deposit 5769
46 *Lds Merc*
47 WRQS, Wakefield, January 1775
48 Land Tax Assessments, County Hall, Wakefield
49 WRRD, BR 244 316
50 Leeds City Archives Department, Sheepscar Library
51 WRRD, DY 494 620; WRQS, Pontefract, August 1799
52 WRRD, FI 564 684
53 Leeds City Archives Department, Sheepscar Library
54 *Lds Merc* (18 May 1844)
55 Copies of conveyances at WRRD
56 Supplement to Valuation List, Hunslet, 1824. Leeds City Archives Department
57 *Lds Merc* (13 August 1842)
58 *Lds Merc* (28 October 1843)
59 *Lds Int* (7 and 14 July 1848)
60 WRRD, SK 572 630
61 WRRD, BZ 210
62 WRRD, BE 611 835
63 Information obtained from WRRD and directories
64 Map at Leeds Reference Library, Hunslet Field Book listing occupants, etc. Leeds City Archives Department
65 WRRD, CP 716 1039 and DC 723 958
66 Information from WRRD and directories
67 I am indebted to Mrs E. Blatch for this extract
68 Hunslet Township Valuation List, supplement for 1827. Leeds City Archives Department
69 Information from WRRD and directories
70 I am indebted to A. Collinge for bringing this piece to my attention
71 WRRD, EG 421 556 and EP 329 425
72 Land Tax Assessments, County Hall, Wakefield
73 Information principally from WRRD, Land Tax Assessments and directories
74 Gilbert, Christopher. 'Portrait of a Yorkshire Pottery', *Country Life*, 140 (September 1966)
75 Manuscript at South Yorkshire Museum
76 Information principally from WRRD and directories
77 *Lds Int* (6 April 1782)

78 Mayes, P., Pirie, E. J. E., and Le Patourel, H. E. J. 'A Cistercian Ware Kiln of the Early Sixteenth Century at Potterton, Yorkshire', *The Antiquaries Journal*, Vol XLVI, part 2

79 *Medieval Archaeology*, Vol 9 (1965)

CHAPTER 2: *South Yorkshire*

1 Fitzwilliam Rentals, Sheffield Reference Library
2 Fitzwilliam Bills, Sheffield Reference Library
3 Grabham, Oxley. *Yorkshire Potteries, Pots and Potters* (York 1916), 84
4 Eaglestone & Lockett, 16–31
5 *Lds Merc* (11 March 1926). I am indebted to Mrs E. Blatch for this extract
6 *Lds Int* (31 May 1827). Extracted by Mrs E. Blatch
7 *Lds Merc* (24 August 1833)
8 *Lds Merc* (29 April 1843) and *Sheffield & Rotherham Independent* (7 January 1843)
9 *Lds Merc* (11 June 1843)
10 Rice, D. G. *The Illustrated Guide to Rockingham Pottery and Porcelain* (1971), Plate 38
11 For much of the information on wares I am indebted to Mr & Mrs J. D. Griffin and Mr & Mrs J. G. Evans, and to the books by Eaglestone & Lockett and Rice, mentioned above
12 *Newsletter No 4*, Northern Ceramic Society
13 WRRD, EK 485 651 and EK 486 652
14 WRRD, EQ 147 167
15 Eaglestone & Lockett, 26
16 *Doncaster, Nottingham & Lincoln Gazette* (14 February 1834). I am indebted to J. D. Griffin for this extract
17 Rice, 183–5
18 *Sheffield Mercury & Hallamshire Advertiser* (17 January 1835)
19 *Sheffield Mercury & Hallamshire Advertiser* (20 June 1835)
20 WRRD, NE 758 674
21 *Rotherham Advertiser* (5 August 1893). I am indebted to J. D. Griffin for this extract
22 Jewitt, Llewellynn. *Ceramic Art in Great Britain* (1878)
23 Coysh, 99
24 Tomlinson, John. *Doncaster Into Hallamshire* (Doncaster 1879)

25 I am extremely grateful to J. D. Griffin for much background information on the Don Pottery
26 WRRD, FL 143
27 I am indebted to W. G. Matthews for this information
28 WRRD, RH 643 243 and RH 660 258
29 *The Connoisseur* (May 1929)
30 South Yorkshire Industrial Museum
31 Land Tax Assessments, County Hall, Wakefield
32 WRRD, SM 245 299
33 Eaglestone & Lockett, 29
34 WRRD, FE 460 640
35 WRRD, FO 553 705 and 554 706
36 WRRD, NZ 520 395
37 Early deeds and map at Rotherham Reference Library. Diary extracts from Kiddell, A. J. B. 'John Platt of Rotherham', *English Ceramic Circle Transactions*, Vol 5, part 3
38 WRQS, Barnsley (October 1777). I am indebted to John Goodchild for drawing my attention to this
39 WRRD, DN 566 719
40 *Lds Merc* (16 July 1826). I am indebted to Mrs E. Blatch for this extract
41 *Sheffield Mercury* (13 January 1838)
42 Much of the background information on this pottery is taken from *The Glass Works, Rotherham 1751–1951* (Rotherham), researched by Miss D. Greene
43 WRRD, RG 500 582
44 WRRD, SU 717 779
45 I am indebted to the staff of the Rotherham Reference Library for making available much of the background information and also to Miss P. Hawley and T. Hawley for their help on the Hawley family potteries
46 WRRD and directories
47 WRRD, DB 507 571
48 Sheffield Reference Library
49 Land Tax Assessments, County Hall, Wakefield
50 *Sheffield Mercury & Hallamshire Advertiser* (6 January 1838)
51 WRRD, UR 546 603
52 WRRD, 1904.29.105
53 WRRD, DT 609

54 *Rotherham & Masbrough Advertiser*
55 WRRD, and as No 45
56 I am grateful to Messrs Parker, Rhodes & Burgess for allowing
    me to see these deeds
57 Chiefly WRRD
58 WRRD, NU 235 270
59 WRRD, EU 154 196
60 Milefanti, H. C. & Brears, P. C. D. 'Pottery Kilns at Rawmarsh,
    near Rotherham, Yorkshire', *Post-Medieval Archaeology*, Vol 5
    (1971)
61 WRRD and directories
62 WRRD and directories
63 *Post-Medieval Archaeology*, Vol 5 (1971); excavations by Miss P.
    Beswick for Sheffield City Museums
64 Sheffield Reference Library
65 Information on the early history and wares taken from Kenworthy,
    J. *Early History of Stocksbridge and District* . . . *Midhope Potteries*
    (1928)
66 *Yorkshire Archaeology* (1972), Council for British Archaeology,
    Group 4, 12

CHAPTER 3:   *Ferrybridge, Pontefract and Castleford*

1   Manuscript at South Yorkshire Industrial Museum
2   Wedgwood Archives, Josiah Wedgwood & Sons, Barlaston
3   Land Tax Assessments, County Hall, Wakefield
4   *Lds Merc* (21 May 1842)
5   Manuscript at South Yorkshire Industrial Museum
6   As No 5
7   I am greatly indebted to T. G. Brown of the Ferrybridge Pottery
    for making the deeds of the pottery available to me. Much of the
    information has been taken from them
8   Wedgwood Archives
9   WRRD, 852 9 5
10 WRRD, 1899 28 165
11 WRRD, 875 484
12 Manuscript at South Yorkshire Industrial Museum
13 As No 12
14 WRRD, CZ 667 952

15 Land Tax Assessments
16 WRRD, DG 189 264 and DG 190 265
17 Manuscript at South Yorkshire Industrial Museum
18 As No 17
19 *Lds Int* (21 May 1821)
20 Information chiefly from WRRD and Mr Goodchild
21 *Lds Merc* (20 March 1841)
22 As No 20
23 As No 20
24 WRRD, MY 359 338
25 WRRD, 1886 18 72
26 WRRD, SU 488
27 Excavations by H. K. Bowse on behalf of the Borough Council of Castleford
28 WRRD and directories
29 WRRD, ON 692 670
30 *Lds Merc* (24 February 1844)
31 Conveyances WRRD
32 WRRD and Mr Goodchild
33 WRRD, TU 661 772

CHAPTER 4: Halifax, Huddersfield and Bradford

1 Walton, James. 'Some Decadent Local Industries', *Halifax Antiquarian Society Trans* (1938)
2 Excavated by G. F. Bryant. *Post-Medieval Archaeology*, Vol 1 (1967), 116
3 As No 1
4 As No 1 and directories
5 As No 1 and Hanson, T. W. 'The Ovenden Heights', *Halifax Antiquarian Society Trans* (1913–14), 270
6 WRRD, TH 245 294
7 WRRD, 658 755 877
8 WRRD, 1897 42 285 136
9 WRRD, 1944 11 593 289
10 WRRD, 1885 30 238
11 WRRD, 1918 38 777
12 Trigg, W. B. 'The Halifax Coalfield', *Halifax Antiquarian Society Trans* (1932)

13 WRRD, TI 60 61
14 Excavated by R. Varley for Halifax Archaeological Research Group
15 I am indebted to John Bradley for this information
16 WRRD, 1886 4 542 335 and 1886 22 467
17 WRRD
18 WRRD, FN 731 901
19 As No 1, directories and WRRD. I am grateful to Mr Ormrod for his recollections of the pottery
20 WRRD, ME 678 649
21 Land Tax Assessments
22 WRRD, GT 499 498
23 WRRD, RY 318 367
24 WRRD, BT 322 421
25 Maltby, H. J. M. 'The Wibsey Pottery', *The Connoisseur* (April 1929)
26 As No 25
27 WRRD, SM 432
28 Tolson Museum, Huddersfield

CHAPTER 5: Wakefield and District

1 Walker, J. W. *Wakefield, Its History and People* (1934), 102
2 Charlesworth, J. (ed). *Wakefield Manor Book 1709* (1939), 184. Yorkshire Archaeological Society Record Series
3 Leeds City Archives Department
4 I am indebted to P. C. D. Brears for the information on Potovens
5 Woodrow, K. J. 'Cistercian Ware from Silcoates School, near Wakefield', *Post-Medieval Archaeology*, Vol 5 (1971), 185
6 Bartlett, K. S. 'Excavations at Potovens, near Wakefield, 1968', *Post-Medieval Archaeology*, Vol 5 (1971)
7 Kiln mentioned in deed of 1743, WRRD, SS 358, could refer to maltkiln; 1768 deed—WRRD, BL 4 6
8 My attention was drawn to this pottery by manuscript notes for a History of Oulton by the Rev G. H. Mercer in Rothwell Public Library
9 I am indebted to John Goodchild for this information

CHAPTER 6: Burton in Lonsdale

1 WRRD, AH 647
2 WRRD, CS 461 and Land Tax Assessments
3 WRRD, 1889 16 118
4 WRRD, EL 64 85
5 WRRD, 1886 7 695
6 All conveyances WRRD
7 As No 6
8 As No 6
9 As No 6

CHAPTER 7: North-east Yorkshire and Scarborough

1 Background information from Lillie, William. *History of Middles-brough, 1926-51*, and Le Vine, J. R. A. *Teesside Potteries*, a Teesside Museums & Art Galleries Service Research Publication
2 For further information see Le Vine, J. R. A. *Linthorpe Pottery*, a Teesside Museums and Art Galleries Service Research Publication, from which these notes have been drawn
3 *Lds Int* (2 December 1848)
4 Information chiefly taken from Vine. *Teesside Potteries*
5 As No 4
6 As No 4
7 I am indebted to John Mallet for this information
8 I am indebted to M. Y. Ashcroft for these searches
9 Conveyances and mortgages, WRRD. Other information from P. C. D. Brears
10 Bellamy, C. V. and Le Patourel, H. E. J. 'Four Medieval Pottery Kilns at Woodhouse Farm, Winksley, Near Ripon, West Riding', *Medieval Archaeology*, Vol 14 (1970)
11 Excavated by S. Brooke. 'A late Medieval Pottery Site near Yearsley', *Yorkshire Archaeological Journal*, Vol 37 (1951)
12 Excavated by R. A. Varley for the North Riding Research Committee. *The Dalesman* (17 June 1971)
13 *Post-Medieval Archaeology*, Vol 5 (1971), 216
14 Excavation report in *Yorkshire Archaeological Journal*, Vol 40
15 I am indebted to J. G. Rutter for this information

16 Rutter, J. G. 'Medieval Pottery in the Scarborough Museum, 13th and 14th Centuries', *Scarborough and District Archaeological Society Research Report No 3* (1961)

17 Rutter, J. G. 'Ayton Castle: its History & Excavation', *Scarborough and District Archaeological Society Research Report No 5* (1967)

18 As No 16, and Brewster, T. C. M. 'Staxton Ware' an Interim Report, *Yorkshire Archaeological Journal*, Vol 39

19 As No 16

CHAPTER 8: Hull and District

1 *Lds Merc* (24 July 1841)

2 Sheppard, T. 'The Belle Vue Pottery, Hull', *The Transactions of the British Ceramic Society*, Vol 40 (1941)

3 As a result of research into the history of the pottery by Mrs E. Blatch, the site was excavated by the East Riding Archaeological Society

4 Background information taken from Bartlett, John, and Brooks, Derek. 'Hull Pottery', *Kingston Upon Hull Museums Bulletin No 5*

5 I am indebted to Mrs E. Blatch for her advice on the Belle Vue Pottery

6 Directories and as No 2

7 Grabham, Oxley. *Yorkshire Potteries, Pots and Potters* (York 1916)

CHAPTER 9: York and South of York

1 Brears, P. C. D. *The English Country Pottery* (1971), 231

2 Jewitt, Llewellynn, *Ceramic Art in Great Britain*, Vol 1 (1878)

3 Rice, D. G. *The Illustrated Guide to Rockingham Pottery and Porcelain* (1971), 125

4 Tyler, E. G. 'Francis Place's Pottery', *English Ceramic Circle Transactions*, Vol 8, part 2

5 Mayes, P. *Medieval Archaeology* (1964), 297, and other sources

6 Directories and WRRD

MARKS

LEEDS POTTERY

1 Impressed. In various forms, often slightly curved; an asterisk, dash or full stop sometimes separates or follows the words. Sometimes the mark was impressed twice in the form of a cross. *c* 1775–1850. NB. A neat straight version of this mark was used by the Seniors on reproduction Leeds Pottery

2 Impressed. *c* 1780–*c* 1810. Rare

3 Printed. Occasionally included in the print. Late eighteenth century

4 Incised. Found on a creamware vase candlestick, Pattern Book No 116. *c* 1785. Rare

5 Impressed. Found on red stoneware. Eighteenth century. Rare.

5A Incised. Found on a red stoneware coffee pot. Eighteenth century. Very rare

6
7 } Impressed. Found in a variety of forms, sometimes impressed twice in the form of a cross. *c* 1800–30
8

9 Impressed. Richard Britton. 1850–72. Rare

10 Printed. Richard Britton & Son. Often included in pattern mark. 1872–8. Rare

HUNSLET HALL POTTERY

11 Impressed. 1800–17. Fairly rare. See p 49

12 Impressed. Found on plate illustrated on p 51, the only known design. 1817–46. Rare

13 Impressed. Found on identical plate to one bearing mark no 12 and excavated on the site of the pottery

14 Printed. Found on unglazed waster in Hunslet. Probably Joseph W. Taylor, who worked Petty's Pottery *c* 1875–81, Leathley Lane Pottery 1867–*c* 1885, and the Leeds Old Pottery 1881

HUNSLETESQUE POTTERY

15 Impressed. 1884–90. Rare. See p 39

LEEDS POTTERY

1

LP

2

Leeds Pottery

3

£

4

5

L.P.

5A

HARTLEY GREENS & Cº
LEEDS POTTERY

6

HARTLEY GREENS & Cº
LEEDS POTTERY

7

HARTLEY GREENS & Cº

8

9

R.B. & S.

10

RAINFORTH & C(o.)

11

PETTYS & Cº. LEEDS.

12

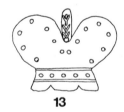

13

J TAYLOR

14

ESQUE POTTERY
HUNSLET
LEEDS

15

LEEDS
ART POTTERY

16

LEEDS
AP

17

L.A.P.
LEEDS

18

P

LEEDS ART POTTERY

16
17 } Impressed. 1890–*c* 1900. See also no 22
18

REPRODUCTION LEEDS POTTERY

19 Impressed. Only one known piece. Senior, twentieth century. See p 39 and mark no 1

W. WILKS

20 Impressed under brown glazed jelly mould. Probably William Wilks 1866. See p 72

WOODLESFORD ART POTTERY

21 Impressed. 1893–6

LEEDS

22 In relief. Only one example known, on a pink lustre decorated vase *c* 1900. Probably the Leeds Art Pottery or the Leeds Fireclay Co (see pp 56 and 67)

WORTLEY

23 Impressed. Probably used by William Ingham & Sons or Joseph Cliff & Sons (see p 71). *c* 1890

MORTON

24 Incised. Sometimes the year was included. 1933–9 or 1945–7. If 'Filey' is not included *c* 1910–14 or 1947–*c* 1953. See p 39

MIDDLETON FIRECLAY COMPANY

25 Impressed on highly glazed art wares. *c* 1895. See p 72

JACK LANE POTTERY

26 Impressed. Found on stoneware. 1848–66. See p 61

BURMANTOFTS, LEEDS FIRECLAY CO (LTD)

27
28 All impressed. Burmantofts. 1882–9. Pattern numbers often
29 impressed. See p 67
30

31
32 } Impressed. Leeds Fireclay Co. 1889–*c* 1912

33 Impressed. Trademark of Leeds Fireclay Co 1905

19 GEO
W
SENIOR
LEEDS POTTERY

20 W.WILKS
LEEDS

WOODLESFORD
ART POTTERY
21 Nr. LEEDS

22 LEEDS

23 WORTLEY

24 J T Morton
Filey

25 MIDDLETON
LEEDS

26 ROBINSON
JACK LANE POTTERY
LEEDS

27 BURMANTOFTS
FAIENCE

28 B

29 B F

30 B.F.

31 L.
F. C.

32 LEEDS FIRECLAY COMPANY

33 LEFICO

34 GRANITOFTS

35 LFC Lᴰ
HIPPERHOLME

36

37

38

34 Impressed. Trademark of Leeds Fireclay Co 1906
35 Impressed on tobacco jar dated 1920, see p 71

SWILLINGTON BRIDGE POTTERY

36 Printed. Found on glazed waster of 'Willow Pattern' design on the site. Probably 1820–33, but could be up to 1842. See p 73
37 Printed. Pattern mark (also used at other potteries) found on glazed waster on the site. *c* 1820–42
38 Impressed. On same waster as no 37. Broadest width 11mm
39 Impressed. Found on site on glazed waster. Also seen on plate bearing no 43. Probably used by Reed & Taylor
40 Printed. Found on site, but waster was broken, giving only the top of the crown
41 Impressed. The top half only of this mark was found on the site, but the complete mark has since been seen together with mark no 44
42 Printed. Found on the site, and since seen on 'Willow Pattern' plates. Not to be confused with no 110
43 ⎫ Printed. Found on 'Willow Pattern' plates. No 43 appears with
44 ⎭ no 39, and no 44 with no 41. Probably used by Reed & Taylor
45 Impressed. Found on unglazed waster on the site. Probably a workman's mark. Similar marks found at Swinton and elsewhere

HUNSLET NEW POTTERY

46 ⎫ Printed. Found on 'Willow Pattern' plates. Possibly G. & S.
47 ⎭ Taylor, Jack Lane, Hunslet. 1837–87. See p 58

YATES

48 Printed or painted. Relates to a china and earthenware dealer William Yates, 12 Bond Street, Leeds. *c* 1835–76

SWINTON POTTERY, ROCKINGHAM WORKS

49 Impressed. Recorded by Hurst but not seen by any modern writer. 1778–85. Very rare
50 Impressed. Often followed by a numeral or sign. Used on earthenware 1806–42. See p 93
51 Impressed. Found on a green glazed Cadogan pot. Rare
52 Painted. Found on painted creamware jug. Rare
53 Embossed. Found on caneware and without the outer rim on earthenware, and rarely on early porcelain

39

40

41

42

43

44

45 ⊕

46

47

YATES
LEEDS
48

BINGLEY
49

BRAMELD
50

BRAMELD & CO.
51

BRAMELD & CO
SWINTON POTTERY
52

53

Brameld
54

MORTLOCK
55

CADOGAN
56

54 Painted. Found on two earthenware vases and early porcelain. Rare

55
56
57 } Impressed. Found on tea, coffee, chocolate and Cadogan pots
58 exclusively. Sold by the London retailers
59

60
61
62
63
64 } Printed pattern marks peculiar to Swinton Pottery. Often found
65 in conjunction with nos 50 or 53
66
67
68

69 Impressed. Found on cane-coloured kitchen ware waster during excavations on the site

70 Printed. Found on the site

71 Impressed. Found on brown glazed earthenware 1826–42

72 Painted in gilt on some high quality porcelain. 1826–42. Rare

72A Impressed in script. Found on brown glazed earthenware. It is questionable whether this is a Rockingham mark. Other firms used the name to describe the type of ware

73 Painted in script on a cup at Rotherham Museum

74 Griffin mark printed in red with 'Rockingham Works Brameld' below. The commonest mark of the period 1826–31. An example is known printed in puce

75 Griffin mark printed in red with 'Rockingham Works' over the mark and 'Brameld' beneath. Fairly rare. 1826–31

76 Griffin mark printed in puce with 'Royal Rockingham Brameld' beneath. 1831–42

77 Griffin mark printed in puce with 'Rockingham Works Brameld Manufacturer to the King' beneath. The commonest mark found for the period 1831–42

78 Griffin mark printed in puce with 'Royal Rock^m Works Brameld' beneath. 1831–42

79 Griffin mark in puce with 'Rockingham Works' beneath and 'Brameld Manufacturer to the King Queen and Royal Family' in a cartouche below. Used particularly on porcelain made for Royalty. Rare

MORTLOCK'S
CADOGAN

57

NORFOLK

58

MORTLOCK'S
ROYAL
ROCKINGHAM

59

60

61

62

63

64

65

66

68

67

69

70
(CH)INA SKETCHES

71
ROCKINGHAM

80 Griffin mark impressed. Occasionally the words were used alone. Found on biscuit ware figures and some glazed figures. On some early models it is printed in red

BAGULEY

81 Griffin mark printed in red. Found on earthenware and porcelain. Several variations in the wording are recorded: 'Baguley' alone, 'Baguley Rockingham Works' in two lines, and 'Royal Rockingham Works Baguley' in three lines. Sometimes the griffin stands alone with no writing. 1842. It is likely that these marks were no longer used after 1865 when Alfred Baguley moved to Mexborough, but this is not certain

82 Printed. 1865–91. See p 94

DON POTTERY

83 Impressed. Found on all types of ware. 1801–34. See p 99

84 Painted in red in script. Found on Orange Jumper Jugs. *c* 1807

85 Printed, generally in blue, occasionally black. *c* 1810–34. Usually on printed wares

86 Impressed. Found on all types of ware except creamware. *c* 1805–34

87 Printed in blue with 'GREEN DON POTTERY' in the garter. Found on printed wares, but uncommon. *c* 1810–34

88 Incised on back of plaque (see plate, p 103). Rare

89 Embossed. Found on daisy jugs and rarely on other jugs. *c* 1820–34. See p 103

90 Impressed. The attribution of this mark is not certain. Godden records a printed mark used by a London retailer, J. Green & Sons. However, Coysh illustrates a plate with the impressed mark which is identical to the plate illustrated on p 88, which has the Don Pottery mark no 85. See p 102

91 Impressed. The attribution of this mark is uncertain. It may relate to the London firm of wholesalers or the Don Pottery. Rare.

92 Printed. Found on several pieces of Don Pottery, both with other marks or known Don patterns. 1815–34

93 Impressed. Probably the first mark used by Samuel Barker. *c* 1840–55

94 Printed. Samuel Barker & Son. *c* 1850–55. Uncommon

95 Printed. Samuel Barker & Son. Sometimes the name of the pattern is included in the garter. The commonest mark of the period. *c* 1855–93

Rockingham

72/72A

Rockingham
China Works
Swinton 1826

73

Rockingham Works Brameld

74

Rockingham China Brameld

75

Royal Rockingham Brameld.

76

Rockingham Works Brameld Manufacturers to the King

77

Royal Rockm Works Brameld

78

Rocking ham Works Brameld Manufacturers to the King and Royal Family

79

ROCKINGHAM
WORKS
BRAMELD

80

Rockingham Works Manufacturers to the Queen

81

ROCKINGHAM WORKS MEXBRO
BAGULEY

82

DON POTTERY

83

Don. Pottery,

84

DON POTTERY

85

DON POTTERY

86

GREEN DON POTTERY

87

88 *Don. Pottery. July. th 21 1829.*

DON

89

J GREEN & SON

90

GREEN
LONDON

91

96⎫
97 ⎬ Printed pattern marks found on wasters on the site. *c* 1860–93
98⎭

99 Printed. Found on wares decorated by Wilson's. The name of the manufacturer was sometimes included

100 Recorded on earthenware plant pot with applied ornamentation of flowers in colours on blue ground. Registered 1893

NEWHILL AND KILNHURST

101 Impressed. Found on green glazed 'Thistle' plates, blue painted and printed ware. Probably used by Joseph Twigg at Newhill *c* 1820–40. The pieces of Don Pottery origin would be dated after 1835 (see p 108)

102 Impressed. Found on blue printed plates with Italian scenes· Joseph Twigg, Newhill, 1834–*c* 1860. The mark may have been used earlier, but there are no known examples of earlier wares with the mark

103 Impressed. Found on all types of printed and painted pottery. Possibly used at Newhill, but certainly used at Kilnhurst Old Pottery. *c* 1840–84

104⎫ Impressed. Found on all types of wares. Sometimes with only
    ⎬ one G
105⎭ Kilnhurst Old Pottery. 1840–84

106 Printed. Found with no 104 on 'Willow Pattern' plate. Kilnhurst Old Pottery

107 Printed. Found with no 103 on 'Willow Pattern' plate. Kilnhurst Old Pottery

108 Printed. Found with no 104 on 'Willow Pattern' plate. Kilnhurst Old Pottery

109 Printed. Found on 'Willow Pattern'. Kilnhurst Old Pottery

110 Printed. Found with no 103 on 'Willow Pattern' plate. Kilnhurst Old Pottery. Not to be confused with no 42

111 Printed. Found on dinner service in 'Albion' design, together with no 104. Kilnhurst Old Pottery

112 Printed. Found on 'Asiatic Pheasant' design plate with no 104. Kilnhurst Old Pottery

113 Impressed. Found on child's plate illustrated on p 159. Kilnhurst Old Pottery

114⎫ Printed. Used on plates with 'Eton College' pattern. Kilnhurst
115⎭ Old Pottery. Pre-1877

D

92

BARKER
DON
POTTERY
93

IRONSTONE CHINA
S.&G.
94

95   S. B. & S

Asiatic Pheasants
S.B.&S.
96

THE
XARP
97

GEM
98

D & JS
WILSON
DON POTTERY
SWINTON   99

DON ART WARE
100

TWIGG
101

TWIGG
NEWHILL
102

TWIGG'S
103

TWIGG
104   KP

TWIGG
105   K-P

STONE CHINA
T
K 9 P
106

STONE-CHINA
T
14
107

STONE CHINA
14
108

STONE CHINA
T
(K.P.)
109

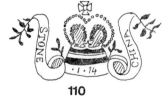

STONE CHINA
· 1 · 74
110

116 Printed on plate depicting the Mormon Temple at Nauvoo. Kilnhurst Old Pottery *c* 1846

117 Impressed. Hepworth & Heald, Kilnhurst Old Pottery 1884–1924. Rarely seen

MEXBOROUGH POTTERY

118 Impressed. Found on transfer-printed earthenware in 'Willow Pattern' design. 1800–8. Rare

119 ⎱ Attributed to Sowter & Co by earlier writers, although there
120 ⎰ seems to be no conclusive evidence. See p 115

121 Impressed. There is no conclusive evidence that this mark was used by the Barkers at Mexborough. Could also relate to Peter Barker in Rawmarsh or to a Staffordshire firm. See p 116

MEXBOROUGH ROCK POTTERY

122 Printed. Reed & Taylor often used printed marks of patterns which included their initials. These could have been made at Mexborough *c* 1830–8, at Ferrybridge 1832–*c* 1838, or at Swillington Bridge 1833–*c* 1838

123 ⎱ Printed pattern marks used by Reed & Taylor. See remarks,
124 ⎰ no 122

125 Printed. Incorporated in various printed pattern marks. Reed, Taylor & Co at the Mexborough Rock Pottery *c* 1838–*c* 1843, at Ferrybridge, or at Swillington Bridge, same date

126 ⎫
127 ⎪ Printed pattern marks used by Reed, Taylor & Co. See remarks,
128 ⎬ no 125
129 ⎪
    ⎭

130 Impressed. Seen on earthenware whose patterns were bought at the Brameld's sale in 1843. Fairly rare

131 ⎱ Printed. Two variations of Reed's mark, one found on a jug and
132 ⎰ the other on a bowl in the 'Boy Playing the Pipes' pattern. 1844–70. Rare. No 132 also found with no 126

EMERY

133 Incised. Rare

DENABY POTTERY

134 ⎱ Printed. 1864–6. Rare
135 ⎰

136 Printed. 1866–8. Rare

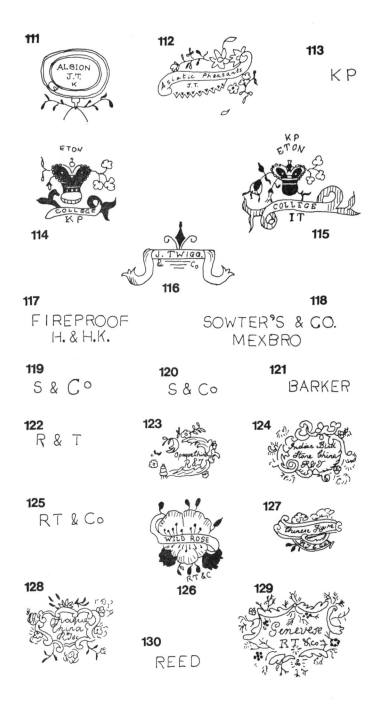

111 ALBION J.T. K

112 Asiatic Pheasants J.T.

113 K P

114 ETON COLLEGE KP

115 KP ETON COLLEGE IT

116 J. TWIGG. & Co

117 FIREPROOF H. & H.K.

118 SOWTER'S & CO. MEXBRO

119 S & Cᵒ

120 S & Co

121 BARKER

122 R & T

123 Opaque China R&T

124 Indian Birds Stone China R&T

125 RT & Co

126 WILD ROSE RT&C

127 Chinese Figure R&T&Co

128 Opaque China RT&Co

129 Genevese R.T. &co

130 REED

HAWLEY POTTERIES

137 Impressed. Found on teapot illustrated p 69. *c* 1800–15. Used either by William Hawley at the Top Pottery, Rawmarsh, or by Thomas Hawley at Kilnhurst Old Pottery (see pp 111 and 135). Rare

138 Impressed on teapot illustrated p 69. *c* 1800–15. Remarks as for no 137. Rare

139 Impressed. Recorded under busts of John Wesley. Thomas Hawley. Kilnhurst Old Pottery. *c* 1780–1808. Rare

140 Printed. Sometimes incorporated in pattern mark. George Hawley at the Low Pottery, Rawmarsh, *c* 1844–63; his son George at the same works, *c* 1868–82; the Northfield Pottery, Rotherham, 1855–63; or, though less likely, the Top Pottery, Rawmarsh, 1844–58. See pp 127, 134 and 135

141 Printed pattern mark. George Hawley, as no 140

142 Printed. George Hawley, as no 140

143 Printed. Usually incorporated in pattern mark. William and George Hawley, Northfield Pottery, Rotherham, 1864–8. Rare

144 Printed mark of HB intertwined, in a shield with 1790 below. Ltd added after 1897. Recorded by Grabham, but never seen by the author. Hawley Brothers, Northfield Pottery, Rotherham. 1864–97

145 Printed. 'Leyland, Walker & Hornsey', the Low Pottery, Rawmarsh. 1882–4. Only one piece known (see p 134)

146 } Painted on porcelain made by Hawley Brothers, under Sydney
147 } Hawley at the Northfield Pottery, Rotherham *c* 1890

148 Impressed. Trademark of Hawley Bros Ltd and the Northfield Hawley Pottery Co Ltd. Northfield Pottery 1898–*c* 1915 or the Low Pottery, Rawmarsh, 1898–1904

149 Printed. Found on a copper plate in the possession of John Hawley's daughter. No known examples. Rare

149A Impressed. Northfield Pottery, Rotherham. Found on unglazed sherd on the site of the pottery. No known examples. Rare

HOLMES POTTERY

150 Printed. John Jackson & Co. Initials included in printed pattern marks. *c* 1860–87. Rare

151 Printed. George Shaw & Sons, *c* 1887–*c* 1935. Ltd was added after 1909. Rare

FERRYBRIDGE or KNOTTINGLEY POTTERY

152 Impressed. Recorded by Jewitt (see p 157). 1793–8. Tomlinson, Foster & Co. Rare

131

132

133

134

135

136

137

HAWLEY

138

HAWLEY

139

THO HAWLEY

140

GEO. HAWLEY

141

142

G.H.

143

W. & G. HAWLEY

144

H.B.

145

Hawley Bros.

146

147

HAWLEY BROS

148

149

149A

153 ⎱ Impressed. 1798–1800. Tomlinson, Foster, Wedgwood & Co.
154 ⎰ Also used by Ralph Wedgwood in Burslem *c* 1790–6. The same marks were used again by a Staffordshire firm *c* 1860. See p 157

155   Impressed. Godden suggests this may have been used by William Tomlinson & Co, 1801–4. It could also have been used by William Taylor & Co; Taylor worked the Rothwell Pottery 1780–5, W. Taylor & Co worked the Castleford Pottery 1785–90, and Taylor alone worked the Swillington Bridge Pottery 1791–5. The mark may have been used elsewhere. See p 166

156   Impressed. Used by successive occupants 1801–70. The commonest mark of the pottery. Occasionally the D was reversed

157   Impressed. Benjamin Taylor & Son, Ferrybridge. *c* 1845–50. See p 252 for other marks used by Reed & Taylor and Reed, Taylor & Co at Ferrybridge

158   Printed. Initials included in printed pattern marks. 1851–*c* 1877. Lewis Woolf

159   Printed. Pattern mark of Lewis Woolf. 1851–*c* 1877

160   Impressed. Note the definite edge to the shield on the right. *c* 1845–84. B. Taylor & Son and Lewis and Sydney Woolf. Note similarity to no 39

161   Printed. Found on plate bearing mark no 160. Sydney Woolf, *c* 1860–87, but probably after 1877

162   Printed pattern mark. Sydney Woolf, Ferrybridge or Australian Pottery. *c* 1860–84. Found with no 156

163   These words on a shield, supported by a lion and unicorn and surmounted by a crown, impressed, are recorded by Jewitt, but have not been seen by any modern writer

164   Printed pattern mark. Found on plate bearing mark no 156

165   Impressed or printed. Poulson Brothers, at the Ferrybridge Pottery 1884–95, the West Riding Pottery 1882–1945, and the Calder Pottery *c* 1877–93

166   Printed. Often included in pattern marks. Remarks as for no 165

167   Printed. As no 166

168   Printed on Tyke mug which also bears mark no 165 impressed

169   Printed pattern mark. Poulson Brothers, Ferrybridge. *c* 1890

170   Impressed or printed. Sefton & Brown, Ferrybridge. Often included in pattern marks. 1895–1919

171   Impressed. Thomas Brown & Sons Ltd. 1919 to present. Rarely used

150
J. J. & CO.

151
G. S. & S.

152
TOMLINSON & CO.

153
WEDGWOOD & CO

154
Wedgwood & Co.

155
W T & C°

156
FERRYBRIDGE

157

158
L. W.

159

160

161

162

163
Ferrybridge
and
Australian
Potteries

164

165
P. B.

166
P. BROS

167
POULSON BRO'S

168

169

170
S B
F B

TB & S
F B

171

CASTLEFORD

172
173 Impressed. Found on felspathic stoneware, creamware, painted
174 and transfer-printed ware. David Dunderdale & Co. 1790–1820.
175 See p 166
176

177 Printed. Recorded by Jewitt. T. Nicholson & Co. *c* 1854–*c* 1869.
Castleford Mere Pottery, p 171

178 Printed. Pattern mark given by Jewitt, as no 177

179 Impressed or printed. Included in pattern marks. Clokie &
Masterman, Castleford Mere Pottery, 1869–85. Recorded by
Godden, not seen by the author

180 As no 179

181 Printed. Clokie & Co. Castleford Pottery 1885–1961. Likely to be
182 twentieth century. 'Ltd' may have been added after *c* 1940

183 Printed. Found on engraved copper plate of 'Willow Pattern'. No
known examples. William Gill, Allerton Bywater Pottery 1859–
c 1870, or Providence Pottery *c* 1874–80

184 Printed. William Gill & Sons, Castleford. England added after
1891. Providence Pottery 1880–*c* 1929

185 Printed. Godden records this mark and suggests it could relate
to Taylor, Harrison & Co, *c* 1835–41. See p 172

186 Printed. H. McDowall & Co, Eagle Pottery 1856–61+. See
187 p 177

188 Printed or impressed. Often included in pattern mark. Robinson
Brothers. Allerton Bywater Pottery *c* 1887–*c* 1902; Eleven Acres
Pottery 1892–*c* 1902

189 Impressed. John Robinson & Son. Eleven Acres Pottery *c* 1902–
33

190 Printed. Trade name used by Hartley's (Castleford) Ltd. 1953–60
Found on decorative wares

191 Printed. Found on unglazed waster in Castleford. May relate to
the Albion Pottery or to the name of the pattern made elsewhere

HALIFAX AND HUDDERSFIELD

192 Impressed. Isaac Button jr. Soil Hill Pottery. *c* 1947–65. See p 188

193 Impressed. Joseph Morton & Sons (Lindley) Ltd. *c* 1900–45.
See p 192

194 Printed. Found on cheese stand in 'Asiatic Pheasant' design.
Relates to china and earthenware dealer in Lister Lane, Halifax,
1861–77

D·D & CO
CASTLEFORD
POTTERY
172

D·D & C°
CASTLEFORD
173

D.D. & Co
174

CASTLEFORD
POTTERY
175

CASTLEFORD
176

T N & Co
177

178

C.& M.
179

180
CLOKIE &
MASTERMAN

181

182

183

184

186

185
T.H. & CO.

187

188
R.B.

189
J.R. & S.

190
HARTROX

191
ALBION

192
I BUTTON   SOIL HILL POTTERY   HOLMFIELD

193
LINDLEY WARE

194A Impressed. Woodhead, Davison & Cooper, Eccleshill. *c* 1845–60. Rare

MIDDLESBROUGH POTTERY

195 Impressed. Middlesbrough Pottery Co. 1834–44
196 Impressed. As no 195. See p 210
197 Impressed. As no 195
198 Impressed. Used by both the Middlesbrough Pottery Co and the Middlesbrough Earthenware Co. 1834–52
199 Impressed. Middlesbrough Earthenware Co and Isaac Wilson & Co. 1852–87
200 Impressed. As no 195
201 Impressed. Middlesbrough Earthenware Co. 1844–52
202 Printed. Printed pattern mark. Middlesbrough Pottery Co. 1834–44
203 Printed. As no 202
204 Printed. Appears with nos 197 and 198. 1834–52
205 Printed. Appears with no 198. 1834–52
206 Printed. As no 205
207 Printed. Appears with nos 199 and 216. *c* 1852–87
207A Printed. Appears with nos 199 and 210
208 Printed. Appears with no 198. 1834–52
209 Printed. Appears with nos 199 and 216. 1852–87
210 Impressed. Isaac Wilson & Co. 1852–87
211 ⎫
212 ⎬ Impressed. As no 210
213 ⎫
214 ⎬ Printed. Appears with nos 199 and 216. Isaac Wilson & Co. 1852–87
215 Printed. Isaac Wilson & Co. 1852–87
216 Impressed. Isaac Wilson & Co. 1852–87
217 Impressed. Recorded by Le Vine

LINTHORPE POTTERY

218 Impressed. 1879–*c* 1884
219 Impressed. Several variations in which the size of the bowl varies. *c* 1882–90

194

WOODHEAD . DAVISON
. & COOPER .
ECCLESHILL . MANOR
POTTERY
194A . YORKSHIRE .

195
MIDDLESBRO
POTTERY CO.

196
M.P. CO.

197

198

199

200
MIDDLESBROUGH
POTTERY   CO.

M. E. & CO.
201

202

203

204

205

206

207

207A
RHINE
M. P. Cº

208

209

220 Stamped with raised letters. Found on tiles. 1884–90

221 Impressed. Includes the signature of Christopher Dresser and the monogram of Henry Tooth. 1879–*c* 1882

222 Impressed signature found in various forms. Dresser was art director and superintendent at the Linthorpe Pottery. 1879–*c* 1884

223 Impressed. Monogram of Henry Tooth, the pottery manager, 1879–*c* 1882

224 Printed. In various forms. Wardle was a retailer in Middlesbrough, *c* 1860–1910

225 Printed. In various forms. Relates to firm of retailers in Middlesbrough, *c* 1860–1910

STAFFORD POTTERY

226 Impressed. William Smith. *c* 1825–1830s

227 Impressed. William Smith. *c* 1825–7

228 Impressed. William Smith & Co. *c* 1825–55

229 Impressed. William Smith & Son. *c* 1825–30

230 Impressed. William Smith & Co. *c* 1825–47

231 Impressed. As no 230

232 Impressed. William Smith & Co. Found with other factory marks. *c* 1825–47

233 Impressed. Found with no 228. William Smith & Co. 1825–47

234 Impressed. As no 233

235 Impressed. William Smith & Co. 1825–55

236
237 } Impressed. As no 235
238

239 Impressed. George & William Skinner. 1855–*c* 1860

240 Impressed. George Skinner & Co. 1855–70

241 Impressed. George Skinner & Walker. 1875–7

242 Impressed. Skinner & Walker. 1875–7

243 } Impressed. Ambrose Walker & Co. 1877–1890s
244

245
246
247 } Printed. Pattern marks used by William Smith & Co. *c* 1840–50
248
249

I. W. & CO.
210

I.W. & CO.
MIDDLESBRO'
211

I.W. & CO.
MIDDLESBROUGH
212

213

214

215

216

217
XL
ALL

218
LINTHORPE

219
LINTHORPE

220
LINTHORPE

221
H LINTHORPE
Chr: Dresser

222
Chr: Dresser

223
H

224
J WARDLE

225
LLOYD & Co

226
W. Smith

227
W.S.
STOCKTON

228
W.SMITH & CO.

229
W.S.& S.

230
W. S. & CO'S
WEDGEWOOD

231
W.S & CO'S
WEDGWOOD
WARE

232
WEDGEWOOD

250 Printed. William Smith & Co at a branch of the pottery in Brussels. *c* 1850

251
252
253 }Printed pattern marks used by William Smith & Co. *c* 1830–55
254
255

COMMONDALE POTTERY

256 Impressed. 1872–82. See p214

257 Impressed. 1872–84

YARM POTTERY

258 Impressed. 1927–*c* 1938. See p 215

LITTLETHORPE POTTERY

259 Impressed. Present day. See p 217

BELLE VUE POTTERY

260
261 }Impressed. William Bell. 1826–41. See p 222

262
263 }Printed. William Bell. 1826–41
264

265 Printed. Thought to be used by William Bell. 1826–41. See p 223

NAFFERTON POTTERY

266 Impressed. Samuel Longbottom. *c* 1875–99

WEDGWOOD
233

WEDGEWOOD
WARE
234

W. S. & CO'S
QUEEN'S WARE
STOCKTON **235**

236
W. S. & CO'S
QUEEN'S WARE

W. S. & CO'S **237**
QUEEN'S WARE
SOUTH STOCKTON

238
STAFFORD POTTERY
SOUTH STOCKTON

239
G. & W. S.
PEARL WHITE

240
G.S. & CO.

241
G. S. & W'S
QUEEN'S WARE
SO. STOCKTON

242
S. & W'S
QUEEN'S WARE
SO. STOCKTON

243
A.W. & Co
SO. STOCKTON

244
A.W. & Cº Lᴰ
THORNABY

245

246

247

248

249

250

251

253
PAUL
and
VIRGINIA

252
FRUIT
BASKET
W. S. & Co.

254
Tourist
WS & C°

255
65
NAPOLEON
WS&C

256
·COMMONDALE·
POTTERY

257
CROSSLEY
COMMONDALE

258
J. H. CLARK
THE POTTERY
YARM-ON-TEES

259
LITTLETHORPE POTTERY
CURTIS
RIPON

260
BELLE. VUE. POTTERY
B. HULL.

261
BELLE VUE POTTERY
HULL.

262
BELLE VUE POTTERY.
HULL.

263
Belle Vue Pottery
B. Hull.

264
Belle vue Pottery
Hull.

265
Chinese
Marine
OPAQUE CHINA

266
S L

POTTERS
NOT INCLUDED IN TEXT

The following list aims to include known potters, decorators, and allied workers who worked in Yorkshire but are not included in the text of the book. The dates given are merely a guide and do not necessarily cover the whole period of work in an area. Where the pottery is specified in the reference, it is listed, but when a person is described as of Swinton, for example, he could equally well have worked at any of the Swinton, Don, Mexborough, Kilnhurst or Newhill Potteries.

The names come from various sources, including parish registers, West Riding Quarter Sessions Rolls, directories, newspapers, and the West Riding Registry of Deeds. Abbreviations are used as follows:

> p   = potter
> ew mf = earthenware manufacturer
> ptr   = painter
> decr   = decorator
> C   = century (as C19)

ADAMSON, Henry, 1875, pottery manager, Knottingley, at Swinton; 1880, pottery manager, Swinton
ADAMSON, John, 1848–52, p, Swinton
ALLEN, John, 1793, p, Castleford Pottery
ALLON, William, 1745–52, p, Rotherham; 1758, p, Hoyland Swaine, Silkstone; 1763, p, Pittsmoor, Sheffield; 1766, p, Hoyland Swaine

AMBLER, Richard, 1803, p, Swinton

ANDERSON, 1834, p, Hunslet

ANDREWS, Richard, 1605, p, Potovens

APPLEYARD, William, 1853, Castleford Pottery

ARMITAGE, John & Son, *c* 1890s, Deepcar, Sheffield, terracotta manufacturers

ARMITAGE, William, 1680, p, Potovens

ASBURRY (ASHBURY), William, 1774–8, 'Hunslet Pottery', 'Pottery' and 'Pottery, Leeds'

ASHTON, flower modeller, Rockingham Works

ASKAM, Robert, *c* 1800–56, Ferrybridge Pottery

ASTBURY, Benjamin, 1854, p, Rotherham

ASTBURY, Mrs Mary, 1893, pottery mould mf, 4 Sheffield Road, Rotherham

ASTBURY, William, modeller and mouldmaker for Hawley's for 63 years

ASTBURY, William, 1770–1, p, Rothwell (may be same as William Asburry or Ashbury)

ASTBURY, William, 1842, p, Swillington Bridge

ASQUITH, John, 1793 and 1807, p, Castleford Pottery

ATHERTON, James, 1822, ew mf, Mexborough

AUTRY, James, 1848, p, Mexborough

BAGALEY, George, 1806, p, Burton in Lonsdale

BAGGALEY, Edward, 1804, p, Mexborough Old Pottery

BAGLEY (BEGLEY), Thomas, 1772, 'Pothouse' Leeds; 1774, Hunslet Pottery

BAILEY, William W., 1830s, ornamental ptr, Rockingham Works; 1841, china mf, Wath on Dearne. NB: porcelain known inscribed 'China Works, Wath', 'W. W. Bailey, Wath', 'Wath', and 'Wath China Works'

BALGEY, George, 1805, p, Pontefract

BALL, Jesse, 1773, 'Pottery', Leeds

BALL, Enoch, 1770–3, p, Rothwell; 1777–85, Hunslet (d 1806)

BALL, Richard, 1805, p, Swinton; 1814, Don Pottery

BALL, Sylvanus, artist, Swinton Pottery

BAMETT, James, 1804, p, Rawmarsh
BARKER, Charles, 1789, p, Rawmarsh Low Pottery
BARKER, Charles, p, Swinton, father of Enoch Barker
BARKER, Enoch, p, Swinton, died 1878
BARKER, John, 1875–83, p, Swinton
BARRACLOUGH, Elizabeth, 1809, ptr, Swinton Pottery
BARRACLOUGH, John, 1817, p, Leeds
BARTON, William, 1839, Don Pottery
BATESON, Christopher, 1769, p, Burton in Lonsdale
BATESON, George, 1795 and 1806–11, p, Burton in Lonsdale
BATESON, John, sr, 1808, p, Burton in Lonsdale
BATESON, John, jr, 1795, p, Burton in Lonsdale
BATESON, Robert, 1763, p, Burton in Lonsdale
BATESON, Thomas, 1765, p, Burton in Lonsdale
BATESON, William, 1797, p, Burton in Lonsdale; died 1811. NB: there were several William Batesons, potters, in Burton in Lonsdale
BATTY, Samuel, 1804–11, p, Burton in Lonsdale
BAWLIN, William, of Shelton, 1855, china gilder, Swinton
BEARD, James, 1857, p, Cindar Hill, nr Ecclesfield
BEDFORD, John, 1868, p, Strensall, nr York
BEDFORD, 1823, lived at Leeds Pottery
BEEDEL, John, 1834–62, p, Fletcher's Pottery, Castleford
BELL, Timothy, 1823, lived at Leeds Pottery
BENNET, Joseph, 1830, Don Pottery
BENNETT, H. T., 1904, p, Grange Farm, Goole
BEST, William, 1753, p, Rawmarsh
BETNEY, Joseph, 1793, p, Knottingley
BEVITT, Benjamin, 1709, p, Potovens, son of William Bevitt
BEVITT, William, 1650s, p, Potovens
BILSBROUGH, James, 1808, Ferrybridge Pottery
BILSBROUGH, Thomas, ptr, Castleford, early C19
BINNER, Roger, 1773, p, Wibsey
BIRCH, J., 1870–6, ew mf, 109 Sweet Street, Leeds
BLACK, George, 1821, p, Castleford Pottery
BLOOR, James, 1830–40, p, Woodlesford

BLOOR, James, 1854, p, Rotherham

BOOTH, Ward, 1814, Don Pottery

BOOTH & WALKER, 1904, potters, Tyrell Street, Bradford

BOOTHROYD, Emanuel, 1775, p, Lindley, Huddersfield

BOWATER, James, 1855, salesman, Leeds Pottery

BRAGG, John, 1754, p, Potovens; 1788, p, Langside, Penistone, late of Potovens

BRAIM, John, 1808, Ferrybridge Pottery

BRAIM, John, 1817, manager to 'Hartley & Co', lived Leeds Pottery House

BRAIM, Thomas, 1791, Castleford Pottery; 1807+, Ferrybridge Pottery; 1810, agent for Ferrybridge Pottery

BRIANT, Henry, 1797, p, Knottingley

BRAITHWAITE, Edmund, 1887, p, 427 High Street, Attercliffe

BRAMMER, Thomas, 1808, p, Swinton

BRANDESBY, Thomas de, 1284, p, York

BREAR, John, 1847–53, p, Bradshaw Lane, Ovenden

BREARTON, Thomas, 1804, p, Mexborough Old Pottery

BRENTNALL, Thomas, 1831–3, ptr, Rockingham Works

BROADHURST, James, 1804, p, Mexborough Old Pottery

BROOK, T., 1861, p, Brackenmoor, Bolsterstone, Sheffield

BROOKE, Edward, 1861, p, Fireclay Works, Fartown, Huddersfield

BROOKE, William, 1830, p, Castleford

BROWN, George, 1808, Ferrybridge Pottery

BROWN, William, 1904, p, Station Road, Sherburn in Elmet

BRUIN, William, 1789–90, p, Rawmarsh

BRUNT, Ephraim, 1837, overlooker, Samuel Barker's Manufactory

BRUNT, Job, 1837, p, Swinton; 1846, ew mf, Mexborough; 1850, p, Don Pottery

BRUNT, R., 1830–40, potter printer, Oulton

BULLOCK, Charles & James, 1870s, ew and glass bottle mfs, Mexborough

BULLOUGH, Benjamin, 1808, Ferrybridge Pottery

BULLOUGH, James, 1809, ptr, Swinton Pottery; an earthenware

tobacco jar is inscribed 'James Bullough Hunslet September 4 1810'

BULLOUGH, John, 1820, Leeds Pottery

BULLOUGH, Joseph, 1817, ew printer, Hunslet Hall, Leeds

BULLOUGH, Joseph, 1829, sorter of biscuit ware, Rockingham Works

BYFORD, Daniel, 1844–6, p, Castleford

BYFORD, William, 1844, p, Castleford

BYRAM, William, 1793, p, Castleford Pottery

CARTER, Charles, 1793, p, Castleford Pottery

CARTLEDGE, Ralph, 1773–6, 'Pottery', Leeds

CARTRIDGE, William, 1769–73, p, Swinton

CAVE, Stephen, 1783, Castleford Mere Pottery

CAVE, William, 1807, Castleford Pottery

CHADWICK, John, 1894, pottery mould mf, 93 Byram Street, Leeds

CHALLINER, Samuel, mid-C19 pottery press printer, Swinton

CHAPPEL, John, 1801–5, p, Swinton

CHARLESWORTH, William, 1801, p, Swinton

CHILD, Thomas, 1783–6, p, Stanley, Wakefield

CLARK, John, 1804, p, late of Woodlesford

CLEGG, John, 1802–7, p, Castleford Pottery

CLIFFE, Robert, 1680, p, Potovens

CLOUGH, Francis, 1765, potseller, Clayton, Bradford

COLLINSON, George, 1817, enameller and repairer of china, Hunslet

COLLINSON, flower ptr, Rockingham Works

COLLIS, John, 1891, ew and brickmaker, Mexborough

COOKE, John, mid-C19, printer, Newhill Pottery

COOPE, William, 1771, p, Swinton; 1772–8, 'Pottery', Leeds

CORDON, William, ptr, Rockingham Works

COUP, Jesse, 1772–3, 'Pottery', Leeds

COWAN, Richard, 1838, Mexborough Pottery

COWEN, William, ptr, Rockingham Works

COX, Mannassah, 1803, p, Swinton

CRAVEN, Thomas, 1817, ptr, Leeds Pottery; 1834, enameller, Hunslet
CRESWELL, John, 1826, ptr, Rockingham Works
CROHAM, J., 1872–6, p, 34 Upper Cross Street, Leeds
CROSSLEY & Co, 1936, ew mfs, The Common, South Heindley, Barnsley

DALE, George, born 1845, p, at Wedgwoods, Don, Northfield and New Jersey (USA)
DALMER, J., 1872, p, 6 & 12 Holbeck Lane, Leeds
DAWSON, Paul, 1822, p, Pontefract
DEKYNE, Thomas, 1371, p, York
DENNISON, John, 1788, p, Hunslet
DENNISON, 1830, p, Oulton
DOBSON, William, 1895, p, Mexborough
DICKINSON, Thomas, 1852, ew mf, Castleford
DICKINSON, William, 1850, ew mf, late of Mexborough
DUFFY, Patrick, 1891–3, china & ew decorator, Masbrough, Rotherham
DUNWELL, Christopher, 1848, Leeds Pottery

EASTWOOD, Joseph, 1831, p, Mexborough
EATON, Thomas, 1879, p, Tocketts, Guisborough
ELEY, John, 1839, p, Newhill, previously at Rockingham Works
ELEY, William, modeller, Rockingham Works
ESHALL, Richard, 1608, p, Potovens

FAZACKALEY, William, 1807–17, ew ptr, printer and potter, Hunslet
FENTON, Elizabeth, 1834, gilder, enameller and repairer of glass and china, Leeds
FENTON, Miss, early C19 agent to Leeds Pottery
FERRY, Esther, 1880s–90, artist, Linthorpe and Burmantofts
FIELDHOUSE, Benjamin, 1830s, p, Oulton; 1834–59, p and mould-maker, Hunslet, connections in Swinton
FIRTH, Edward, 1738–9, p, Rawmarsh

FIRTH, John, 1782, p, Rawmarsh
FIRTH & GLADDERS, 1897, potters, Methley Road, Castleford
FORSTARD, William, 1830s, p, Woodlesford
FOXTON BROS, 1904, p, Church Fenton, near Leeds

GARNER, Thomas, elder and younger, 1772, p, Rotherham
GARNTHWAITE, John, 1796, waggoner, Swinton Pottery
GARTHWAITE, Richard, 1834, p, Hunslet
GATER, Daniel, 1787, p, Castleford
GILL, Joseph, 1807, p, Methley
GLASBY, George, 1817, p, Swinton (son-in-law was Jonathan Taylor)
GLEDHOW, Alexander, C14, p, Cowick
GLOBE, George (son-in-law of Isaac Lee), ptr, Holmes Pottery; son Isaac, presser, Holmes Pottery; Isaac's son Charles, presser; Isaac's other son Henry, p, Northfield, Rawmarsh, and Swinton then opened pot shop in Rotherham. Henry's son John, thrower in Staffordshire
GLOVER: many potters of this name worked in Potovens from early C17–mid-C18. One family comprised four generations of Roberts; another consisted of Daniel, son Caleb, and grandson Daniel
GOLDWAITE, Joseph, 1808, p, Castleford Pottery
GOTHARD, John, 1808, clerk to Castleford Pottery
GREATOREX, William, 1834, p, Hunslet
GREAVES, John, 1830s, p, Oulton-
GREAVES, Thomas, 1797, p, Knottingley
GREEN, Henry, 1879, p, Strensall
GREEN, Joseph William, 1892, p, Boroughbridge, York, and Stonefall, Knaresbrough
GRETRIX, German, 1781, p, Elland
GRETRIX, John, 1781, p, Longwood, Huddersfield

HAIGH, George, 1895, p, Mexborough
HARLING, Jo., 1830s, p, Oulton-
HARRISON, G., 1872, p, 8 Cross Green Lane, Leeds

HARRISON, William, 1830, p, Castleford
HATHER, Joseph, 1834, p, Hunslet
HATTONS, Thomas, 1766, p, Burton in Lonsdale
HAWLEY, John, 1846, ew mf, Silkstone
HAWLEY, Richard, 1788–9, p, Rawmarsh
HENTIG, A. W., agent to Leeds Pottery
HINTON, James, 1787, p, Castleford
HIRST, J., 1861, p, 98 York Street, Kirkstall, Leeds
HIRST, Mrs, 1823, ew mf & coal dealer, Denholme
HOBKINS, William, 1808, Ferrybridge Pottery
HOBSON, John, 1808, Ferrybridge Pottery, previously Castleford
    Pottery
HOBSON, Michael, 1820, p, Woodlesford
HODGSON, Dinah & Ann, 1809, ptrs, Swinton Pottery
HOLDON, Joseph, 1792, p, Woodlesford
HOLGAT, John, 1653, p, Rawmarsh
HOLLAND, James, 1788, p, Burton in Lonsdale
HOLLIDAY, Richard, 1699, p, Potovens
HOLROYD, James, 1887, pottery manager, Burmantofts
HOLYDAY, Richard, 1765, p, Northowram
HOPKINS, artist, Rockingham Works
HORNCASTLE, Joseph, Newhill and Denaby Potteries
HORNCASTLE, William, 1829, in charge of ornamental warehouse,
    Rockingham Works
HOUGHTON, Thomas, 1834, p, Hunslet
HOYLAND, Anna, and daughter, ptrs, Rawmarsh Low Pottery
HOYLAND, Joseph, 1839, Swinton Pottery
HULME, Jesse, 1801, engraver, Swinton; 1825, Newhill, gent
HULME, John, 1800 and 1816, Swinton Pottery, 1822, ew mf,
    Swinton
HURDAS, John, 1807, Castleford Pottery; 1830s, p, Woodlesford
HURDAS, Peter, 1807, p, Ferrybridge

INMAN, Joseph & William, 1848, lived Leeds Pottery
ISSETT, John, 1853, Castleford Pottery

JACKSON, Ann, ptr, Newhill Pottery

JACKSON, M., agent to Leeds Pottery
JACKSON, William, 1379–83, p, Cowick
JARVIS, 1793, p, Rotherham
JARVIS, John, 1798, p, Rotherham
JEBSON, W., 1840, p, Castleford
JENKINSON, James, 1804, p, Mexborough Old Pottery
JESSOP, John, 1787, inkpot maker, Eccleshall Brierlow

KEELING, Samuel, pre-1821, Castleford Pottery
KELLIT, Joseph, 1801, p, Beeston, Leeds
KEMP, George, 1853–62, engraver, Swinton
KEMP, Mathew, 1852, ew mf, Castleford
KENT, Rockingham Works
KNOWLES, Robert, 1810, p, Burton in Lonsdale

LAKIN, Thomas, c 1815, probably Leeds Pottery
LAWSON, William, 1839, p, Knottingley
LAX, S., 1872–6, p, 10 Green Lane, Leeds
LEATHLEY, John, 1894, p, Moor View Road, Leeds
LEATHLEY, William, 1836, p, Hunslet Moor
LEE, Isaac (father of Joseph), 1816, ew mf, Swinton; 1842, p, Rotherham
LEE, James (brother of Joseph), modeller, Kilnhurst Pottery
LEE, Timothy, 1813, p, Rawmarsh
LEES, William, 1792, p, Wath on Dearne
LENG, Isaac, 1893, pottery mould mf, Byrom Street, Leeds
LETHLEY, William de, 1321, p, Conisbrough
LEYLAND, Richard, 1838, Mexborough Pottery
LEYLAND, ptr, Rockingham Works
LIVERSIDGE, Alfred, 1887–9, p, Swinton
LIVERSIDGE, George, 1816, began apprenticeship as printer, Swinton Pottery; 1829, overlooker and manager of printing department, Rockingham Works
LIVERSIDGE, Isaac, 1833, engraver, Swinton
LLANDIG, ptr, Rockingham Works
LOFTHOUSE, Thomas, 1807, p, Wakefield

LONGBOTTOM, Joseph, 1798, p, Castleford
LONGLEY, John, 1805, p, Castleford Pottery
LOWTHER, J., 1830s, p, Oulton
LUCAS, ptr, Rockingham Works

MACDONALD, John, 1807, p, Ferrybridge
MALKIN, Samuel, 1770, p, Swinton
MALKIN, Samuel, p, reputedly at Woodman House, early C18
MALKIN, William, 1763–70, p, Swinton
MALTKILN, Samuel, 1779, p, Thornton, near Bradford
MALTON, Charles, 1839, Rockingham Works
MANSFIELD, Joseph, 1829–37, gilder and chaser, Swinton
MARCH, Richard, 1770–4, p, Rothwell
MARSDEN, James, pre-1821, Castleford Pottery
MASTERMAN, Thomas, 1808, Ferrybridge Pottery
MAYER, Paul, 1755, p, Burton in Lonsdale
MEDLEY, Miss, 1822, of 'The Pottery', Hull
METCALF, George, 1814, p, Hunslet
MIDDLETON, George, 1850, p, Mexborough
MORRIS, Robert, c 1675, potseller, Halifax
MORTON, Joseph, 1839, Rockingham Works
MYAHE, Michael, 1781, p, Longwood, Huddersfield
MYATT, Charles, pre-1821, Castleford Pottery

NADIN, Miles, 1803, p, Swinton
NADIN, Thomas, 1795, p, Rotherham
NEWTON, Joseph, 1801, 'pot painter', Swinton
NEWTON, Thomas, 1822, Don Pottery
NICHELS, Thomas, 1771, p, Rothwell
NICHOLSON, Abraham, 1809, ptr, Swinton Pottery
NIXON, John, 1808, p, Swinton
NUNNS, Thomas, 1845–8, p, Hunslet

OLDFIELD, James, 1882–3, p, Jack Lane, Hunslet
OLDFIELD, John, 1823, ew mf, Mexborough; 1841, ew mf, Chesterfield
OLIVER, Thomas, 1608, p, Potovens

OXLEY, Joseph, 1839, Rockingham Works

PALISIER, BAILEY & ROWE, potters, 1898, 158 Hills Yard, Meadow Lane, Hunslet
PARIGE, Elisha, 1802, book-keeper, Hunslet, concerned in Leeds Pottery
PARKER, Thomas, 1853, Castleford Pottery
PARKS, Joseph, *c* 1810, Castleford Pottery
PARPOINT, John, 1767, p, Thornton, near Bradford
PAWSON, William, 1830, Russell's Pottery, Castleford
PEARSON, Joseph, 1834, p, Hunslet
PEOVER, Frederick, 1848, lived Leeds Pottery
PILLEY, Nicholas, printer, Newhill Pottery
PINDAR, Mark, 1830s, ew mf and shopkeeper, Holbeck, Leeds
POLLARD, John, 1826, ew mf, Idle
POOL, Hanley, 1783 to d 1789, p, Rothwell
POOL, Hanley, 1790–3, p, Castleford Pottery; 1808, p, Ferrybridge
POOL, William, 1808, Ferrybridge Pottery
POOL, William, 1804–7, p, Hunslet
PORTER, Philip, 1778, p, Rothwell
POTMAKERE, Richard le, 1297, Alverthorpe, Wakefield
POTTER, Nicholas, 1321, p, Conisbrough
PRINCE, pre-1806, Leeds Pottery agent at Swinton

RADLEY, Joseph, 1808, Ferrybridge Pottery
RANDALL, John, 1830–3, ptr, Rockingham Works
RAPER, Thomas, p, buried Gilling near Helmsley, 1697
RASTRICK, G., 1861, p, 82 Thornton Road, Pudsey
REDMAN, Thomas, 1808, Ferrybridge Pottery
REDMAYNE, Thomas, 1840, p, Burton in Lonsdale
RHODES, J., 1861, pottery mould mfs, Lidget Hill, Pudsey
RIGG, John, 1649, p, Potovens
RIGG, Robert, 1707–10, p, Potovens
RIGTON, George, 1680, p, Potovens
RILEY, 1882, p and grocer, Hunslet Hall Road, Hunslet

RIPLEY, John, 1821, p, Don Pottery
RIPLEY, Thomas, 1822, ew mf & dealer, Westgate, Wakefield
RIPLEY, William, pre-1821, Castleford Pottery
ROBERTS, G., 1861, p, Westgate, Cleckheaton
ROBERTSHAW, J., 1830s, p, Woodlesford
ROBINSON, 1823, 'The Pottery', Hull
ROBSON, Thomas, 1876, p, 2 Moorville Street, Beeston, Leeds
RODDIS, Charlotte, 1830, Russell's Pottery, Castleford
ROPER, John, 1649–56, p, Potovens
ROSS, James, ptr, Rockingham Works
RUSHTON, John, 1743, p, Rotherham

SAILES, Mary, 1809, apprentice, Swinton Pottery
SCHOFIELD, Edward, 1776, Pottery, Leeds
SCHOFIELD, John, 1799, p, Hunslet
SCHOFIELD, William, 1830s, p, Oulton
SCHROEDER, John, 1774–6 and 1813, Hunslet Pottery (previously of Liverpool)
SCORAH, George, 1833, engraver, Swinton Pottery
SCORAH, William, jr, 1803, Swinton Pottery
SCORAH, William, 1822, farmer, Don Pottery
SCORAH & LIVERSIDGE, engravers, Canal Bridge, Swinton; partnership dissolved 1835
SCOTT, James, 1819, Leeds Pottery
SEWARD, William, 1778, p, Burton in Lonsdale
SHACKLETON, George, 1842, p, Swillington Bridge
SHACKLETON, Samuel, 1814, p, Halifax
SHARP, James, 1824–8, ew ptr, Castleford
SHAW, John, 1809, ptr, Swinton Pottery
SHAW, Joseph, 1801, p, Swinton
SHAW, Stephen, 1801, p, Swinton
SHAW, Thomas, 1825, p, Mexborough
SHENSTON, John, decr, Swillington Bridge
SHERWOOD, 1827, agent from Brameld's, 44 Briggate, Leeds
SHILLITO, Francis, 1801, p, Swinton
SHILLITO, Richard, 1829, overlooker, Swinton Pottery

SIMPSON, John, 1797–1808, p, Ferrybridge Pottery
SIMPSON, John, 1844–55, p, Rawmarsh Top Pottery
SIMPSON, Ralph, 1797, p, Knottingley
SIMPSON, Richard, 1804, p, Mexborough Old Pottery
SIMPSON, Samuel, 1763, p, Burton in Lonsdale
SIMPSON, William, 1807, p, Knottingley
SIMS, George, 1829, p, Castleford
SMITH, Jeremiah, 1777, 'Pottery', Leeds
SMITH, John, 1804, p, Mexborough Old Pottery
SMITH, Rachael, 1880s, Linthorpe and Burmantofts
SMITH, Robert, 1801, 'potter painter', Swinton
SMITH, William D., 1893, pottery mould mf, Johnson Square, Charles Street, Leeds
SPEIGHT, Christopher, 1771, labourer at Pothouse, Rothwell
SPEIGHT, George, 1826–39, ornamental ptr, Swinton; 1853, artist, Shelton, Staffordshire; 1857, 1861 and 1865, china ptr and gilder, Rockingham Works; 1862, artist, Swinton
SPEIGHT, Godfrey, c 1812, Don Pottery
SPEIGHT, James, 1834, p, Hunslet
SPEIGHT, John, 1829, p, Rockingham Works
SPEIGHT, William, 1801 and 1826, p, Swinton; 1826, ptr, Swinton Pottery; 1829, in charge of flint mill, colours and glazes, Swinton Pottery. Married Mary Kemp; 1853, engraver, Swinton
STANTON, John & Samuel, 1781, potters, Holbeck, Leeds
STEEL, Thomas (1772–1850), c 1830, ptr, Rockingham Works
STEELE, Edwin (1804–71), son of Thomas Steel; 1828–32, ptr, Rockingham Works
STENTON, William, c 1854–c 1870, Newhill Pottery
SWALES, George, 1818, p, Burton in Lonsdale
SWALES, John, 1755, dealer in pots, Burton in Lonsdale
SWALES, John, 1804, p, Burton in Lonsdale
SWETMAN, John, 1830, p, Oulton
SYKES, Richard, 1808, Ferrybridge Pottery
SYKES, Thomas, 1776, p, Leeds Pottery

TAYLOR, Benjamin, 1771, Rothwell Pottery

TAYLOR, Benjamin, 1820–2, Don Pottery
TAYLOR, Richard, 1775, p, Rothwell
TAYLOR, Thomas, 1817–23, Don Pottery
TAYLOR, William, 1773, 'Pottery', Leeds
TEMPEST, Henry, 1814, p, Holbeck, Leeds
TEMPEST, John S., 1817, ew printer, Hunslet
THACKERY, Thomas, 1790s–1850, p, Ferrybridge Pottery
THOMAS, Joseph, died 1829, Don Pottery
THOMPSON, Henry, 1891, pottery painter, Swinton
THOMPSON, J., 1861, p, Westgate, Bradford
THORNTON, William, 1853, pot mould mf, Cooper Bridge, Huddersfield
TILBURY, Henry, ptr, Rockingham Works
TODD, Joseph, 1804, p, Hunslet
TOWERS, Elizabeth, 1765, p, Leeds; 1767, china seller, Leeds
TOWNSEND, John, 1850, p, York

WAGG, John, 1804, Mexborough Pottery
WAGSTAFF, John, 1772, p, Rothwell
WALKER, Benjamin, 1857, p, Woodlesford
WALKER, Jesse, 1850, p, Knottingley
WALKER, William, 1808, p, Swinton
WALKER & CRAWSHAW, late C19, ew mfs and brickmakers, Sheffield Road, Conisbrough
WALMSLEY, James, 1805–10, p, Burton in Lonsdale
WALMSLEY, John, 1799, p, Burton in Lonsdale
WARBURTON, Joseph, 1826, china ptr and enameller, Hunslet
WARD, Isaac, 1831, p, Doncaster, son of Richard Ward
WARD, John, 1797, 1813, 1818 and 1855, p, Rawmarsh
WARD, Richard, 1811 and 1817, p, Rawmarsh
WATTS, William, 1834, p, Hunslet
WEBSTER, Thomas, 1830s, p, Oulton
WELSMAN, John R., 1881, p, 26 Simes Street, Bradford
WHITAKER, Ralph, 1804, p, Mexborough Old Pottery
WHITAKER, Thomas jr, pre-1801, Castleford Pottery
WIGGLESWORTH, John, 1829, Fletcher's Pottery, Castleford

WILD, Thomas, 1808, p, Whitwood

WILD, 1823, lived Leeds Pottery

WILKINSON, George, 1817, ew ptr, Leeds Pottery

WILLANS, Jacob, 1625–56, p, Potovens; son Thomas, grandson Robert, 1709–23, also potters, Potovens

WILLANS, Thomas, 1869–76, manager, Don Pottery

WILSON, George, 1771, p, Burton in Lonsdale

WILSON, Thomas, 1808, engraver, Knottingley

WINTERBOTTOM, J., 1872, p, 95 Bewerley Street, Leeds

WOOD, Charles, 1769, p, Swinton

WOOD, Edward, artist, Swinton Pottery

WOOD, John, 1830s, p, Oulton

WOOD, John, 1850–4, ew mf, Castleford; 1855, of Birmingham, china painter now of Sheffield, gent

WOOD, Joseph, 1817–23, ew turner, Hunslet

WOOD, Thomas, 1768–70, p, Rothwell

WOOD, William, 1808, p, Swinton

WOODGER, George, 1841, china mf, Wellgate, Rotherham

WOODGER, John, 1841, china mf, Masbrough, Rotherham

WOOLF, Benjamin, 1814, Don Pottery; 1833, china ptr, Swinton

WOOLF, John, 1772, 'Pottery', Leeds; 1792, p, Hunslet

WOOLF, John, 1807–12, p, Hunslet, son of above

WRIGHT, George, died 1807, of Leeds Pottery

WRIGHT, George, c 1820, Castleford Pottery

WRIGHT, John, died 1798, p, Hunslet

WRIGHT, John, son of Matthew Wright, p, Newcastle under Lyme, Staffordshire

WRIGHT, John, p, Methley

WRIGHT, Matthew, 1772, 'Pottery', Leeds, died 1804 after 34 years at Leeds Pottery, aged fifty-six. Father of Matthew and Thomas below

WRIGHT, Matthew, p, Hunslet, died 1807

WRIGHT, Thomas, 1809, p, Leeds

YATES, Thomas, 1769, p, Burton in Lonsdale

YOUNG, Robert, 1853–9, ew mf, Bateson's Pottery, Castleford

SUPPLEMENTARY
LIST OF POTTERIES

There is archaeological and/or documentary evidence of further potteries having existed at the following places:

Aberford	Long Marston
Altofts	Loversall
Askwith	Middlestown
Blaxton	Oulton
Bradford	Pittsmoor
Bradsby	Potter Newton
Bramham	Pudsey
Branton	Rawmarsh
Burley	Ripley
Church Fenton	Roundhay
Cleckheaton	Ryther
Cold Coniston	Sherburn in Elmet
Conisbrough	Silsden
Ecclesfield	Skelton
Eccleshall Bierlow	South Heindley
Gilberdike	Strensall
Gilling East	Tankersley
Guisborough	Templehurst
Holme on Spalding	Thirlby
Moor	Thorner
Idle	Thorpe
Kelk	Todmorden
Lastingham	Wetherby

BIBLIOGRAPHY

Bartlett, J. and Brooks, J. 'Hull Pottery', *Kingston Upon Hull Museums Bulletin*, No 5 (1971)

Bartlett, K. S. 'Excavations at Potovens, near Wakefield', *Post-Medieval Archaeology*, Vol 5 (1971)

Beatson, Clark & Co Ltd. *The Glass Works, Rotherham*, researched by Miss D. Greene

Bellamy, C. V. and Le Patourel, H. E. J. 'Four Medieval Pottery Kilns at Woodhouse Farm, Winksley, near Ripon, West Riding', *Medieval Archaeology*, Vol 14 (1970)

BREARS, P. C. D. *Catalogue of the English Country Pottery Housed In The Yorkshire Museum, York* (1968)

——. 'Excavations at Potovens, near Wakefield', *Post-Medieval Archaeology*, Vol 1 (1967)

——. *The English Country Pottery* (1971)

Brewster, T. C. M. 'Staxton Ware, An Interim Report', *Archaeological Journal*, Vol 39

Brooke, S. 'A Late Medieval Pottery Site at Yearsley', *The Yorkshire Archaeological Journal*, 37 (1951)

Castleford Pottery Pattern Book (reprinted 1973). With a brief history of the Castleford Pottery by Heather Lawrence

Christie, Manson & Woods Ltd. Sale Catalogue of the Collection of Leeds Creamware and Allied Wares formed by Alistair Sampson (1967)

Eaglestone, A. A. and Lockett, T. A. *The Rockingham Pottery* (Rotherham 1964)

Gilbert, C. 'Portrait of a Yorkshire Pottery', *Country Life*, 140 (September 1966)

Godden, G. A. *Encyclopaedia of British Pottery & Porcelain Marks* (1964)

———. *Illustrated Encyclopaedia of British Pottery & Porcelain* (1966)

Grabham, O. *Yorkshire Potteries, Pots & Potters* (1916, reprinted Wakefield 1971)

Hanson, T. W. 'The Ovenden Heights', *Halifax Antiquarian Society Transactions* (1913–14)

Hurst, A. *A Catalogue of the Boynton Collection of Yorkshire Pottery* (York 1922)

Jewitt, L. *The Ceramic Art of Great Britain* (1878)

Kenworthy, J. *The Midhope Potteries* (Sheffield 1928)

Kiddell, A. J. B. 'John Platt of Rotherham, Potter and Mason Architect', *English Ceramic Circle Transactions*, Vol 5, part 3 (1962)

Kidson, J. R. and F. *Historical Notices of the Leeds Old Pottery* (Leeds 1892, reprinted Wakefield 1970)

Lawrence, Heather. 'Wedgwood & Co', *The Connoisseur* (June 1974)

Leeds Arts Calendar, No 56 (1965), includes 'The Leeds Pottery and Its Wares, A Bibliography', compiled by D. S. Thornton

Leeds Arts Calendar, No 67 (1970), includes 'Mr Greg's Leeds Ware' by M. R. Parkinson, 'Some Trifles from Leeds' by D. S. Thornton and 'A Leeds Collector's Notebook' by P. Walton

Leeds Arts Calendar, No 73 (1973), includes 'The Rothwell Pottery and Its Wares' by Heather Lawrence and Peter Walton, and 'A Leeds Collector's Notebook' by Peter Walton

Le Vine, J. R. A. *Linthorpe Pottery, an Interim Report* (Teesside 1970)

——— *Teesside Potteries* (Teesside 1972)

Rice, D. G. *Rockingham Ornamental Porcelain*

———*Rockingham Pottery & Porcelain* (1971)

Rutter, J. G. 'Ayton Castle: Its History & Excavation', *Scarborough & District Archaeological Society Research Report No 5*

———. 'Medieval Pottery in the Scarborough Museum', *Scarborough & District Archaeological Society Research Report No 3*

Sheppard, T. 'The Belle Vue Pottery, Hull', *Transactions of the British Ceramic Society*, Vol 40 (1941)

Sotheby & Co, Sale Catalogue of English Creamware, the property of D. C. Towner (1968)

Towner, D. C. *English Cream Coloured Earthenware* (1957)

——. *The Leeds Pottery* (1963)

Tyler, E. G. 'Francis Place's Pottery', *English Ceramic Circle Transactions*, Vol 8, part 2 (1972)

Walton, J. 'Some Decadent Local Industries', *Halifax Antiquarian Society Transactions*, 19 (1939)

Woodrow, K. J. 'Cistercian Ware from Silcoates School, near Wakefield', *Post-Medieval Archaeology*, Vol 5 (1972)

Most of the facts in the text are taken from or confirmed by source material, including deeds, directories, maps, rate assessments, inclosure awards, parish registers, newspapers, wills and other original material, the majority of which are housed in the following depositories:

Borthwick Institute of Historical Research, St Anthony's Hall, York
Halifax Reference Library
Leeds City Archives Department, Sheepscar Library, Leeds
Leeds City Reference Library, The Headrow, Leeds
Rotherham Reference Library
Sheffield City Reference Library
South Yorkshire Industrial Museum, Cusworth Hall, Doncaster
West Riding County Council Records Office, Wakefield
West Riding County Library, Balne Lane, Wakefield
West Riding Registry of Deeds, Newstead Road, Wakefield
Yorkshire Archaeological Society, Clarendon Road, Leeds

ACKNOWLEDGEMENTS

My grateful thanks go to the many individuals who have helped and advised me in compiling this book, and to the librarians and curators, too numerous to mention individually, who have assisted me in my research. Particular thanks go to John Goodchild of the South Yorkshire Industrial Museum (whose suggestion it was that I write the book) for making available so much documentary material; to John Griffin for material on the Don Pottery; to A. A. Eaglestone for correcting the manuscript; to Miss B. J. Hawley and T. Hawley for advice on the Hawley potteries; to T. G. Brown for making available the deeds of the Ferrybridge Pottery; to Mrs E. Blatch for advice on the Belle Vue Pottery; to Miss M. G. Pyle of the Castleford Museum, B. Tattersall of the Wedgwood Museum and P. C. D. Brears, Mrs F. V. Crowder, Mr and Mrs J. G. Evans, P. Littlewood, W. G. Matthews, D. C. Towner, P. Walton and the staffs of the depositories listed at the end of the Bibliography.

INDEX

Main entries in the text are in italic, numbers in italic refer to illustrations